Fantasy Sports
Real Money

Fantasy Sports
Real Money

The Unlikely Rise of Daily Fantasy
How to Play–How to Win

Bill Ordine

HUNTINGTON PRESS
LAS VEGAS, NEVADA

Fantasy Sports Real Money
The Unlikely Rise of Daily Fantasy
How to Play–How to Win

Published by
Huntington Press
3665 Procyon St.
Las Vegas, NV 89103
Phone (702) 252-0655
e-mail: books@huntingtonpress.com

ISBN: 978-1-935396-65-9
$19.95US

In chronological order, photographs appear courtesy of: ©johanley2015 (Nigel Eccles); United States Office of Humanities; DraftKings; FanDuel/Scott & Danielle Hanson; Rob Gomes; Corinne Green; Andy Mousalimas; Arthur Bovino/Daniel Okrent; Paul Charchian; Adam Krejcik/Eilers Research; Anita Marks; ©Steve Marcus (Floyd Mayweather); ©Winslow Townson-USA TODAY Sports/Reuters (American Pharaoh).

Front Cover Photos: @Vladyslav Starozhylov (money); ©Photo Alto/ Alamy Stock Photo (Football Player)
Book/Cover Design & Production: Laurie Cabot

Dedication

To Emily, who on her own Author's Day graciously put aside her accomplishments to ask, "So how's the book going?"

Acknowledgments

When I started this book, I checked Amazon to survey the literature written about games of skill. Chess, for instance, had more than 26,000 titles. Poker, more than 7,700. This new field of daily fantasy sports had less than 20. Yet, that there were any at all illustrates that ground had already been plowed and to all those who went before, I offer recognition of their work, along with the humble hope that what is found in these pages will be of help to those who come after.

Individual acknowledgments (no specific order) are offered gratefully with the trepidation that some who generously gave their time are missed. To those, I offer apologies and a rain check on the beverage of their choice.

Thank you for historical, legislative, legal, scholarly, business, media, gaming, and other types of guidance, suggestions, and counsel to: the estimable Jim Leach, former U.S. Rep. (Iowa); Bob Bowman, MLB; Sal LaRocca, NBA; Trent Dilfer, ESPN; Dan Okrent; Sue Schneider; Frank Fahrenkopf; John Pappas; Jason Ader; Adam Krejcik; Zak Gilbert; I. Nelson Rose; Andy Mousalimas; David Safavian; Anita Marks; Ed Miller; Steve Fezzik; Dan Walsh; Ellen Souchak, Richard Schuetz; David G. Schwartz; Joris Drayer; Andy Billings; Brendan Dwyer; Jay Kornegay; Seth Palansky; Matthew Gavin;

Chris Moneymaker; Ryan Davis; Glenn Clark; Steve Dannenmann; Stan Charles; Matthew Gould; John Acunto; Patrick Guinan; Chris Grove; Kim Darrell; Jeff Hwang; Bill Mandry; Marc Edelman; Glenn Guzzo; Brody Ruihley.

DFS dignitaries: Nigel Eccels, FanDuel CEO; Matt Kalish, DraftKings co-founder; Kevin Bonnet; Jonathan Bales; Drew Dinkmeyer; Chris Raybon; Adam Levitan; Vin Narayanan; Renee Miller; Al Zeidenfeld; Paul Charchian; David Gomes; Rob Gomes; Scott Hanson; Sabrina Macias; Femi Wasserman; David Copeland; Christy Keenan.

Numbers experts: David Appelman; Jared Cross; Dave Hall.

The 34th Street Irregulars: Steve Grantz; Sam Chambers; Doug Donovan; Akim Reinhardt; Kevin Osten; Adam Sheingate; Andrew Wolfe; Andrew Stephenson; Hugh Ivory; Peter Armitage.

The indispensables: publisher Anthony Curtis; editor Deke Castleman; Jessica Roe; Laurie Cabot.

Contents

Prologue

Just a few years ago, most sports fans had never heard of daily fantasy sports. That includes the most rabid of them, even long-time participants in the traditional fantasy sports leagues that have been around for ages. Today, by contrast, it's nearly impossible for any sports follower not to notice this new thing called daily fantasy sports.

But what is it?

Briefly, daily fantasy sports (DFS) websites offer Internet contests in which players throughout most of North America can stake real money on the performances of real athletes in order to win real cash prizes.

Anyone who watches sports on TV can't miss the constant commercials. The two biggest operators, FanDuel and DraftKings, have saturated the airwaves with their message, which, simply put, is: "Play and win big money!"

But the marketing reach has gone far beyond TV. Daily fantasy companies have spent big bucks to have their logos behind home plate in major league ballparks, plastered on the walls at NFL stadiums, and decorating NBA arenas.

Almost overnight, DFS has become an inescapable reality on the American sports landscape. Caught by surprise, legions of fans wonder: Is it legal? If so, how can it be? How do I play these contests? Can I really win big money? Is it gambling? Where did it come from? And where is it all going?

This book answers all of those questions—and many many more.

In the early chapters, I explain how the journey to DFS' legal status has taken it through the labyrinth of lawmaking and is a prime example of the law of unintended consequences. As for the future, while it's still uncertain, it does have the potential to establish a new normal in spectator sports by changing how fans see themselves and express their enthusiasm for the games. Also yet to be determined are the roles public policymakers will play in shaping daily fantasy's future.

The bulk of the book is a primer for fans interested in testing their own sports acumen in DFS contests. With the strategies I reveal, you can approach the cash games conservatively and earn a little extra money on a regular basis. Or you can take a shot at the lottery-type jackpots that are routinely up for grabs and, unlike the lottery, improve your chances with the skillful tactics presented in these pages.

Whatever your ambitions regarding DFS, *Fantasy Sports, Real Money* is meant to give you an edge on the competition, so that when the actual football, baseball, basketball, and hockey games are over, no matter what sports teams emerge victorious, you'll be the real winner.

Chapter 1

All-Star Fantasy Protest

Down on the diamond at Coors Field, the brightest luminaries in baseball were getting ready for the 69th All-Star Game, being held for the first time ever in Denver, Colorado.

For the baseball fans at Coors Field that day in July 1998, it was clear that a jubilant carnival had come to Denver. The stadium, named after the brewery responsible for Colorado's famous amber export, had opened three years earlier and the All-Star Game was a reward for the Mile High City delivering a sparkling new ballpark to Major League Baseball.

Seattle superstar Ken Griffey Jr., Baltimore's 37-year-old ironman Cal Ripken Jr., and 24-year-old New York Yankee sensation Derek Jeter were among the game's glitterati that fans from all over the country had come to see. Barry Bonds, Roger Clemens, Mark McGwire, and Rafael Palmeiro—all players whose career accomplishments would be smudged by the suggestion of PED use—ceremoniously lined up along the baselines for introductions at the Midsummer Classic. Faith Hill sang the National Anthem, a military flyover underscored the pervasive patriotic feel-good, and Coors Field, a hitter's paradise, would give the crowd what it always wants: offensive fireworks that were a match for the real pyrotechnics that are *de rigueur* at such events.

The American League won, 13-8, then a record for All-Star scoring, and the game featured 31 hits screaming like tracers through Denver's thin air.

Zak Gilbert, who was working in public relations for the Colorado Rockies at the time, was in the press box at Coors Field for both the All-Star Game and the exhibition Home Run Derby the day before. At one point, Gilbert looked up from the hoopla below and spotted a small airplane towing a banner.

"It said something about Congress and sports, and I was thinking, 'What's this all about?'" Gilbert said years later. "I figured it was just the latest political stunt."

In a sense, it was. The airplane banner was a warning, a call-to-arms on behalf of fantasy sports, and it was targeting those thousands of fans below and any politicians that may have been among them.

The subplot to the celebration drew zero interest from the assembled media at the time, but that day would be a seminal moment for both sports fans and the games they love. And the plane towing the banner "about Congress and sports" that the PR fellow had spotted was part of that subplot.

As fans arrived at Coors Field, they were greeted by one of those giant inflatable gorillas, the kind whose only purpose is to draw a glance, to capture the attention of passers-by, if for only a moment—a moment long enough to impart a quick message. And the message was something that would certainly resonate with baseball fans: "Stop Congress from Taking Away Our Fantasy Baseball." This was essentially the line spotlighted by folks handing out flyers warning of still another attempt by those bums in Washington, D.C., to butt in where they didn't belong.

And if the fans missed the message being pushed by the

gorilla or the foot soldiers distributing brochures, there was the air campaign overhead, the flying banner also warning of Washington's intrusion where it wasn't wanted.

Today, the banning of traditional fantasy sports—whether baseball or any other sport—seems so far-fetched, the proposal of such a thing seems utterly absurd.

By 2015, traditional fantasy sports had been around for more than a half-century and its legions of devotees had grown to more than 50 million in the U.S. and Canada, according to the Fantasy Sports Trade Association, which represents the activity's interests. But even more significant, a newer version of fantasy sports, one that was born in the new millennium and called *daily* fantasy sports, had burst onto the scene and was turning what was once a hobby for sports nerds into big business.

Daily fantasy sports, as a business, began getting noticed in mainstream media in 2010, and from a standing start its early growth was exponential. The two largest daily fantasy sports companies, FanDuel and DraftKings, reported combined revenues of about $97 million in 2014. And that was just part of the story. The two major daily fantasy sports websites, again combined, saw year-over-year revenue growth of 570% from 2013 to 2014. The 2014 data also reflected that customers had spent $926 million in total entry fees, with most of that being returned in prize money.

By 2015, those numbers were being *obliterated*. In one month—October 2015—FanDuel and DraftKings combined for about $173.8 million in entry fees in their larger football contests, according to tracking website SuperLobby.com.

FanDuel made its financial information public from the beginning of 2011 through the end of 2014. The numbers illustrate the exponential growth of FanDuel as it went from a virtually unknown company with an equally unknown product to become the number-one DFS company in the world (at least through the end of 2014). By 2015, competitor DraftKings would catch up.

FanDuel Annual Growth			
	Entry Fees	**Revenue**	**Paid Actives**
2011	$11.50 mil	$1.15 mil	17,251
2012	$51.66 mil	$9.96 mil	69,061
2013	$159.38 mil	$14.26 mil	192,942
2014	$621.72 mil	$57.26 mil	1,012,265

Meanwhile, the relatively recent concept of daily fantasy sports was the beneficiary of a credibility boost when Major League Baseball and the National Basketball Association took equity positions in the emerging industry's major companies—MLB with Boston-based DraftKings and the NBA with New York-headquartered FanDuel. About the same time, the National Hockey League jumped into an advertising partnership with DraftKings. Soon, 16 National Football League teams had signed on to accept DFS advertising from FanDuel. Also, FanDuel signed on 15 NBA teams to advertising deals. Not to be outdone, DraftKings signed 12 NFL teams, 9 NBA teams, 8 NHL teams, and 27 MLB teams to advertising deals.

By spring 2015, daily fantasy brands seemed to be everywhere a major sports event was happening. When Floyd Mayweather Jr. beat Manny Pacquiao in the "Fight of the Century" in May 2015, the winner wore daily fantasy website FanDuel's logo on his trunks. And when American Pharoah won horse racing's first Triple Crown in 37 years about a month later, the race featured the advertising branding of DraftKings, with the

Ad Blitz

After raising hundreds of millions of dollars in venture capital earlier in 2015, both DraftKings and FanDuel launched massive commercial crusades as the NFL season began. Overnight, the barrage of TV spots that aired during pro and college football games propelled the two companies to household-name status. During the seven-day period that ended Sept. 10, 2015, DraftKings was the number-one television advertiser, spending an estimated $21.8 million on 5,800 commercials. FanDuel spent $11.8 million during the same week on 2,600 commercials.

The pace remained frenetic over the next two weeks, and as the NFL headed toward its third weekend, DraftKings had spent an estimated $17 million during a seven-day period on nearly 2,800 commercials and FanDuel was close behind with an estimated $15.8 million, also on almost 2,800 commercials. News reports indicated that DraftKings, with its initial burst of advertising, had attracted more than one million new fantasy sign-ups.

While immediate brand recognition was achieved and customer gains were impressive, TV viewers quickly grew weary of the incessant hammering about winning millions by playing daily fantasy sports, and all the huckstering caught the attention of a suspicious mainstream media and prying politicians.

company's trademark emblazoned on the history-making colt's saddle blanket.

But long before any of that happened, back when it was beyond anyone's imagination to even conceive of such a thing, there were the folks at that Denver All-Star Game in 1998, tugging at the sleeves of baseball fans warning about a piece of legislation being pushed by Arizona Sen. Jon Kyl.

The bill that Kyl introduced to the Senate in the late 1990s had the potential to put the brakes on fantasy sports contests where prizes were given out. At the time, fantasy sports was generally considered a harmless hobby that lots of fans enjoyed mainly for fun and bragging rights.

By then, most sports fans knew at least a little about fantasy baseball and football.

Or Did They?

If you were like some of the more rabid sports fans, you and a bunch of your friends picked a roster of players from the ranks of major leaguers or the NFL at "The Draft," the annual ritual marked by beer, pizza, and trash talk. You and your pals gave your teams goofy-pun names like Scared Hitless and Victorious Secret (real team names, by the way). Then, the old gang each tossed $10 or $20 or even $100 into the pot. The real baseball or football players were accumulating points for all those fantasy rosters with their real home runs and RBI and touchdowns. As the season dragged on, you dropped some stinkers; you added some guys who might do better; you tried to hornswoggle your pals in some trades. At the end of the year, the fantasy team "owner" whose fictitious team had accumulated the most points got the lion's share of the pot.

Of course, someone in your group had to keep track of the stats and the records and make sure the trades were according to the league's rules. That guy may have held the honorary title of Commissioner, but the job was still a pain in the neck.

By the 1990s, a handful of small-time businesses had sprung up around the country that gave fantasy sports enthusiasts a little more structure and organization in their contests. They charged a fee to keep track of the stats, give the participants periodic updates, and, in general, make sure the leagues ran smoothly. Some of them also collected the entry fees and sorted out the winnings. In time, the cottage industry of daily fantasy sports administration started making the transition from old-school methods, like paper-and-pencil and the U.S. mail, to the Internet.

So back when the early version of Kyl's anti-Internet gambling legislation was chugging through Congress, there was money involved in some traditional season-long fantasy sports contests. Even so, very few saw fantasy sports as a threat to the moral fiber of America.

And at the 1998 All-Star Game, fans from around the country arriving at Coors Field were getting the word that stuffy old politicians in Washington with nothing better to do were trying to ruin it all.

At least, that was the message.

Banning Online Gambling

The bill being pushed by Kyl in 1998 was actually meant to stamp out something not a lot of folks were paying attention to back then—Internet gambling.

This was five years before a young fellow from Tennessee named Chris Moneymaker won the World Series of Poker Main Event and millions of dollars in Las Vegas after qualifying for the prestigious tournament, with its $10,000 buy-in, on an Internet poker website for just $39.

In 1998, the idea of Internet gambling was of little concern to most Americans. After all, who would ship money to some sketchy website operators in the Caribbean, then place a bet on a football game, hoping that they'd get paid if they won?

But Kyl, an old-school conservative Republican and a ferocious opponent of legalized gambling of any kind, saw the potential for something much more insidious. In his view, Internet gambling amounted to turning every living room or den or rec room in America into a virtual casino.

"Click a mouse, lose the house" was the anti-Internet gambling slogan.

To nip that kind of threat in the bud, Kyl had been introducing bills to halt Internet gambling for a few years and when the All-Star Game in Denver was played, the latest Kyl effort was the Internet Gambling Prohibition Act of 1998. It was take-no-prisoners legislation that, if passed, would have wiped out just about every contest imaginable where someone could risk money via the global computer network, although policing such a law would have been a daunting task.

Frank Fahrenkopf, at the time the head of the America Gaming Association, an umbrella group that represents commercial, and now tribal, casinos in the United States, said the bill was inspired by work done by a pair of state attorneys general with an unlikely coupling of last names, Nixon and Humphrey. Skip Humphrey III was the attorney general in Minnesota and the son of former Vice President Hubert Humphrey, who ran for president in 1968 and lost to Richard Nixon. Jay Nixon (no relation to Richard) was the AG from Missouri. Alarmed by the Wild West of Internet gambling in the 1990s—no legal statutes, no regulatory controls, no taxes—Humphrey and Nixon inspired a suggested remedy that helped frame Kyl's early attempt at the Internet Gambling Prohibition Act.

As written, said one Capitol Hill insider who was involved in the issue at the time, Kyl's anti-Internet gambling bill "would have made a Pillsbury bake-off illegal." That may have been an exaggeration, but the bill was certainly the most aggressive and restrictive piece of anti-Internet gambling legislation anyone has ever seen make any headway in Washington. Average bettors could be fined as much as $500—and go to jail. Although some states had laws penalizing the placing of an online wager, the Kyl bill would have escalated betting by an individual on the Internet to a federal crime.

Those who accepted online-gambling advertising could also be penalized. Internet service providers would be tasked with helping to enforce the law. And there were no exceptions for games of skill, such as fantasy sports.

As a result, many fantasy sports businesses that offered contests with cash prizes—businesses just making the transition from pencil-and-paper operations to the Internet—were in danger of being killed by Kyl's bill. This wasn't necessarily apparent to the millions of folks playing fantasy sports at the time or even to the handful of mom-and-pop companies conducting fantasy games with cash prizes. However, it *was* apparent to a lobbying firm with ties to one of Washington's most canny and successful lobbyists, a man named Jack Abramoff.

Ironically, Abramoff was often a peddler of Republican causes himself. He'd helped campaign for Ronald Reagan in 1980 on college campuses in, of all places, Massachusetts, where Reagan pulled off an upset win, according to a profile of Abramoff in the *Washington Post*. Over the years, Abramoff became friendly with the most conservative elements of the GOP, such as anti-tax anti-big-government stalwart Grover Norquist, and Ralph Reed, whose Christian-values-inspired brand of politics has fueled his influence in conservative ranks.

But when Kyl introduced the Internet Gambling Prohibition Act in 1998, a Washington lobbying group that shared some clients with Abramoff (as well as being broadly Republican in tone) was representing Internet gaming interests. In a strange twist, these otherwise conservative-leaning lobbyists were tasked with derailing the Kyl bill. They knew they needed persuasive and sympathetic supporters, and they found the allies they needed in those earnest and rabid fantasy sports folks. To dramatize the threat to fantasy sports, the lobbyists hired a firm skilled in the behind-the-scenes political art of "astroturfing." (Astroturfing is creating the appearance of a grassroots effort on behalf of some issue.)

Conveniently, the chairmen of both the Democratic and Republican national committees were from Colorado and the All-Star Game in Denver provided the perfect stage for the theatrics cooked up by the professional "grassroots" organizers who adroitly portrayed Kyl's anti-Internet gambling legislation as an attack on the cherished and innocent institution of fantasy sports, the origins of which are discussed later on in this chapter.

The Carve-Out

Kyl's bill, despite winning 90-10 approval in the Senate, never got a vote in the House of Representatives that year.

Reasons for the 1998 Kyl bill failing probably went beyond merely the pushback from fantasy sports interests. At the time, Congress was obsessed with the Bill Clinton-Monica Lewinsky scandal. But the lobbying group representing the fantasy sports industry wasn't shy about taking credit. When the Kyl bill failed to pass, there was a celebratory message on the fledgling Fantasy Sports Trade Association website.

But more to the point was this fact: Ever since that 1998 attempt to halt Internet gambling was met by protest at the All-Star game, every subsequent piece of anti-online gambling legislation has included some exemption or "carve-out" for fantasy sports, though admittedly, the specific carve-out language might have differed in various instances.

In 1999, Kyl came back with another version of the Internet Gambling Prohibition Act that was pushed by Virginia Rep. Bob Goodlatte in the House of Representatives. And this time, the bill included a carve-out for fantasy sports.

Already, fantasy sports had become a third rail for anti-Internet gambling legislation. If gambling opponents wanted an anti-online gambling bill, they knew they had to steer clear of fantasy sports. In addition, fantasy sports was getting popular in Washington. Sue Schneider, founder and longtime leader of the Interactive Gaming Council, a gambling trade association, testified countless times about Internet gambling in front of Congress and state legislatures.

"Every time I went up to the Hill, you'd go in the offices and all the Congressional staffers had their fantasy games up on their computer screens," Schneider said. "It seemed like that's all they were doing."

The attempt at an Internet gambling prohibition in 1999 was destined to fail, too. This time, Abramoff was more directly involved and the lobbying efforts were far more aggressive, even sinister. To sabotage the bill, Abramoff artfully turned conservative against conservative and managed to frame the anti-Internet gambling legislation as a vehicle that actually expanded gambling, thanks to exemptions for horse racing, dog racing, and jai alai. The idea was to stir opposition among social conservatives, and it worked by convincing the most rabid anti-gambling groups that the latest anti-Internet gambling legislation was too soft and no bill at all was better than this weak one.

Meanwhile, Rep. Bob Goodlatte, a staunch conservative

himself, had taken on Internet-gambling abolition as a personal crusade, and he'd been spearheading the 1999 version of IGPA in the House of Representatives. The bill was voted on in July 2000. Largely due to Abramoff's machinations, the vote was held under suspension rules, meaning it needed a two-thirds majority; it failed to muster the necessary votes.

Abramoff's camp celebrated over quashing the 1999 Internet Gambling Prohibition Act, but the good times were soon over for the powerful lobbyist, whose problematic tactics on other issues led to his downfall and imprisonment. There were also criminal convictions for more than a dozen of Abramoff's associates on Capitol Hill, including a Congressman.

To the dismay of online gambling interests, Abramoff's work to undermine the 1999 anti-Internet gambling proposal later became ammunition for people aiming to ban online gaming.

Internet Gambling Foes Press the Attack

As the issue of Internet gambling simmered, powerful institutions were planning on raising the heat to the boiling point. Among them were the major professional and amateur sports organizations, especially the most powerful of these, the National Football League, whose red-white-and-blue trademark shield makes it look as if it's a government agency.

Leading the NFL's lobbying efforts was Marty Gold, a respected figure on Capitol Hill and one of Washington's foremost experts in Senate procedures and parliamentary strategies. Among the senators Gold served as a senior staffer was Majority Leader Sen. Howard H. Baker Jr., a Tennessee Republican; significantly, in 2003, Gold was an adviser and counsel to another GOP Senate Majority Leader who was also from Tennessee, Sen. Bill Frist. By 2004, Gold was with a law firm that represented the pro football league, Covington & Burling, and was so respected by the league that when he switched law firms in 2015, the NFL followed him.

Abramoff's shenanigans in sabotaging the 1999 Internet Gambling Prohibition Act stiffened the resolve of anti-Internet gambling crusaders such as Frist, Goodlatte, and Republican Rep. Jim Leach of Iowa, all of whom would be involved, to some degree, in what became the quintessential anti-Internet gambling legislation: the Unlawful Internet Gambling Enforcement Act of 2006, commonly called UIGEA (pronounced You-Gee-Ah).

As various legislative means to stop Internet gambling were being crafted, Goodlatte, the staunch conservative, favored mounting a frontal assault to make Internet gambling explicitly illegal. Leach, a relatively more moderate Republican, reasoned that even with such a law on the books, enforcement would be difficult, if not impossible. So, Leach went a different route. His approach was to choke off the financial pipeline between the bettors and the betting websites. It was Leach's strategy of blocking financial transactions to offshore gambling companies that would be the de facto enforcement mechanism of UIGEA.

Frist, as Senate majority leader, was a key player. Because he could work the upper chamber of Congress, he could, if need be, help attach anti-Internet gambling legislation to a must-pass bill.

In September 2006 in Iowa, Leach's home state—where Frist needed to make headway for a run at the GOP presidential nomination two years later—the Tennessee senator announced at a hearing chaired by Leach that he wanted to do something about the scourge of Internet gambling, and he embraced Leach's approach.

By this time, Abramoff's misdeeds were making sensational headlines. The rogue lobbyist's questionable tactics in undermining previous anti-Internet gambling legislation, along with the corruption that followed, was used by Leach and others as further evidence of why online gambling needed to be stopped.

Despite even that momentum, it wasn't easy sledding for the anti-Internet gambling lawmakers and in the fall of 2006, the clock was running out on the 109th Congress. If the session expired without passing UIGEA, the anti-Internet gambling forces would be back to square one the following year. Initially, Frist wanted to attach UIGEA to a must-pass defense-appropriations bill, but tough-minded Senate Armed Services Committee Chairman Sen. John Warner, a Republican centrist from Virginia, was having no part of unrelated legislation being hitched to that bill.

Some within the Internet gambling industry, including the offshore companies making millions from online poker, thought they'd survived another legislative scare.

The SAFE Port Act

But Frist wasn't finished. After being rebuffed by Warner, he targeted legislation known as the SAFE Port Act (an acronym for Security and Accountability for Every Port). This was a piece of legislation that probably never would have come about had it not been for the 9/11 terrorist attacks that spawned heightened homeland-security concerns.

In the years following the attacks, a British firm controlled the operating contracts for a half-dozen major U.S. seaports, including in New York, New Jersey, Baltimore, New Orleans, Miami, and Philadelphia. In 2006, the UK firm was purchased by a company under the control of Dubai in the United Arab

Emirates, a Persian Gulf country that was allied with America in the war on terror.

Some moderate Republicans, including President George W. Bush, approved of the change in ownership. But more conservative elements of the GOP and some Democrats were unhappy about the prospects of ceding management of strategic American assets to foreign—especially Arab—control.

Clearly, opponents of the change in port control were drawing a distinction between a company with a British pedigree and one from the Middle East. Besides, there was also the fact that the Dubai company was actually state-controlled.

Bush tried to save the deal and went so far as to say that opposing the shift of port management to the Dubai company delivered a bad message to America's allies. "It sends a terrible signal to friends around the world that it's okay for a company from one country to manage the port, but not a country that plays by the rules and has got a good track record from another part of the world," Bush said.

But 9/11 was still fresh in the country's consciousness and Congress wasn't swayed by the president's rhetoric. Instead, the SAFE Port Act was hammered out to stop the Dubai deal.

11th-Hour Maneuvering

As the 109th Congress neared its conclusion, Senate Majority Leader Frist and his former floor counsel, ace NFL lobbyist Marty Gold, had their opportunity to finally get the anti-Internet gambling law known as UIGEA passed by attaching it to the port-security bill. However, tucked inside of UIGEA was a subsection that described activities that didn't fall under the definition of "bet or wager" and, as a result, were exempted from the financial-transaction restrictions (and consequently, the enforcement measures) faced by Internet-gambling operators.

One such exempted endeavor was "any activity governed by the securities laws ... for the purchase or sale of securities."

Insurance contracts also got a green light.

And just a few a sentences later, there was this: "... participation in any fantasy or simulation sports game."

To be sure, several important conditions had to be met in order for fantasy sports to remain clear of the enhanced enforcement mechanisms under UIGEA.

Some of the more important elements are:

- "All winning outcomes reflect the relative knowledge and skill of the participants and are determined predominantly by accumulated statistical results of the performance of individuals (athletes in the case of sports events) in multiple real-world sporting or other events."
- Prizes that go to the winners are established before the contest starts and the prizes are "not dependent on the number of participants or the amount of any fees paid by those participants."
- The winning outcomes are not based on the "score, point-spread, or any performance or performances of any single real-world team or any combination of such teams."
- The winning outcomes are not based "solely on any single performance of an individual athlete in any single real-world sporting or other event."

There's no question that the NFL was a driving force behind the passage of UIGEA. Indeed, Iowa Congressman Jim Leach called NFL lobbyist Marty Gold one of his "most important allies."

"I'd say the support for the bill was eighty-five percent the

NFL and fifteen percent the other leagues and the NCAA," Leach said.

So, pro football ostensibly led the push for UIGEA. Sports leagues—especially the NFL—were concerned about gambling activities that could corrupt game outcomes and their interest was, mainly, in stopping offshore sports wagering. But fantasy sports wasn't viewed as a danger. Indeed, sports leagues have viewed fantasy sports as imposing none of the existential threat of sports wagering, where rigged outcomes could jeopardize the league's very existence.

The benign attitude toward fantasy sports comes from the belief that such games are dependent on so many combinations of various athletes' performances on so many teams in so many contests that the fears of fixing or point-shaving attached to regular sports betting simply do not apply to fantasy sports.

However, those close to the NFL, along with Leach, the bill's sponsor, say that the pro football league had no strong feelings about the fantasy sports carve-out and did not advocate for it.

"That happened toward the very end," Leach said of the fantasy sports carve-out. "I had staffers come to me who said they had been told by other Congressional staffers that we needed to include [the carve-out] to get the bill passed. At the time, it seemed fairly innocent and certainly not the end of the world."

The rise of "daily fantasy sports betting," as Leach calls it, now gives him serious pause. "If I knew then what I know now," he said, "I would have tried to say something that made it more like it was the end of the world."

The NFL's reaction to the carve-out in 2006 was similar to that of Leach. The league acquiesced to the fantasy sports exemption, because the carefully constructed carve-out language didn't appear to substantially impact on UIGEA's overall objective, which was to eliminate most, if not all, risks that sports betting held for major league sports, never mind the arguably billions of dollars that benefit the leagues thanks to sports betting, legal and illegal.

So who or what group pushed for the fantasy sports carve-out in UIGEA?

Leach, now a visiting professor of law and a senior scholar at the University of Iowa School of Law, said in an interview that he simply doesn't know. All Leach claims to have known back in 2006 when he agreed to the carve-out was that staffers from other Congressional members had made it clear that it was an essential inclusion in UIGEA in order to get the bill to President Bush for a signature.

"I don't think you'll ever get beyond that," Leach said of trying to solve the mystery of who was behind the all-important carve-out for fantasy sports.

"Beyond-That" Possibilities

Prior to the passage of UIGEA in October 2006, there had been skirmishing over Internet gambling on the floor of the House of Representatives. Even as those arguments went on, it was evident that fantasy sports was being protected, just as it had been ever since the late 1990s.

Rep. John Conyers, a Michigan Democrat, entered into the Congressional record a news article that laid the fantasy sports carve-out at the feet of Major League Baseball and the fantasy sports industry—without attribution. More recently, in 2015, a *Washington Post* article also asserted that MLB advocated for the carve-out.

Paul Charchian, president of the Fantasy Sports Trade

Association, said his organization wasn't involved.

Bob Bowman, President and CEO of MLB Advanced Media, has been the baseball executive overseeing MLB's partnership with daily fantasy baseball. Bowman said he was unaware of a specific lobbying effort by MLB for the fantasy sports carve-out in UIGEA.

"It could have happened without my knowledge, but I was never part of any meeting or any discussion of any kind where I heard us discussing a unique and solitary lobbying effort in this capacity, either by management, meaning people who work in baseball, or by the owners," Bowman said.

It would have been more likely that a coalition of sports organizations would have pushed for such a carve-out, he said. "Obviously by 2000, fantasy sports had become part of the fabric of our land and obviously, it's not gambling, so a carve-out is appropriate. We'd be remiss if we didn't say a carve-out is appropriate. It certainly is."

In the absence of either a smoking gun or an admission on the fantasy sports carve-out, at least the question can be asked: What would be the motivations for any major sports organization to push for the fantasy sports language in UIGEA?

Well, there's no doubt that as the popularity of fantasy sports was growing (and it was in the midst of a surge by 2006), professional sports leagues recognized the synergy between their games and the fantasy sports "hobby." It didn't take a genius to intuit that fantasy sports encourages greater fan interest. And greater fan interest means higher TV ratings, more time spent on all kinds of sports websites (including those run by the leagues), and more money all around.

For example, sports news websites, such as CBS SportsLine, were rolling out editorial products aimed at the fantasy football crowd as early as the late 1990s. In 2009, the NFL launched a television channel, NFL RedZone, which unabashedly catered to fantasy interests by running non-stop game action of teams about to score.

Major League Baseball had introduced its own game called Beat the Streak in 2002 that was a precursor of daily fantasy sports. In Beat the Steak, fans are invited to pick one or two hitters a day and keep a hitting streak going that would eclipse Joe DiMaggio's legendary streak of 56 games. Anyone who could pull off the feat would win a huge prize. (In 13 years, no one has topped Joltin' Joe and the prize, at the time of this writing, has climbed to $5.6 million.) At one point, a variation of the Streak game shrank the contest to just one day as fans were challenged to pick 57 players who would all have to get a hit on the same day. Although Beat the Streak is a free game, MLB gets a healthy payback in fan interest and engagement.

The Legal Question

While Jim Leach has pointed out that the UIGEA carve-out does nothing to specifically legalize fantasy sports, the inference that many have taken from the carve-out has had tremendous impact. On daily fantasy websites, UIGEA is consistently rolled out to help answer the simple question: Is this legal? For instance, in its frequently asked questions, FanDuel says this:

In 2006, the Congress passed the UIGEA, which was designed to prevent financial institutions from accepting or sending payments related to illegal gambling over the Internet. The law includes a carve-out that clarifies the legality of fantasy sports. Specifically, it exempts entry fees for contests that meet the following definition from being considered bets or wagers.

FanDuel then quotes the law's exemption language.

Leach argues that UIGEA didn't "legalize" fantasy sorts as a gambling proposition. According to Leach, the bill simply did not subject fantasy sports to the enhanced enforcement mechanisms that apply to other activities; if a state attorney general or a federal prosecutor wants to use existing law to pursue a case against fantasy sports, nothing in UIGEA precludes that.

However, the reality is that because of the carve-out, UIGEA is viewed as having planted the seeds from which daily fantasy sports sprouted, despite the fact that UIGEA's overarching intent was to curb what Leach calls "a growing gambling ethos in America." And to a great extent, UIGEA was effective in eventually halting Internet poker.

As financial restrictions grew tighter and tighter after UIGEA's passage, some poker websites and the intermediaries that helped move cash between players and the gambling companies engaged in illegal subterfuges. That chicanery led to the famous federal crackdown on Internet poker on April 15, 2011, known in poker circles as Black Friday, the day that the major Internet poker sites in the United States were essentially put out of business.

Years after the passage of UIGEA, Leach said he was surprised when he started getting calls from reporters asking about daily fantasy sports. He was unaware that such for-cash daily contests existed to the extent that they do, and he was startled to find out the companies running those games had formed partnerships with major sports leagues.

And while many observers have credited UIGEA with providing fantasy sports with the famous carve-out that eventually led to an emergent DFS industry—as it surely did—it should not be forgotten that it was also the theatrics at that 1998 All-Star Game in Denver that helped alert lawmakers to how passionately fantasy sports fans felt about their beloved hobby.

Why Daily Fantasy Sports is *Not* Sports Gambling

Many comparisons have been made between DFS and traditional sports betting, but there are two significant differences between the two.

Outcome vs. Performance

Traditional sports wagers are determined by the *outcome* of an event—who wins and who loses. The bets are essentially binary in nature (it's a win-or-lose result), even in parlays that involve wagering on several teams and the one-off proposition bets on, say, whether a football player gains a certain number of yards.

How DFS differs: DFS results are determined by a combination of *performances* of several players participating in several events.

Betting against the House vs. Peer-to-Peer

In traditional sports wagering, the bettor plays against "the house." The bookmaker sets odds that, in the long run, assure that the house will make a profit.

How DFS differs: DFS is a peer-to-peer contest in which the participants are trying to win one another's money—much like poker and horse-race betting. The DFS website takes a percentage of the total amount of entry fees, with the remainder comprising the prize pool. It's true that a DFS company can lose money on a contest if it guarantees a payout that exceeds the total buy-ins, but that doesn't change the nature of the contest.

DFS as a peer-to-peer activity also contributes to the argument that it's a game of skill, because better players prevail over less accomplished opponents in the long run.

Perturbed Poker Players

At the time UIGEA was passed in 2006, poker enthusiasts were obviously upset over the trouble it portended. It took five years to come to pass and in 2011, the U.S. Department of Justice used UIGEA, in conjunction with bank-fraud and money-laundering laws, to shut down the major online poker websites on Black Friday.

Since then, online poker has been trying to make a comeback.

A reversal in the Department of Justice's reading of the Interstate Wire Act of 1961, which resulted in the DOJ narrowing its interpretation to pertain exclusively to sports betting, opened the door to states being able to offer online gambling under certain conditions. By 2015, three states had done so—New Jersey, Nevada, and Delaware. New Jersey and Delaware offer Internet poker and casino games, while Nevada allows online poker only. In all three cases, the revenue growth has been lower than initially projected. Also, expansion to other larger states has been slow. The glacial pace of more states adopting Internet poker has dampened hopes that there could someday be inter-state Internet poker playing through cross-state compacts.

Recently, with the uncertain trajectory that online poker has experienced in contrast to the exponential growth enjoyed by daily fantasy sports, the poker crowd often expresses strong resentment that daily fantasy sports has been given a free pass to operate in most of the country, largely without any regulation. At the same time, getting individual states to adopt online poker has been a Sisyphean effort—rolling a big rock up a steep hill.

When UIGEA was passed, poker advocates—angry about the 11th-hour maneuvering that led to the passage of the ban—

argued that the NFL's motivations were more about self-interest than righteousness. The league, some poker advocates claimed, viewed online poker as competition for the growing business of fantasy sports. So UIGEA, the poker argument went, was a way of eliminating one of its rivals.

Meanwhile, even before the Department of Justice dropped an anvil on online poker in 2011, daily fantasy sports websites had been trying to gain a foothold in the skill-games space. Their job was a tough one, because even though the term "fantasy sports" was familiar to the public, this new iteration was a far cry from its forbearers.

The Birth of Fantasy Sports

Like the source of the Nile River, the origin of fantasy sports engenders debate.

The now-accepted lore of fantasy sports identifies the original sport as football, its birthplace as a Manhattan hotel, and the time of delivery Nov. 3, 1962.

The godfather-midwife was the late Wilfred "Bill" Winkenbach, a minority owner of the Oakland Raiders, then in the upstart American Football League. With Winkenbach in the hotel that day were *Oakland Tribune* sportswriter Scotty Stirling and Raiders public relations man Bill Tunnell. The three were in New York because the Raiders were listlessly slogging through a three-game East Coast road trip that had seen them already lose in Buffalo to the Bills and in Boston to the Patriots. The next day, the Raiders would lose their eighth straight to the New York Titans on their way to a 1-13 campaign. However, all that would be insignificant compared to what the minority owner, the sports writer, and the PR guy were cooking up on a dreary day in the Big Apple.

The three wise men devised a set of rules that would become the template for untold numbers of fantasy sports leagues, which, in turn, would command billions of hours of attention from tens of millions of sports fans for generations.

In fact, it can be argued that Winkenbach had actually predated his own fantasy football league, which would become known by the long-winded moniker of the Greater Oakland Professional Pigskin Prognosticators League (GOPPPL). Before Winkenbach and company codified the rules for fantasy football in 1962, he'd already dabbled in fantasy-style games for baseball and golf in the late 1950s. But none of those make-believe sports notions had the organizational framework of Winkenbach's football-based brainchild.

The first draft of Winkenbach's new game was held in 1963 in his rec room in the Bay Area; it took eight hours and it set the tone for countless drafts to follow. The team owners with the first pick were the sports writer, Stirling, and a bar operator named Andy Mousalimas. They made then-Houston quarterback-kicker George Blanda the No. 1 overall pick in the first-ever fantasy football draft. In doing so, the sports writer and the bar operator passed up a running back named Jim Brown—thus suffering the first instance of buyers' regret in fantasy draft history.

Because of Winkenbach's connection to the Raiders, the first fantasy league had actual football people involved. And one of the participants in the league was a 24-year-old Raiders first-year talent scout named Ron Wolf. Wolf's team drafted quarterbacks Frank Ryan (Cleveland Browns) and Dick Wood (N.Y. Jets). Later as general manager of the Green Bay Packers, Wolf showed he'd learned a little something about picking quarterbacks when he swung a trade with Atlanta for a backup QB named Brett Favre. (Wolf, a member of the first-ever fantasy football league, was inducted into the Pro Football Hall of Fame in Canton, Ohio, in August 2015.)

The first fantasy football league didn't exactly catch on like wildfire, perhaps because it was a little unwieldy. The original draft was 18 rounds and included kick returners and defensive linemen. Its complexity probably strained the attention spans of casual fans, so its spread was slow.

As mentioned, the origins of fantasy sports are debatable and there's an alternate version of fantasy sports' genesis that predates the Winkenbach league. That version makes its way eventually to baseball's fantasy origins, the Rotisserie League.

In the baseball-based account of fantasy's birth, Harvard sociologist William Gamson, along with some friends, formulated a game called the National Baseball Seminar in 1960. The Gamson game was fairly streamlined. The only statistics it measured were RBIs and batting average for hitters and earned-run average and games won for pitchers.

The lineage of Gamson's invention features the involvement of original National Baseball Seminar team owner and noted cinema historian Robert Sklar, an academic adviser to a student named Dan Okrent. Sklar exposed Okrent to Gamson's concept.

Okrent, a celebrated author whose works include *The Ultimate Baseball Book*, later said in an oral history of fantasy baseball that ran in *ESPN the Magazine* that he wasn't much taken with Gamson's game at first, but that it "probably buried itself somewhere deep in my cerebellum and became the germ of my idea."

About two decades later, between the 1979 and 1980 baseball seasons, Okrent came up with the legendary baseball fantasy game known as The Rotisserie League, named after a Manhattan restaurant La Rotisserie Francaise. Okrent's goal was to allow owners to take charge of their teams with trades and roster moves.

Sklar, who died in 2011 in Spain, also became an original owner in the Rotisserie League.

"In the Gamson game, all you wanted were sluggers and high-average hitters," Sklar said in the ESPN fantasy sports oral history. "There were no trades. You just sat back and watched your numbers. Dan's intent was to make you a virtual GM."

More recently, Okrent has comically tried to distance himself from his imaginative creation, having said numerous times that he feels like J. Robert Oppenheimer, the father of the atomic bomb. In this case, you can call it inventor's regret.

From a personal point of view, Okrent said, his association with fantasy baseball has become far too strong. He quit participating in fantasy baseball twice. "The first time was in 1995 or '96 when people started following me into the men's room to talk about their fantasy baseball teams," he said. He got back into fantasy baseball in about 2000 or 2001. "But after seven or eight years, I found myself one day at the draft, sitting across from three people who were the offspring of guys who were in the original league, and I just said the heck with it."

Today, Okrent's affection for the game is stripped of fantasy involvement entirely and he's now merely a fan of his adult son's favorite team, the Chicago Cubs. "I think I'm reverting to my childhood when I was a Tigers fan," said Okrent, a Michigan native.

Whether it was Bill Winkenbach's football-based GOPPPL or Okrent's alternate baseball universe, the Rotisserie League, the main driver of participation in those early iterations of fantasy sports was pure love of the games, and the reward was mainly bragging rights—or conversely, avoiding the good-natured heckling of fellow league owners.

Thomas Hobbes, the 17th century English philosopher, wrote, "Every man is wont to please himself most with those things which stir up laughter ... by comparison of another man's defects and infirmities." And nowhere do folks seem to take more delight in a friend's shortcomings than in fantasy sports.

In the Winkenbach league, the last-place finisher got something that was a harbinger of the Lombardi Trophy given to the Super Bowl winner: a gleaming silver football, but with an ironic twist: The Winkenbach cellar-dweller trophy was a carved wooden football with a dunce cap.

In recent times, the stakes have been raised in terms of the bragging rights, or the opposite, mementoes of ignominy. One Omaha, Nebraska, fantasy football league recognizes its last-place finisher by requiring the loser to get a tattoo of the winner's, or the league's, choosing. The images have ranged from unicorns to Care Bears to Justin Bieber, all accompanied by the shameful tag, "Fantasy Loser."

However, for many fantasy participants, the rewards and penalties for fantasy triumph or defeat are more conventional—money either won or lost.

After creative minds like Bill Winkenbach and Dan Okrent provided the platforms for a new kind of sports-fan competition, the stage was obviously set for cash to become part of the equation. Even before the explosion in the daily fantasy sports play-for-cash phenomenon, season-long fantasy leagues were offering money contests. As previously mentioned, those contests of an earlier era required time-consuming statistics gathering, old-fashioned calculations and record-keeping, and communication was via telephone and the U.S. mail.

Those businesses banded together in 1998 to form the Fantasy Sports Trade Association. Also, some folks in that segment of the fantasy sports business were recruited as allies to fend off the early version of the Internet Gambling Prohibition Act, the law that could have stopped for-cash fantasy sports in its tracks long before UIGEA came along and helped insulate fantasy sports (if not inoculate it) from legal challenges.

One of the more prominent evolutionary descendants of the season-long cash fantasy games is the Fantasy Football Players Championship (FFPC). In its own words, the organization is "the old-fashioned kind [of fantasy football] where you draft your team at the beginning of the season and follow the action each week."

Some of the entry fees are decidedly low-stakes: $35, $77, $150, and $250. So-called mid-stakes are $350 and $500. It gets more serious with buy-ins at $750, $1,250, and higher. And finally, high-roller leagues have $5,000 and $10,000 buy-ins. For the FFPC's main event, the 2015 draft was scheduled to be held at Caesars Palace in Las Vegas, and the grand prize was advertised as $300,000.

However, even with that kind of glitz and big money now attached to season-long football fantasy, the admittedly "old-fashioned kind" of fantasy sports pales in comparison to the growing appeal and skyrocketing prize money that has been up for grabs in daily fantasy sports.

From UIGEA Springs Daily Fantasy

The short-duration iteration of fantasy sports, which involved picking a new team for each contest and having the outcome decided in as little as one day, was conceived shortly after President George W. Bush signed the legislation that enacted the Unlawful Internet Gambling Enforcement Act, along with the fantasy sports carve-out, in October 2006.

Kevin Bonnet, who coined the phrase "daily fantasy sports," launched the first short-duration fantasy sports website in June 2007. Prior to the passage of UIGEA, Bonnet had played online poker and was blogging about poker, but his experience in fantasy football was casual.

In his book, *Essential Strategies for Winning at Daily Fantasy Sports*, Bonnet wrote how he created Fantasy Sports Live in June 2007 as the first UIGEA-compliant DFS website after a careful reading of the Act.

"Suddenly there was an 'Ah Ha' moment for me, and the concept of Daily Fantasy Sports was born," Bonnet wrote in his book. "It hit me that the multiple players and multiple game requirements could be met with as little as two games held on the same day. Congress was thinking that this requirement would require a full season of traditional fantasy sports to be met. I was realizing that it actually allowed for a new type of legal sports betting based on fantasy sports."

Some of the operators now running the huge DFS websites would blanch at Bonnet's declaration that daily fantasy sports constitutes "legal sports betting based on fantasy sports." They try to distance themselves conceptually from gambling on actual games, but Bonnet had certainly discovered what would be the appeal of DFS to lots of potential participants.

Unfortunately for Bonnet, although he had the right idea, he wasn't effective in raising the sort of venture capital needed to sustain his business in the long run. Complicating matters was the rush of competition that entered the market as Bonnet was trying to get traction. Some of the early competition had backers with deeper pockets, but they saddled themselves with consumer-unfriendly elements, such as an extremely high rake, and those handicaps proved fatal.

However, daily fantasy sports did start to gain a foothold

and attract media attention. The odd twist of UIGEA setting the stage for this new type of fantasy contest was a delicious storyline and, through increased notice, the road was being paved for more companies to enter the market.

In 2009, Scotland-based FanDuel made its move into the U.S. and formed partnerships with mainstream media companies, such as Philly.com, the news website affiliated with the *Philadelphia Inquirer, Philadelphia Daily News*, and separately, the *New York Post*. Eventually, FanDuel established a New York headquarters.

In the first few years, from 2010 through 2013, a number of daily fantasy websites tried to establish beachheads and all of them were scrambling for funding. In 2012, Boston-based DraftKings made its arrival and was aggressive in capturing a substantial, if still minority, marketplace share.

Meanwhile, Fantasy Sports Live—the website that had started it all—was foundering and in June 2013 the website and customer base were sold to a competitor. "In hindsight, we needed to be much more aggressive at fundraising," Bonnet wrote.

While Fantasy Sports Live's Bonnet had a terrific idea that never got enough financial backing to make headway, FanDuel CEO Nigel Eccles managed to recover from a startup that was a flop.

In the years after UIGEA had opened the door to fantasy sports innovation, Eccles was running a company called Hubdub. Hubdub was a predictions website that allowed users to forecast future events in entertainment, politics, sports, and other areas. It wasn't a for-cash game; participants used play money. If there was a viable business model for Hubdub, it was in simply generating web traffic, which drove ad revenue. In 2009, Eccles and his partners were scrambling for a new idea when he was attending the South by Southwest Conference (SXSW), an ongoing music, film, and interactive festival, in Austin, Texas.

"Not a lot of people know that," Eccles said speaking on a panel at SXSW in 2015.

"The story was that myself and my four co-founders were here," Eccles continued. "We had a failing start-up. And we came out here and we said we need to come up with another idea. And we literally stood in front of a ... well, we stood in front of a shed. This is Austin. And we stuck Post-it notes on that shed until we came up with one that we kind of liked and that one was FanDuel."

Actually, a Hubdub fan helped open Eccles' eyes to the potential in something like fantasy football. But having the idea was one thing. Getting it financed was another.

If Bonnet's genius had been seeing the opening in UIGEA that allowed for something with the potential of daily fantasy sports, it was Eccles' gift that he was undaunted in making other people (with money) see the same thing. Eccles admitted he was lucky in so quickly getting the angel money that led to Hubdub, which, although a failure, led to FanDuel.

He struck up a fortuitous relationship with U.K.-based investment group PenTech Ventures that, along with the Scottish Investment Bank, helped with FanDuel's Series A funding in 2009. PenTech came through again in 2011 in a $4 million Series B round of funding when FanDuel was suffering through player lockouts in both the NFL and NBA.

FanDuel's Series B funding was especially difficult. Eccles said FanDuel pitched 85 investors in more than 100 meetings over nine months.

"I remember meeting a frog and thinking, 'Maybe I should kiss it. ... Who knows? He might turn into a [venture capitalist] and give me money," Eccles said in a talk at an Edinburgh technology conference.

Eccles received 50 turndown emails and no responses from another 35. "The experience was demoralizing," he said. "We closed the money a day before we would have gone bust."

In 2013, when FanDuel went looking for more investment cash, the proof of concept for DFS was well-established, at least as far as Eccles' company was concerned. Revenues had grown 500%. FanDuel had a better idea of how to acquire customers. And investors who'd flat-out turned down the DFS company two years earlier were saying, "Wow, this is a great business!"

Eccles had much less difficulty raising $11 million this time around. PenTech and Scottish Investment Bank were still standing with FanDuel, but a new investor raised eyebrows, Comcast Ventures, the venture-capital outfit associated with American communications powerhouse Comcast Corporation.

Having that type of association with a major U.S. media company—and one that coincidentally is heavily invested in sports programming—gave FanDuel substantial credibility that may have been even more valuable than the money.

A year later, just before the start of the 2014 NFL season, investment capital was raining on FanDuel and its new major competitor, DraftKings. FanDuel raised $70 million from Shamrock Capital Advisors and NBC Sports Ventures. That news came only days after DraftKings reported it had raised $41 million. When the cumulative VC money had been tallied in fall 2014, FanDuel had raised about $88 million in venture funding and DraftKings had attracted $75 million.

Boston-based DraftKings' rise has been mercurial. It started in 2012 with co-founders Matt Kalish and Paul Liberman and CEO Jason Robins. Robins has said the company began in Liberman's spare bedroom. Three months after launch,

DraftKings announced a $1.4 million investment in seed money.

DraftKings also has one of the most high-profile employees in the daily fantasy sports business, former professional poker player Jonathan Aguiar, who's cashed more than 30 times in World Series of Poker and World Poker Tour events.

When Aguiar joined DraftKings in 2012 as director of customer experience overseeing live events and VIP customer programs, it was clear that DraftKings was reaching out to a world that's often compared to daily fantasy sports—the Internet poker universe that had been badly damaged by the federal crackdown in 2011.

Ever since online poker was largely shut down in the United States, many players who enjoyed Internet poker have been looking for a replacement. Some became part of a poker diaspora that migrated to Mexico, Canada, and other countries where online poker was legal, allowing them to continue playing for a living. But many others couldn't make such a dramatic life change.

For some of them, daily fantasy sports holds a similar appeal. Many of the skills used in poker, in a broad sense, are translatable to DFS, such as numbers-crunching, game selection, and bankroll management. In addition, it can be played from the comfort of one's own home.

DraftKings has been unabashed in making the point that poker players and daily fantasy sports players fall in the same demographic pot. It has been a television sponsor of the World Poker Tour, whose broadcasts feature poker tournaments from exotic locales around the world. Draft Kings has offered seats in WPT events as prizes in some of its DFS contests. And in 2014 and 2015, the company was one of the major sponsors at the World Series of Poker in Las Vegas; it even had its own branded event as one of the more than 60 tournaments that make up the entirety of the WSOP.

As of this writing, the two major DFS websites, FanDuel and DraftKings, accept customers from 44 states. Both websites block potential customers in Arizona, Iowa, Louisiana, Montana, Washington, and very recently, Nevada. Some smaller websites block users from a handful of other states. In addition, StarsDraft, a division of online poker giant Amaya, operates in just four states. More recently, a number of states began reviewing their stances on DFS.

The combined $97 million in revenue for 2014 for the two major DFS companies broke down to $57 million for FanDuel and $40 million for DraftKings. While those were impressive numbers in a vacuum, some in the legal Internet gaming industry in New Jersey and Nevada scratch their heads as to why the DFS industry was held in awe for its $97 million, when in the same year, New Jersey's still-young Internet gaming industry grossed about $123 million and was considered an enormous disappointment.

The disparate perceptions regarding DFS and online gaming were tied to expectations. Among the three states with legal Internet gambling, New Jersey, because it has the largest population and offers both poker and casino games, has banked the most online gaming revenue, by far. But revenue projections for New Jersey when it started in 2013 were unrealistically high, so when the reality fell short of those forecasts, there was enormous disappointment.

In contrast, the DFS revenue numbers came out of the blue, so they were perceived as a smashing success. And in terms of percentage gains, they *were* fantastic.

DraftKings' revenue shot from $3 million in 2013 to $40 million in 2014. FanDuel also had astronomical growth in revenue, going from a little more than $14 million in 2013 to $57 million in 2014. It was estimated that about 2 million people participated in daily fantasy sports in 2014. Revenue and participation numbers for 2015 are sure to be much higher.

However, despite all the glowing reports regarding daily fantasy revenues and the swelling ranks of customers eager to play, there was still one thing that DFS websites lacked.

In 2014, neither of the two major daily fantasy sports websites had reported making a profit.

Chapter 2

Getting Started

This book doesn't require you to start at the beginning and read through to the end, like a novel or persuasive non-fiction. Certainly, you can read it cover to cover in beginning-to-end fashion. But you can also dip in to take from it only what you need most to become a more informed fantasy sports player.

For instance, if you just picked up this book after winning, say, a $50,000 DFS contest (and congratulations if you did!) in order to learn about the tax implications of the prize money, without wading through the chapters on specific sports, you can do so (see the Appendix). Or if you've been reading the DFS forums online and you're wondering about some of the lingo being slung (such as GPPs and FPPGs and MPEs), you can go right to the Glossary for a quick interpretation.

Subsequent chapters contain in-depth discussions about how to tackle specific sports, along with tips that can give you an advantage when competing against other DFS players. NFL football is, by far, the most popular sport for daily fantasy sports; since the NFL attracts the most players, this book places the greatest concentration on pro football. Football is followed by Major League Baseball and the National Basketball Association. Most DFS websites offer NHL contests and some include golf, college football, and college basketball. You can even occasionally find mixed martial arts, Premiere League

Soccer, and auto racing. But participants who venture into the niche segments of daily fantasy should be versed in those sports if they hope to survive.

Before you worry about strategy, though, you have to know how to play the game. This brief chapter provides a quick overview of the participation process. It's presented step by step, in the proper order to follow. All of these areas are covered in depth later in the book.

Website

The first order of business is choosing a website and that probably means either DraftKings or FanDuel (though other credible alternatives exist and will materialize). My recommendation is that after you experience one, try the other, then stick with whichever seems to fit your style.

Register

The next step is signing up. You may be asked to provide your name, and you'll definitely have to provide an email address, username, and password, and verify your state and age.

Deposit (Optional)

Unless you deposit money into an account on the website, you'll be able to play only free games, which is okay if that's what you want to do—many novices try a few free contests first to get a feel. However, if you're ready to play for real, you should be prepared to deposit money. As of this writing, you can make deposits with major credit cards and PayPal. Like most online accounts, you can see how much money you have on deposit.

There's other information, such as a log of your transactions.

Promo Codes

It's been routine for the larger websites to offer sign-up bonuses, so when you deposit, be sure to use one of the promo codes mentioned in the advertisements. Often, you can get the bonus only when you deposit for the first time. Go to LasVegasAdvisor.com to find promo codes for all major DFS websites and explanations of how they work.

Contests

Next stop, the lobby. Each website has a lobby where the contests offered are listed. It tells you what contests are available to play, along with other important information—in the example below, the entry fee, the amount of the prize pool, and the number of entries in the contest.

Featured	NFL	NBA	CFB	SOC	NHL	PGA	NAS	MMA
Create a Contest	Create a Lineup		Strategy & Research		Refer a Friend			

Contest	Entry Fee	Total Prizes	Entries
NFL $6M Millionaire Magic ($1M to 1st)	$20	$6,000,000	150.5K/343.5K
NFL MASSIVE $25 Double Up ($800,000 Guaranteed)	$25	$800,000	18.5K/36.2K
NFL $700K Blitz ($100,000 to 1st)	$300	$700,000	796/2590
NFL $1.25M Gridiron-Action ($1.25 Million Guaranteed)	$3	$1,250,000	235.3K/479.1K
15M Fantasy Football World Champ 2x Qualifier #85 & #86	$3	2 Prizes + $17,000	23.2K/68.6K
NFL $500K Slant [$500,000 Guaranteed]	$9	$500,000	21.5K/63.8K
NBA $1M Return to the Court [$100,000 to 1st]	$20	$1,000,000	57/57.2K

The array of games can be overwhelming, but take your time and study what's available. Later, you can decide how much you want to play for and which contests are right for you.

Contest Types

Cash Games
Head-to-head, 50/50, double-up, triple-up: These are best for beginners (but avoid head-to-head).

Multipliers
5x (quintuple-up), 10x, 40x: Intermediates should play sparingly. Beginners should avoid.

Tournaments, Leagues, GPPs
Experts should play multiple entries when permitted, especially if an overlay exists. Beginners and intermediates should play sparingly (as if buying a lottery ticket).

Satellites, Qualifiers, Steps
All should play sparingly with fingers crossed.

The Lineup
Once you pick a contest, the fun begins—assembling a lineup. Study the rules and tinker with different combinations. Typically, you have to stay within a certain salary cap, so it's like putting together a puzzle. The players and their salaries are displayed to start.

| Lobby | Upcoming | Live | History | Earn Cash | Help ∨ |

| ALL | TB@ WAS | CLE @STL | HOU @MIA | NYJ @NE | PIT @KC | MIN @DET | OAK @SD | DAL @NYG | PHI @CAR | BAL@ ARI |

Available Players   Download players list   **Your Lineup**
$50,000
Salary Remaining

| All | QB | RB | WR | TE | K | D | ⚲ Find a Player |

🔒 Lineup locks @1:00PM

NAME		FPPG	Played	Game	▼ Salary
QB	Tom Brady	25.5	5	NYJ@NE	$8,500 ⊕
QB	Andrew Luck	18.9	4	NO@IND	$7,600 ⊕
QB	Ben Roethlisberger	16.8	3	PIT@KC	$6,800 ⊕
QB	Drew Brees	17.2	5	NO@IND	$6,700 ⊕
QB	Carson Palmer	20.2	6	BAL@ARI	$6,700 ⊕
QB	Cam Newton	21.9	5	PHI@CAR	$6,600 ⊕
QB	Matt Ryan	16.5	6	ATL@TEN	$6,500 ⊕
QB	Philip Rivers	20.6	6	OAK@SD	$6,300 ⊕
QB	Eli Manning	17.9	6	DAL@NYG	$6,200 ⊕
QB	Derek Carr	16.9	6	OAK@SD	$6,200 ⊕

QB	Add Player
RB	Add Player
RB	Add Player
WR	Add Player
WR	Add Player
WR	Add Player
TE	Add Player
FLEX	Add Player
DST	Add Player

As you make your selections, your roster forms on the screen with your salary-cap information displayed (in the example below, there are two positions to fill with $8,900 in cap space remaining).

| Lobby | Upcoming | Live | History | Earn Cash | Help ∨ |

| ALL | TB@ WAS | CLE @STL | ATL @TEN | HOU @MIA | NYJ @NE | NO @IND | PIT @KC | MIN @DET | OAK @SD | BAL @ARI |

Available Players   Download players list   **Your Lineup**
$8,900
Salary Remaining

| All | QB | RB | WR | TE | K | D | ⚲ Find a Player |

🔒 Lineup locks @1:00PM

NAME		FPPG	Played	Game	▼ Salary
WR	DeAndre Hopkins	21.8	6	HOU@MIA	$6,200 ⊕
WR	Julio Jones	19.7	6	ATL@TEN	$6,100 ⊕
QB	Tom Brady	25.5	5	NYJ@NE	$6,000 ⊕
WR	Odell Beckham Jr.	15.4	6	DAL@NYG	$6,000 ⊕
RB	Le'Veon Bell	19.2	4	PIT@KC	$5,900 ⊕
QB	Anderw Luck	18.9	4	NO@IND	$5,900 ⊕
RB	Adrian Peterson	14.6	5	MIN@DET	$5,700 ⊕
RB	Devonte Freeman	26.3	6	ATL@TEN	$5,600 ⊕
RB	Arian Foster	13.6	3	HOU@MIA	$5,400 ⊕
RB	Doug Martin	18.4	3	TB@WAS	$5,300 ⊕

QB	Cam Newton	$6,600 salary
RB	Lamar Miller	$5,600 salary
RB	Latavius Murray	$5,400 salary
WR	Brandin Cooks	$4,800 salary
WR	Willie Snead	$4,900 salary
WR	Amari Cooper	$7,000 salary
TE	Rob Gronkowski	$6,800 salary
FLEX	Add Player
DST	Add Player

How Daily Fantasy Points are Earned

How fantasy points are earned differs from sport to sport and site to site and they're covered in detail in the chapters on the individual sports. But here's a representative example.

A wide receiver catches a short pass deep in his own territory, then breaks away and runs 80 yards for a touchdown. If you happen to "own" that receiver (he's in your DFS lineup for a contest), you'd earn points as follows. On DraftKings, it's a 15-point play: 6 points for the touchdown, 8 for the 80-yard run, and 1 for the reception. On FanDuel, it's 14.5 points: 6 for the TD, 8 for the 80 yards, and a half-point for the reception.

Follow Along

As soon as the real games start, you can follow ("sweat") the progress of your fantasy team on a computer or mobile device while the live action unfolds. Your fantasy team's totals change almost instantly as your players accumulate real stats and you can see your fantasy team's progress on your contest's leaderboard.

Withdrawals

Withdrawing funds from DFS accounts has been easy as of this writing. Depending on the website, the money may be returned via credit card, PayPal, or mailed check. You may be asked to supply a Social Security number, depending on your net winnings, and there may be a minimum-amount requirement.

Sweat the Bet

One of the entertainment elements of playing daily fantasy sports is known in gambling parlance as "the sweat."

"Sweating" a game means following the action and awaiting the results. In DFS, as in all forms of sports betting, sweating is the principal adrenaline rush—when the real games begin and the athletes start piling up fantasy points.

In a stroke of amazing technological wizardy, DFS participants can follow the progress of their fantasy players and teams in real time on the websites. For instance, in football, as soon as one of your running backs gains, say, 10 yards (which usually equals 1 fantasy point), you'll see his total, and the total score of your entire lineup, change automatically. You'll also see your team's position in the contest change relative to your competition's.

How does it work? The real-time action (touchdowns, yards, home runs, strikeouts, baskets, assists, and all the rest) is tallied by statistics companies, transferred to the DFS websites where it's converted into fantasy points, assigned to the appropriate athletes, and finally reflected in the standings of each fantasy contest. All within seconds.

The various DFS websites have their own formats for following the action and some are better than others. In fact, the experience of sweating the games can be one of the reasons you choose one DFS website over another.

Not surprisingly, often it all comes down to the last few minutes of the last game and that's when DFS players get the same adrenaline jolt that poker players do when they spike their miracle card on the river or blackjack players feel when the dealer turns over the card that busts the dealer's hand.

Chapter 3

Basic Concepts

In this chapter, we'll cover numerous essential topics that anyone with an interest in participating in DFS needs to know about, regardless of which websites they choose or what sports they decide to play.

Traditional vs. Daily Fantasy Sports

As already mentioned, daily fantasy sports incorporates a twist on the decades-old sports-fan hobby of season-long fantasy contests. Many sports fans are familiar with the older style, where a bunch of friends get together before the NFL or MLB seasons begin and conduct their own draft, similar to the NFL's annual draft of college players, known generically as a "snake draft."

In a season-long NFL fantasy league, if the player with the first draft selection chooses Green Bay Packers quarterback Aaron Rodgers, then no one else can pick Rodgers. The player with the last pick in the first round usually has the first pick in the second round. The draft continues until all the fictional team rosters are filled, then the make-believe teams compete against one another throughout the season.

In season-long fantasy, game scores are determined by

points accrued through player performances—X amount of points are awarded for touchdowns in football or home runs in baseball and so forth. Players can be dropped and added and traded. Sometimes the league participants will ante money at the outset and at the end of the year, the prize pool is divvied according to the league standings. Often, the most cherished prize for winning an old-style fantasy league is bragging rights.

Lately, that older fantasy sports hobby has been labeled "traditional fantasy" to distinguish it from the more recent version, commonly called "daily fantasy sports." As it turns out, the name daily fantasy sports—the term that industry pioneer Kevin Bonnet is credited with coining—in the strictest sense is a misnomer. After all, NFL games aren't played daily, so in the case of the most popular DFS sport, participation is weekly, not daily.

When it comes to baseball, basketball, and hockey, the term daily fantasy sports is more applicable. In trying for a one-name-fits-all generic title, some within the DFS industry use the less-common description of "one-day fantasy sports," but even that's not absolutely accurate; when participating in NFL contests, the fantasy competition could stretch across NFL games being played Thursday through Monday. To be most accurate, DFS should probably be called "short-duration fantasy sports," but, that's not particularly catchy. So, daily fantasy sports or DFS it remains.

Daily fantasy sports apparently made its debut in 2007 with the website Fantasy Sports Live, which later ceased operation. Widely believed to have popularized the DFS concept is the company now known as FanDuel, which began operations in 2009 when it was based in Scotland.

In just about every significant way, the dissimilarities between daily fantasy sports and traditional (season-long) fantasy sports are about as stark as the differences between Caesars Palace and a fire-hall bingo game.

The staging place for DFS isn't someone's rec room where the fantasy football draft is held over pizza and beer. Instead, the daily fantasy universe exists in cyberspace, where participants come together on one of the websites that offer and conduct the contests. The two biggest daily fantasy sports websites, as the DFS industry is reaching its adolescence moving into 2016, are FanDuel and its chief rival, DraftKings. But there are plenty of competitors and more are expected. In 2015, Yahoo launched a daily fantasy website and mobile app.

The Websites

Once a prospective participant reaches a DFS website, he or she is encouraged to register, a process familiar to anyone in the 21st century doing business on the Internet.

If it's you, you'll be asked for a name and email address, then required to set up a username and password, all standard operating procedure in the virtual world. Many DFS websites allow newcomers to participate in for-fun-only contests for free, which is a good way to get a feel for the rules of the games. If you want to play for money, a deposit is required and newbies should find the process relatively straightforward.

Among the ways of funding a daily fantasy sports website account, the most simple is with a major credit card. You can also transfer money through popular online payment systems, including PayPal. The money in your DFS website account is applied toward competing in the contests.

The starting point of a DFS website is its lobby, where the available contests are listed. Often, filters allow participants to narrow the selection of contests by sport, type, amount of money required to play (the buy-in), amount of money offered in the prize pool, and maximum number of players allowed.

Deciding where to play is a fundamental decision. Most of the specific discussions in this book relate to the nuances of the two major DFS websites, FanDuel and DraftKings.

A swarm of smaller DFS websites hold onto tiny fractions of the market. Many of these sites attempt to create some meaningful differentiator in the games they offer that, they hope, gives them some special appeal.

Some newer DFS virtual products aren't websites at all and exist only as mobile-device apps.

Frankly, the best thing many of these smaller websites can hope for is to be bought by a larger company. That has already happened in daily fantasy's short history. For instance, a relatively prominent DFS website, DraftStreet, was absorbed by DraftKings in a fairly high-profile move in 2014. That type of consolidation could continue under any number of circumstances.

Scoring Differences

In mid-2015, FanDuel was offering daily fantasy contests in NFL, MLB, NBA, NHL, and college football and basketball. At the same time, DraftKings offered contests in the same sports, plus golf, NASCAR, MMA, soccer, and eSports.

It's important to understand that the scoring rules for the two websites differ enough that you should tailor your selection of players according to which website you're playing on. Those differences also have an impact on the information you consider when preparing to select rosters. Thus, you have to be able to distinguish whether the expert advice you're getting, either on TV/radio or the Internet, is equally relevant to both FanDuel and DraftKings, or whether it's more applicable to one than the other.

For example, a major difference between the two for the average participant is in the pricing of the athletes. For the NFL, the total fictional salary cap for assembling a roster of nine positions on FanDuel is $60,000, whereas the total salary cap for assembling a nine-position roster on DraftKings is typically $50,000.

Another difference is in the notional salaries the websites assign to each player. When a player is priced far differently on the two major DFS websites, that may be an indication of a "pricing inefficiency." In other words, one of the websites is underpricing the player or the other one is overpricing him. If he's being underpriced, that's an opportunity to get him at a bargain.

The important takeaway is that the websites each have their own algorithms for valuing players and sometimes those algorithms produce flawed player values. After all, if a player is the fifth-highest-priced receiver on one website and the 10th-highest on another (and it does happen), one of those websites has missed the correct value on that player. All you have to do is figure out which one.

Which Website is for You?

Newer DFS participants should try out both FanDuel and DraftKings by playing the free games that both offer. However, a more accurate way to get a feel for the two programs is to play real-money contests at the lowest price points. That's generally a better gauge, because your opponents will play more competitively when there's money on the line, even if it's a tiny amount. DraftKings has offered contests for as little as 25¢. FanDuel's lowest buy-in is $1.

There's some evidence about how the websites skew in terms of which is more hospitable for beginning DFS participants and which is considered to have more appeal to experienced DFS players.

FanDuel has expressly held itself out as a website that wants to appeal to a more general clientele and the more casual sports fan. Two policy instances bolster that contention. For one, FanDuel provides a database that shows levels of each customer's participation (DraftKings doesn't provide that information). Arguably, such information helps beginning players more easily identify experienced players in order to avoid highly unfavorable competition. Secondly, FanDuel limits, to some degree, participation in its contests, while DraftKings has no limits. Some DFS professionals submit hundreds, even thousands, of entries in multiple contests over a single NFL weekend to help even out their variance, meaning the ups and downs of outcomes, so that their net profits are more consistent.

As of this writing, FanDuel limits single-user participation to 1,000 contests per day. For the 2015 season in baseball, the FanDuel limit was 750 contests per day. For the 2014-15 NBA season, the daily limit was 500. For the 2014-15 NHL season, there was no limit.

Another circumstance that encouraged experienced daily fantasy players to gravitate to DraftKings, at least during the 2014 NFL season, was its reputation for more equity overlays than FanDuel in large tournaments. An overlay occurs when a guaranteed prize pool exceeds total buy-ins, a condition that gives participants a theoretical edge, assuming they play at an average skill level. Conversely, FanDuel practices extreme prudence in reducing the occasions where overlays may occur, and that's obvious to DFS customers.

While overlays appear to be a good thing for customers on the surface, FanDuel argues that they attract more experienced players to DraftKings and, in the long run, create a less favorable overall climate for the more casual DFS participants.

Anatomy of an Overlay

In a tournament or contest of any kind, the fundamental measure of its playability is equity. If a DFS contest collects $10 from 100 players and distributes $1,000 in prize money, it would be an even-equity contest. If the site takes out 10% (rake), it becomes 90% equity. On the other hand, if a contest has a $1,000 prize guarantee and only 70 players show up, that creates an "equity overlay," in that every player has an average expected return of $14.29 ($1,000/70) for putting up only $10.

To identify an overlay, first add up all the money being paid in prizes. If some of the prizes are non-cash, e.g., a trip somewhere that you want to go, then put a value on that trip and add it into the total. If a non-cash prize holds no value for you, don't include it. Divide the prize total by the number of entrants and if the resulting number is more than the entry fee, it's an overlay.

Overlays show up regularly in daily fantasy contests, especially on smaller sites attempting to build traffic. You can usually identify them easily. Or monitor a website that routinely identifies overlays, such as SuperLobby.com.

Indeed, even some extremely experienced DFS players concede that the competition on DraftKings is more intense. On the other hand, some believe the user experience on Draft-Kings is superior; it's easier to navigate through an in-progress contest to track where you stand during the contest, and re-search information on individual players is a bit more extensive.

A benefit that DraftKings has been offering newer DFS participants has been its "Beginner" contests. A new player can join DraftKings Beginner contests for his first 50 contests in each sport. That would suggest easier competition, at least for a while. FanDuel has had a similar program called "Rookie Leagues," but the eligibility duration has been far shorter than the 50-contest period at DraftKings.

Aesthetically, the FanDuel website has a lean minimalist look, while DraftKings is splashier. Both sites have added features, such as analysis tools and editorial content.

Finally, it's a good idea to try out at least one of the smaller websites, such as Yahoo, FantasyAces, FantasyDraft, or DraftPot. You may find some attractive promotions, softer competition, or a more appealing type of contest.

The Salary Cap

Among the chief differences between season-long and daily fantasy sports is how teams are assembled.

As most sports fans know, the absolute highlight of any season-long fantasy sports league is The Draft. Highly social and sometimes comically competitive, season-long fantasy drafts are often marked by parties and reams and reams of draft cheat sheets and alternative scenarios. A more important point is that season-long fantasy leagues typically use the snake draft, which is exactly the same as fans are accustomed to seeing in the NFL's annual draft of college players.

Daily fantasy sports drafts generally don't, and couldn't, work that way. Snake drafts are too time-consuming and cumbersome and they involve getting a group of people together to go through the pool of players one by one. Instead, DFS contests normally begin with a "salary-cap draft," in which each owner has the same theoretical amount of money to work with—say, $50,000. With that limited amount of money, the player has to assemble a team made up of a certain number of positions. For football, both FanDuel and DraftKings require that nine positions be filled.

Each NFL player (and each entire-team defense/special teams, which you have to buy as a whole) is assigned a salary figure. For example, quarterback Aaron Rodgers might be assigned a salary of $10,000, the highest of any quarterback. Selecting Rodgers would leave $40,000 to spend on the other eight positions, or an average of $5,000 per.

Clearly, the more salary-cap dollars a fantasy owner spends on one or two star players, the less money is available to fill out the lineup. So somewhere in the hypothetical Aaron Rodgers lineup, there has to be some scrimping at other positions, and therein resides the challenge.

A major difference between a snake draft and a salary-cap draft is that more than one team owner can have the same player in his lineup. So if lots of team owners select Peyton Manning in the same contest, the difference between various teams comes down to the other positions. In some respects, playing DFS is like assembling a puzzle where the pieces all have to fit.

Salary-cap management—when to splurge on stars and when to save on players who are good values relative to their assigned salaries—is at the heart of competing successfully in daily fantasy sports.

A term of art in DFS regarding the notional salaries assigned to players is "inefficiencies," a fancy word for mistakes. As mentioned briefly earlier, a pricing inefficiency is the perception that a player is priced either too high or too low. Each website has its own secret recipes, or algorithms, for figuring out how a player should be priced within the overall salary cap, taking into consideration such factors as past performance and the matchup against the next opponent. It's a daunting task and an inexact science.

That the websites will over-value some players and under-value others is a good thing, certainly from a game-playing angle and perhaps even from a legal one. The possibility of inefficiencies in some players' salaries is part of the fun and the challenge of DFS as a game. And importantly, this same possibility, which better DFS participants can recognize and take advantage of, bolsters the argument that daily fantasy sports is, indeed, a game of skill, a key concept in many jurisdictions regarding presumed legality.

You'll learn much more about managing the salary cap to maximize your chances of winning money later in this book.

Types of Contests

As already mentioned, the starting point for most daily fantasy websites is their respective lobbies. That's where you'll find the menu of contests that the websites offer. Often, it's a very full menu and it can be, at first glance, confusing. This section provides a summary of contests offered on the major daily fantasy websites; more extensive explanations regarding contest type are covered in the individual-sports chapters.

True to the name *daily* fantasy sports, some contests do start and end in one day, but that isn't always the case. Many contests run over several days, as in a Thursday through Monday period for an NFL contest. The contests posted in the website lobby can also be for sports events being played at some future date.

While contest duration is the most obvious departure for daily fantasy sports from traditional fantasy, another major difference is the competitors. In traditional fantasy, the participants are often friends who have been battling it out in the same league for years, sometimes for decades. But in daily fantasy, opponents are short-term. They're usually strangers (although frequent players get to know one another as familiar screen names) and the competitors are assembled in cyberspace as they enter a competition. Note, however, that DFS websites offer the option of a group of friends getting together and competing in their *own* league, whether it's a cozy competition for two or some larger number.

Here are brief descriptions of the most common types of contests.

Cash Games—These are the simplest games. The most basic is the head-to-head contest where two DFS participants compete against each other.

Other typical cash games are "50/50s" and "double-ups." In a 50/50 contest, half of the participants with the best scores "qualify for a prize." To qualify for a prize is "to cash" and in a 50/50, the award money is slightly less than double the buy-in. For example, the prize in a contest with a $10 buy-in is typically $18. It doesn't matter how high a participant finishes; everyone who earns a prize gets the same amount. In a double-up, all players who cash also get a flat amount—double the buy-in. Slightly less than half the field will cash in a double-up.

Multipliers—In these contests, the prize for those who qualify is some multiple of the buy-in. For instance, in a triple-up with a buy-in of $25, all entrants who qualify for cash prizes receive $75. Like in the cash games, the prizes in multipliers are a flat amount. Several variations of multipliers include prizes four times, five times, and 10 times the buy-ins.

Tournaments/Leagues/GPPs—These are contests where a smaller percentage of participants qualify for a prize than in cash games, but the top prizes are much larger. For example, in a 10-person league, the prize structure might pay the top three scorers at rates of 50%, 30%, and 20% of the pool. Or a daily fantasy tournament could start with a massive field of 20,000 entrants, the top 20% will cash, and the winner will get a jackpot-sized award.

The initials "GPP" stand for guaranteed prize pool; the website guarantees that the prize pool will be a pre-determined amount regardless of how many entrants there are.

Satellites/Qualifiers—These represent a category of contests—sometimes at modest buy-ins, sometimes at hefty buy-ins—where the prize is an entry into another contest in which the eventual prize is of substantial value.

For instance, a satellite with a $2 buy-in and a total of 11 participants might feature a top prize for a single winner that is a virtual voucher, ticket, or token worth $20. Moving ahead, that $20 virtual voucher might be good for an entry into yet another qualifier where the top finishers receive a second virtual voucher into a still larger-buy-in tournament: Perhaps the grand-finale tournament with a $200 buy-in and a top prize in the thousands or tens of thousands of dollars. And it all started with a $2-buy-in satellite.

Satellites played a big part in the explosion of online poker, as thousands of players put up small buy-ins for a chance to climb the ladder and win entry into big tournaments, such as the Main Event of the World Series of Poker. Just such a scenario played out for everyman poker player Chris Moneymaker, who parlayed a $39 online qualifier into $2.5 million when he won the WSOP Main Event in 2003. Moneymaker's victory is credited (along with other factors, including the Internet, televised poker, and the hole-card cam) with setting off the poker boom.

A similar story unfolded in 2015 with Max Steinberg, who entered a $27 online satellite, won it, and rode it all the way up to win entry into the WSOP Main Event. The satellite wasn't on a poker site; it was a qualifier at DraftKings, which had a cross-promotion arrangement with the WSOP. Amazingly, Steinberg emerged from a field of 6,420 players to make the "November Nine" final table and eventually finished fourth for a prize of $2,615,361. While Steinberg possesses a decidedly more impressive gambling résumé than did Moneymaker—his reputation is that of a very competent DFS *and* poker player— his ascension through daily fantasy sports to nearly become a poker World Champion provides another valuable marketing hook for the DFS industry and DraftKings, in particular.

While satellites are generally thought of as a low-cost way to eventually win mega-prizes, some qualifiers can be fairly expensive with buy-ins in the hundreds of dollars.

The Rake

Businesses that specialize in financial transactions often make their money by charging a commission for facilitating a trade or creating a marketplace. When you buy and sell stocks, the brokerage house that helps execute that transaction charges a fee that's added onto the purchase of the stock if you're a buyer or subtracted from the sale proceeds if you're a seller.

Occasionally, the commission is less direct. When you walk into a casino in Las Vegas and place a bet on your favorite team in the sports book, the casino's commission is built into the wager. Here's an example.

Two players stroll into a Las Vegas casino and head to the sports book to bet on a game between the Green Bay Packers and New England Patriots. The game is considered an absolutely even contest, so neither team is giving or getting points. As a wagering proposition, the game is called a "pick" (or "pick 'em") in sports-betting parlance.

One player wants to bet on the Packers and would like to win $100. In placing the bet, the casino requires the bettor to risk $110. Meanwhile, the second bettor wants to wager on the Patriots. He also risks $110 to win $100. Assuming the game doesn't end in a tie, one of them will win $100 (and have the initial $110 returned) and the other will lose $110. The casino profits $10.

In poker, it works a little differently, but the result is the same. Whether in a bricks-and-mortar or Internet poker room, the casino or website takes some amount of money from each pot as a fee for dealing the game.

The fee charged by the stockbroker, the sports book, or the poker room has many names: commission (stocks); juice and vigorish (sports betting); rake (poker); takeout (horse racing). It all amounts to the same thing. Some businesses just use a fancier vocabulary for the appearance of propriety.

The business model for daily fantasy sports is also rooted in collecting a fee from every paid entry. For the record, the DFS companies hate the word "rake," because they desperately want to distance themselves from any association with gambling or its trappings. In some DFS circles, a new term of art has come into the lexicon to reference the house fee; the term is "margin." Makes it sound a little Wall Street-like, doesn't it? But lately, even the highest officials within DFS have lapsed into the habit of calling the fee they charge for their games a "rake," so that's how I refer to those commissions here.

Frankly, it doesn't matter what it's called. For a DFS player, the percentage of cash that's siphoned out of a prize pool is an obstacle to making a profit. The better informed a DFS player is about the rake, the better off he or she will be.

As a rule of thumb, the prevailing rake in DFS is about 10%—a convenient number to remember. It can be a little higher or lower, depending on the type of contest (more on that later), but 10% is a good number to use when considering what you have to do to make money at daily fantasy sports.

On the continuum of skill-based risk-reward activities where some third-party agent facilitates the action, the DFS rake falls in the middle to high-middle range. Among the highest commissions charged are in horse racing, where the takeouts typically run from 16% to as high as 25%. Sort of makes sense that horse players are going the way of the dinosaur, doesn't it? Some of the lowest vigorish rates are found in sports betting, which generally come in at 4.55%, although sports betting is not peer-to-peer. Consider the Packers-Patriots wager described earlier, in which two people wagered a combined $220. One won, the other lost. The house retained $10 ($10 divided by $220 equals 4.55%). In poker, the rake varies according to the game and size of the pot, but it generally ranges from 2.5% to 10%.

What this means for the DFS player is that a win rate of 56% (55.6%, to be more precise) is required to make a small profit in contests where almost half the entrants double their money. The math on what it takes to do a little better than break even is pretty elementary. Let's say you enter a DFS contest with nine other players and each of you pays an entry fee of $10. That's a total of $100 that the players contribute to fund the game. The DFS website takes $10 from the $100 prize pool as its commission, a.k.a. the rake, leaving $90 in the prize pool.

The top five finishers will each get an equal amount of money, $18 (the original $10 fee is returned, plus $8 in winnings). If you play this type of game 100 times and place among the top five finishers 56 times (for a win rate of 56%), your winnings will be $448 (56 times $8). For the 44 times when you fail to cash, your losses will amount to $440 (44 times $10).

Bottom line: Over the course of 100 DFS 50/50 contests in which you cash 56 times and whiff on 44 tries, your profit will be $8—or 8¢ per contest. As those old poker players were fond of saying about their game, "It's a hard way to make an easy living."

Still, as a peer-to-peer game of skill, there really is money to be made in daily fantasy sports, just as there is in stock trading and poker, for those willing to put in the effort to become educated about the athletes, study the statistics, and apply some math in assembling the optimal lineup for the right contest.

Taking a closer look at the DFS rake, on occasion, it can be higher than the usual benchmark of 10%, as well as considerably lower. A good online resource for tracking the rake at various DFS websites is SuperLobby.com. This website serves several functions, including listing the rakes and overlays for all contests on major DFS websites.

You'll learn on SuperLobby that the rake can run from 12% to 15% for contests that feature very small buy-ins and high payouts for the top finishers. For instance, some DFS contests require an investment of no more than 25¢. That's right, just *two bits*, as they say in the old movies. And the highest payout will be $100. Then there are $1-buy-in contests with $500 going to first place. They're meant to attract thousands of entrants and, considering the huge rake, these pie-in-the-sky contests should be considered as something akin to buying a lottery ticket. Still, they serve as good training exercises for anyone who wants to get a feel for what works and what doesn't in assembling fantasy teams for large-field tournaments.

At the other end of the buy-in spectrum, there's a big discount on the rake for the high rollers in daily fantasy. Just about every day of the week, scores of DFS contests are posted with buy-ins of $500, $1,000, even $5,000, in which the DFS equivalent of sumo-sized competitors metaphorically butt bellies in head-to-head match-ups. For those DFS whales, the rake gets ratcheted down to less than 6%. It's not uncommon to see head-to-head contests (known as H2H) set up for $5,300 entry fees with the winner collecting $10,000. The rake on that is 5.7% ($600 divided by $10,600).

Mid-level high-roller events, i.e., $530 buy-ins, also have smaller rakes in the 6% to 7% range. And DFS players willing to get into the $100-buy-in contests can shave a couple of percentage points off the 10% mark.

Rake can also be reflected in the percentage of players who get paid. For instance, contests advertised as double-ups will, indeed, double the money of the players who hit the threshold for cashing in the tournament. But the number of players who make the money cut-off will be slightly less than half the field: A double-up contest that accepts a maximum of 112 competitors will pay just the top 50 finishers. The rake on that is 10.7%.

So, while a double-up may feel like a better deal than a 50/50 (because in the 50/50, the winners get a prize that's below that of a double-up), remember that there's often a higher-percentage rake for the double-up. It's something of a mathematical optical illusion.

Rakeback

Daily fantasy sports players who are also familiar with the world of online poker have raised the question of "rakeback."

When online poker proliferated in the United States, poker websites frequently offered rakeback, a partial rebate on the commission the game hosts took from each pot. Various iterations of rakeback are sometimes offered in bricks-and-mortar casino poker rooms.

During the heyday of online poker, from about 2003 through 2011, rakeback was an important part of the income stream for online-poker regulars, as the poker websites competed for the most active players with various schemes for delivering rakeback. The more a player played, the more rakeback he or she could expect.

Eccles on the Rake

In 2014, FanDuel CEO Nigel Eccles voluntarily faced a barrage of questions from DFS players in a wide-ranging online Q&A session on the popular DFS website, RotoGrinders.

More than once, Eccles was asked about the possibility of lowering the rake on his company's contests. Eccles didn't think it likely that DFS would see a large drop in rake.

"It is unclear what will happen to rake levels," Eccles wrote. "About 4-5 years ago [a competing website] had rake at 20% (!). We came out at around 9-10% and that has become the generally accepted level. We have also reduced the rake level at the higher buy-in levels. Sites that offered reduced rake have generally all sold or folded, which isn't a great sign. Rake in poker stayed fairly constant from the early days so I suspect it will be similar in daily fantasy."

It should be noted that, while rake percentages may have remained fairly constant in online poker, rakeback programs also became standard to a great degree and that has not happened so far with DFS.

As beneficiaries of generous rakeback programs, extremely prolific online poker players could essentially tread water and just about break even in the games, but still make an overall profit from the rakeback. By and large, the tidy bonanza that rakeback provided was killed off when the federal government cracked down on online gambling in 2011, at least for U.S. players.

So, when daily fantasy sports began to gain traction in the U.S. and former poker grinders began migrating to DFS websites where they were once again paying rake, they wondered, "Where's the rakeback?"

Up to this point, the industry hasn't gone down the rakeback road. The major DFS websites have shown that they're willing to spend tens of millions on conventional TV/radio advertising to recruit customers, but routinely offering rakeback hasn't been part of the marketing strategy.

Some DFS websites, including FanDuel and DraftKings, do offer deposit bonuses to new players; they also have modest reward programs pegged to frequency of play. The deposit bonuses (discussed in the next section) can be thought of as an indirect rakeback while a DFS newbie is learning the ropes. And the frequent-player programs are added value for prolific players.

Some smaller websites have offered pure rakeback, depending on level of play, and third-party websites that provide research resources and advice columns have also advertised a form of rakeback for participants who sign up to play through their links.

However, for the majority of DFS participants, prospects for more profitable play lie not with rakeback programs or frequent-play perks, but with a lower rake to begin with.

Unfortunately, DFS websites are reluctant to offer that kind of relief. They have their own profit issues, due in most part to player-acquisition expenses—the cost to recruit a new customer—being so high. If formal regulation comes to DFS, the added expense could be passed on to participants.

The wildcard regarding rake is competition. If competitors with deep pockets and the database resources to direct-market (thus reducing per-player acquisition costs) eventually come into the marketplace, that could be a game-changer. An emerging DFS company that has the ability to achieve market penetration without huge marketing expenses could conceivably offer a smaller rake to recruit and retain customers. It remains to be seen how the current market leaders would respond to such a challenge.

Bonuses and Participation Programs

As some daily fantasy websites imply in their advertising, they're giving away money to new customers. But as you can imagine, there are some catches.

So far, the main incentive DFS websites have used to recruit players has been the sign-up bonus. In fact, trumpeting these bonuses has been a mainstay of TV and online advertising for both FanDuel and DraftKings. A regularly appearing FanDuel ad said, "Get up to $200 free on your first deposit." DraftKings went further with its promise of a "100% bonus up to $600." Some smaller websites have offered similarly attractive bonuses.

In truth, the bonus offers have caused some controversy and, in some cases, sparked lawsuits contending that the prominent advertising claims don't fully spell out the bonus conditions appearing in the fine print.

Generally, the amount of the *potential* bonus is pegged to the amount of the customer's initial deposit. The bonus is placed in what can be described as a separate "pending" account. Then, the bonuses are released only as customers participate in contests that require entry fees. Typically, the pending bonus is released at a rate of 4% of the money spent on contest entry fees.

So let's take a look at DraftKings' "100% Bonus up to $600" pitch.

A customer deposits $600 into a DraftKings account and the 100% bonus match, $600, goes into pending status. To be clear, the new customer cannot request to have that $600 bonus sent to him immediately.

On DraftKings, participation in cash games is translated into Frequent Player Points (FPPs). How many FPPs are earned per dollar of entry fee paid varies and that information is spelled out in the rules for each contest. Frequently, the customer earns 4 Frequent Player Points for every $1 spent on a contest. So if you enter a DraftKings football contest with a $10 buy-in, you receive 40 FPPs. After you accumulate 100 FPPs, $1 is transferred from the bonus account into your cash account.

So what would it take to get the entire $600 bonus released from pending status into a person's actual cash account? At the 4% rate, it would take $15,000 in entry fees to release the total $600. And there's another condition for collecting the sign-up bonus at DraftKings. The pending bonus amount must be earned and released into the customer's cash account within four months of the initial deposit, otherwise it expires.

So if you hope to redeem the entire $600 bonus, you have to play $15,000 of your own money within four months of your first deposit (DraftKings does encourage players with expiring bonuses to contact customer support). That's $125 in entry fees every day for four months! It's easy to see why some players believe they were misled over the terms of this sign-up bonus.

On FanDuel, one of the more frequently advertised maximum bonuses is $200. If your initial deposit is $200 on Fan-Duel, you receive $200 in pending bonus. The FanDuel bonus

---

DFS Comps ...

Casinos, airlines, hotels, credit cards, and other large retailers and service providers have programs that reward loyal customers. In the gambling business, the rewards are known as complimentaries, or "comps." Some DFS websites offer something similar, where players accumulate points above and beyond their sign-up bonuses that can be redeemed for free entries into regular contests.

Here's how the programs currently work for the two majors.

FanDuel: Earn 10 "FanDuel Points" (FDPs) for every $1 of entry fees, e.g., a $10 entry fee earns 100 FDPs. The redemption rate is 2,400 FDPs for $1 in free entry fees.

Comp rate: You have to spend $240 in entry fees to get $1 in free entries. However, there's a second facet to the FanDuel program that adds additional value. When players reach certain monthly thresholds, they become eligible for special freeroll tournaments. The lowest monthly threshold is 1,000 FDPs, which qualifies you for a free tournament with a $2,000 prize pool. Thresholds jump to plateaus of 5,000 FDPs, 15,000 FDPs, and 50,000 FDPs, and players qualify for additional freerolls with increasingly richer prize pools.

DraftKings: At DraftKings, you earn "Frequent Player Points" (FPPs). The number earned per paid contest varies

money is also released at a rate of 4% of entry fees, but the release of the bonus is immediate. Thus, if a customer plays a $1 daily fantasy contest, 4¢ is immediately released into the customer's cash account. More important, the bonus amount doesn't expire on FanDuel.

Both major websites also have player-loyalty programs

... FanDuel vs. DraftKings

(sometimes wildly) and is listed on the draft page for each contest. Typically, lower-entry-fee contests (25¢-$50) accrue points at a rate of 4 FPPs per $1 in entry fees. Interestingly, higher-entry-fee contests often accrue at a lower rate (e.g., a $100 entry fee may earn 330 FPPs and a $1,000 entry fee may earn 2,264 FPPs). But there have also been contests where just a $3 entry fee earned over 100 FPPs. Keep an eye out for those surprises. The accumulated FPPs are redeemed for virtual "tickets" that serve as entries into regular contests. The redemption rate is about 550 FPPs for $1 in free entries.

Comp rate: Lower-level players typically have to spend $138 in entry fees for each $1 in free entries, but that ratio varies, depending on how many FPPs were assigned to each paid contest. In addition, DraftKings logo items—socks, hats, shirts—have also been available in exchange for points.

Bottom Line: The givebacks amount to about a .7% rebate at DraftKings and a .4% rebate plus the freeroll bonuses at FanDuel, which render the two rates about even. Interestingly, these return rates are comparable to what a casino customer earns in comps or free-play using a players club card.

---

that provide some rewards. DraftKings customers accumulate Frequent Player Points (FPPs), while FanDuel customers accumulate FanDuel Points (FDPs). In both cases, the points can be used in place of money to enter regular contests. These programs provide added value for frequent customers after the sign-up bonus is exhausted or has expired.

In addition to bonuses and points, the websites also offer regular freeroll contests. As the name implies, a freeroll has no entry fee, but high finishers win cash prizes or qualify for entry into another contest. The freerolls are usually tied to play frequency.

Combined, the bonus, points, and freerolls act as a favorable mitigating influence on rake. All of these incentives should be considered when evaluating a DFS program.

Some content websites offer added incentives for registering and depositing through their links. Sometimes, that's a good deal. For instance, you might get a free subscription to premium content that otherwise requires a fee. But sometimes those content websites fail to disclose all the details of the bonus conditions. Instead, they provide a link to the destination website and you have to figure it out for yourself. In the end, it's up to you to sort through all the fine print of all the incentives. A good source for accessing bonus codes and links, along with analysis of the pros and cons of each is LasVegasAdvisor.com.

Daily fantasy players familiar with online poker will recall that in addition to sign-up bonuses, it wasn't unusual for poker websites to offer "reload bonuses." Reload bonuses are exactly what they sound like. If an online poker customer deposited additional money into his account (reloaded), another bonus was paid, usually at a lower rate than the initial sign-up bonus, perhaps 75% of the reload deposit.

In the early years of DFS websites, reload bonuses were

sometimes offered, but they've been extremely rare lately. In the Q&A on RotoGrinders in 2014, FanDuel's Nigel Eccles was asked about reload bonuses and the response was basically negative. "There are some discussions about how to better reward our high-value players," Eccles said. "But not general reload bonuses."

Similar to any prospect of a lower overall rake in the future, it would seem that the return of reload bonuses will require increased competition in the DFS industry.

The Buy-In Part One: Free Play

Participating in daily fantasy sports is a risk-reward business. The reward, of course, is the prize money you hope to win. The risk part is the buy-in, the money you invest every time you enter a contest. And though the buy-in represents the participant's cost of doing business, you need to understand a few things about buy-ins that might not be obvious to beginners, and even to some who've been playing DFS for a while.

Buy-ins have a huge range—so huge that the breadth of them will shock people who are just getting to know the game. At the low end, buy-ins are the best you can hope for—zero. And at the high end, they can be for $5,000 and above.

Generally, contests with a zero buy-in aren't for prizes. As has been mentioned, these contests are valuable for beginners just learning about how daily fantasy works. I strongly recommend, if you've never played DFS, that you play the free, no-risk, and no-prize games 10 or 20 times before you start investing money.

Folks who have played for-fun-only poker on the Internet may feel that these types of games are a waste of time, but they're not. Free DFS contests are very different than free poker.

In free poker, common sense and strategy go out the window. People play with any cards they're dealt, no matter how bad, and they never fold. Why not? The wilder the play, the better.

On the other hand, the very nature of daily fantasy sports, because the rules encourage participants to spend up to the salary cap, means that everyone who does so is fielding at least a representative team. Sure, some players will goof around and stick in terrible players, maybe from their hometown team, on a lark. But as a rule, beginners playing the free games are trying to learn and do their best to sharpen their skills. So there's certainly value in playing the free games, even if most of the participants are also beginners, so you won't be facing very stiff competition.

When you play in free contests, use the opportunity to drill into the results. For instance, take a look at what athletes were taken by the top finishers. Another important piece of intelligence that can be gleaned from your opponents' rosters once a contest has started is what percentage of owners draft certain players. That will help you begin to understand a vital element of assembling a DFS lineup: How likely it is that a player you select will be shared with your competitors.

Another type of contest with a zero buy-in also has value attached to it—the aforementioned freeroll. Freerolls offer cash prizes, though they may be meager. For example, some DFS freerolls are set up to accept as many as 100,000 participants with a total prize pool of $10. The prize is shared by, say, the top five finishers, who receive $2 each, or a top prize of $4 and a bottom prize of $1.

Participants who've been around the DFS scene from the beginning grumble that these promotional freerolls, which were used to get people into the habit of playing, aren't as frequent as they once were. That may be true, but they still come up occasionally.

So should you participate in a contest with thousands of competitors and, basically, the price of a cup of coffee as the prize? Yes, and here's a strong basic strategy to follow when you do.

DFS websites allow what's called "exporting" lineups. This means that if you've already assembled a lineup you like for another contest, with just a few clicks you can submit that same lineup to other contests. If you're already putting together line-ups for regular contests when a freeroll is offered, you can get in on it with minimal effort.

There's another reason to play freerolls beyond the shot at free money. Something you don't get to do on all DFS web-sites is what's known in poker as "railing" or "sweating" other players. To rail a poker player means to watch him play, which is often a good learning opportunity. That's what you get to do when you watch poker on TV.

Some DraftKings contests provide a window into a decent number of "live" contests, but sometimes, you don't get to see a DFS player's lineups unless you're in the same contest with him. By joining these massive freeroll fields, you have an op-portunity to scout many opponents and get a look at lineups they imported into the freeroll from more valuable games.

Bottom line: Regardless of whether you just want to take a crack at free money or are using the freeroll for research, ex-porting a lineup that you've already taken a lot of time to com-pile makes sense.

The Buy-In Part Two: Money Plays

DFS websites offer real-money buy-ins as low as 25¢ (DraftKings calls them the "Quarter Arcade" contests) and they can skyrocket to the thousands of dollars. On the same

day that DraftKings has 25¢ games, they also have plenty of
nose-bleeders for north of $1,000 to as high as $5,000. However, most daily fantasy players are playing at ground level—$2
to $20 a contest.

Here's a key fact: The higher the stakes, typically the higher
the point total a participant will need to cash, all conditions being equal. Why? Because the higher the buy-in level, the more
skilled the DFS players are. Conversely, low-stakes contests
have softer fields.

As we've learned, lower-buy-in tournaments have a higher
rake than high-buy-in contests. Usually, it's the standard 10%,
but sometimes the rake in the low-end contests climbs much
higher. So there's a balancing act in deciding what level of buy-
in you're comfortable with, considering how that will affect the
caliber of competition you'll be facing and the rake percentage
you'll be paying. High rake means lower-buy-in, softer competition, and less risk. Low rake means higher buy-in, tougher
competition, and more risk. Also, be mindful that the high-
buy-in/low-rake contests are usually small fields, such as three-
or four-player leagues or head-to-head, so you'll be toe-to-toe
with particularly elite competition.

One way to overcome at least one of these issues—the risk
associated with high buy-ins—is to partner with other players
you trust. Let's assume you and four friends decide to play in
a $215 contest with a 7% rake. Each of you would put up $43
and together you assemble a lineup.

Another way to achieve the smaller rake and reduce outcome variance is for all five people in the partnership to each
enter a $215 contest with each assembling his or her own line-
up. In this instance, the five partners would need to agree to
share any prize money. So, each player in the group would own
20% of each lineup. In that way, the five partners reduce their

individual variance, thanks to the multiple lineups, and they get the added bonus of the lower rake. (See Chapter 4 for more on variance.)

If we were talking about a poker tournament instead of daily fantasy sports, you and your friends would all be buying "pieces" of one another in the tournament. This is an extremely common practice among poker professionals.

Needless to say, it's mandatory that everyone involved is good friends who trust one another's judgments.

Bankroll

Whether putting money into the stock market, setting out to play poker, or heading into the world of daily fantasy sports, you need to know how much money you can afford to play with. It's here that many turn to the idea of "money management."

The old clichés about not playing with the mortgage money apply in DFS—your playing stake should be made up of funds that you can afford to lose. Beyond that, though, there is no magic betting method or system of managing your bankroll that will ensure that you'll win. Long-term winners do so with knowledge and skill—knowledge to be able to identify favorable situations and skill to know how to play those situations optimally—not with betting systems.

It's true that for expert-level gamblers and players in the investment world, there are sophisticated proportional (optimal) wagering approaches that take bankroll into consideration. However, these techniques also factor in the player's advantage in the games he's playing and aren't applicable when an advantage doesn't exist (in which case the optimal wager is $0).

At the outset of your DFS playing career, your main concern should be staying in action. Hence, common sense takes precedence over any sort of advanced wagering technique or bankroll management. It boils down to playing within your means, which brings into play a contradiction to earlier advice.

I've discussed the long-term importance of lowering the rake, but if achieving a lower rake requires playing in bigger-buy-in contests, that's usually not a prudent strategy for smaller bankrolls. Certainly, when you get to the point where maximizing your expected result is paramount and your bankroll can withstand the bigger swings, then playing in the contests with the smallest take-out becomes key. However, in the stage where participating and honing your skills is the primary objective, confining your play to lower stakes makes sense.

For the sake of example, let's assume that an aspiring DFS player has a bankroll of $500 to start, which he deposits into his DFS website of choice. This player should be entering $5-$20 contests until he has more money to risk, possibly from winning, thus reinforcing that his skills warrant competing in bigger games. You can also enforce a limit of how much money you put into action at one time, perhaps 5%-10% of the entire stake, or up to $50 in a day with our example. Some call this a "session bankroll" and there's nothing wrong with using it to limit your overall bankroll exposure.

There are other ways to mitigate risk. One is to focus the majority of your play on cash games, such as 50/50s or double-ups, where 45%-50% of players cash. A lesser percentage of plays is used for contests with more variance, e.g., the large-field guaranteed-prize-pool (GPP) contests where the payoffs are bigger than in a 50/50, but only about 20% of the field cashes. A reasonable allocation might have the DFS player with a $50-per-day limit using 70%, or $35, on cash games and $15 on GPPs. To be even more prudent, the player might not use more than 1% of the total bankroll ($5) on a single GPP.

Another way to reduce volatility is to enter an assortment of lineups in both the cash games and the GPPs. Let's say a DFS player with $35 to invest in cash games divides that money into micro amounts of $1 each. In a couple of multi-entry tournaments (those where a single DFS player can enter multiple lineups), the player could spread 11 lineups with Aaron Rodgers as quarterback, 12 with Tom Brady as quarterback, and 12 with Drew Brees as quarterback. If two of those three have decent days, the DFS player has made a solid decision on the QB position in approximately two-thirds of his cash-game contests.

It's not advisable to have totally different lineups in every contest. Your research should identify a core of players whom you'll want to play in a majority of your contests. But by hedging some percentage of your lineups with a range of players you believe will be successful that day, you avoid the risk of one or two bad choices ruining an entire weekend.

Week to week in football, your bankroll dictates how much you should put in play. If the player who starts with a $500 bankroll is successful over the first few weeks and his account grows to, say, $600, then he can begin moving up in the frequency or amount of buy-ins. On the other hand, if losses erode the bankroll to $400, then downsizing buy-ins will have the desired bankroll-preservation effect.

Skill vs. Luck

When you take up daily fantasy sports, you're engaging in a game of skill. But that doesn't mean luck plays no role. And when bad luck rears its head, you have to keep yours.

As the 2013 NFL playoffs began, Kansas running back Jamaal Charles was at the top of his game. A skilled rusher and excellent pass receiver, Charles was being utilized to his fullest potential by Kansas City coach Andy Reid, as the versatile back racked up rushing yards, receptions, and touchdowns at a clip that had his fantasy owners beaming. In the regular season, Charles rushed for nearly 2,000 yards, caught 70 passes, and scored 19 touchdowns.

The Chiefs' first playoff game was against the Indianapolis Colts and it figured to be a shootout with Charles primed to rack up his share of offensive stats (and fantasy points). However, after just three carries for 18 yards, Charles suffered what appeared to be a minor injury. On the sideline, though, he failed the NFL's concussion protocol. That was it. He was out for the day.

As the game careened to a 45-44 finish with the Colts winning, Charles' replacement, Knile Davis, gained 100 yards, caught seven passes, and scored two touchdowns.

Charles' fantasy owners could reasonably assume that those stats, or something similar, would have gone to their man had he not suffered the unfortunate injury on Kansas City's first possession. Fortunately for Charles, his injury proved not to be serious; the next season he had another Pro Bowl year with more than 1,300 yards and 14 touchdowns. But in that playoff game against the Colts, fate—luck, if you will—went against Jamaal Charles. And it went against the fantasy players who selected him.

In the end, the expectation is that the consistent application of sound judgment will prevail as the instances of luck even out.

Actually, daily fantasy sports shares a characteristic with a game that no one would suggest involves luck—chess. What

---

Skill Wins Most of the Time

Major League Baseball hired a math consultant to help determine the skill factor in daily fantasy sports. The conclusion was that skill trumped random selections.

Nigel Eccles concurs. "We've tested our games and we can show that ... if you put in a random lineup against one of our high-skilled players, you'll not win," the FanDuel CEO said during a panel discussion at the South by Southwest conference in Austin in 2015. "The high-skill player will win eighty, ninety percent of the time."

---

the two games have in common is that both are games of potentially perfect (or complete) information. Unlike poker, where there are unknown variables, such as the cards an opponent holds, chess is without secrets. The game starts on a literally level playing field: the same number of pieces on both sides of the board that both players can observe as they're moved. The outcome is determined solely by acumen.

Daily fantasy is similar in that every participant starts with the same salary cap, drafts from the same pool of players, and can consult the universe of statistics on which to base decisions.

What make chess and DFS different, though, are the instances of luck that can occur once the game begins. It's also possible that hidden facts about players, such as an undisclosed injury, are known by only a few.

The activity to which DFS is most often compared is poker, another contest where skill prevails, but as anyone who has played or watched the game on TV will tell you, lightning can strike. Pocket aces get beaten more than you'd imagine and the so-called one-outer, meaning the single card in the deck that can flip a hand upside-down, does occasionally show up.

There's considerable debate over which type of fantasy sports is most influenced by luck, season-long or daily. Critics of daily fantasy contend that because of the short duration of the contests, random events (meaning luck) play a greater role than in season-long fantasy. Those who press this line of thought also argue that the daily version has none of the personnel gyrations of the traditional version, such as dropping and adding players, benching some players and activating others, and executing trades with fantasy competitors, all of which is to suggest that more managerial skill is involved in season-long fantasy.

However, the flaw in that argument is that it narrowly compares a season-long competition with an individual DFS contest and the true test of DFS as a game of skill is how daily fantasy competitors fare over the long haul. In other words, how effective do a DFS player's judgments prove to be when viewed over the course of hundreds, even thousands, of contests when the decisions have to take into account match-ups against opponents, the ebb and flow of a season on a game-to-game basis, weather conditions, and many other variables?

Meanwhile, a traditional fantasy franchise can be struck by a brand of bad luck that could prove fatal for an entire season. If the star player who was a fantasy-owner's number-one draft selection gets knocked out for the season in the first game (New England QB Tom Brady in 2008), there's minimal opportunity to find a similarly skilled replacement.

The DFS participant, on the hand, forges new teams every day, every weekend, and over the long haul, either his knowledge of the sport and its players is rewarded or his lack thereof is exposed.

Decision Making

Success in daily fantasy is all about decisions: Pick Running Back A for $9,000 or Running Back B for $7,500.

Running Back A has averaged 100 yards per game for the first half of the season; his team is a heavy favorite and likely to be ahead in the fourth quarter, which means he should have a heavy workload until the final gun. But his $9,000 cost is 18% of the total salary cap of $50,000 (on DraftKings) with eight more positions to fill, which means that the average for each remaining position will be just over $5,100, a modest amount.

Running Back B shares his carries with a short-yardage running back and averages 70 yards per game. However, he also averages five receptions, and while he doesn't get goal-line carries, he's a receiving target in the red zone. He scored twice in the last game and his $7,500 salary-cap price leaves more money to spend on the other positions.

Renee Miller specializes in brain and cognitive sciences and teaches at the University of Rochester. She also writes daily fantasy advice columns for ESPN. Her approach to DFS is measured, deliberative, and evidenced-based. "My edge is that I look at everything as a scientist," Miller said. "It comes from a very logical, grounded, rational place where every decision has to be supported by evidence."

Miller relies on research in the cognitive sciences to construct an approach to decision-making that seems to be useful in general, but is remarkably applicable to DFS. She points out that many people make decisions as a result of biases that have some emotional tug.

Here's an example from Miller.

We make a decision and it turns out well. Our brains are now positively reinforced to believe that the decision was a good one. If the decision goes sour, the opposite occurs; there's negative reinforcement. The problem is this: Biases that become fixed based primarily on outcome don't give enough weight to process.

Two others to be aware of are first-impression biases and most-recent-impression biases. That's not to say that a first impression or a most-recent impression will turn out to be inconsequential evidence in making decisions or, in the case at hand, formulating daily fantasy lineups. But it does mean that we need to be aware of how our minds work, so we don't succumb to common biases. Instead, we need to be reliant on the process that we used in building a DFS lineup.

"Bad decisions that lead to anomalous good results, if repeated, will eventually lead to bad results," Miller wrote for ESPN. "Good, sound decisions, even though they may occasionally yield unpredictably bad results, ultimately pay off."

Skilled poker players have their own expression for the same phenomena: "outcome orientation."

You see it at the poker table when a player correctly folds a hand, then sees cards show that would have turned the hand into a winner. He immediately regrets that he folded, ignoring the fact that his play, prior to the outcome, was the best mathematical decision.

To avoid being adversely affected by biases, Miller advises, establish a sound process for assembling lineups and choosing which contests to enter. Whether the outcomes are good or poor, stick with the process.

Miller's sport of choice in daily fantasy is baseball, where a wealth of statistical information is available.

"The thing I like the best is the ability to do [daily fantasy baseball] in a different environment every day," she said. "The environment changes, the context changes, meaning the games and the players. The process remains the same, but you come to different conclusions."

DFS Food Chain

Another important basic is learning to understand the terrain that you're trying to navigate.

Once you enter the lobby of a DFS website, you need to understand that you're not alone.

You may not be aware of them immediately, but they're all there: from DFS regulars who have been studying statistics and matchups and news reports for the last eight hours to the guys just dropping in on their lunch break to get a few bucks down and spice up that night's slate of games.

These players operate under screen names both cryptic and amusing. Some are an unpronounceable string of consonants and others are quite creative: a personal favorite is the fatalistic moniker, probablymylastlogin.

The sheer number of players and the vast range of skill they bring on any given day are reminiscent of the famous opening line from the classic poker film *Rounders*, where Matt Damon's character says, "Listen, here's the thing. If you can't spot the sucker in your first half-hour at the table, then you *are* the sucker."

The fact that daily fantasy sports is a peer-to-peer contest of skill has its advantages and disadvantages.

The advantage is that you're not playing against the house and a built-in house edge that's impossible to overcome in the long run. Rather, you're playing against "the public," and you have every opportunity to become better informed and more skillful than your opponents.

The disadvantage is that your opponents have the same opportunity, and while DFS is still in its adolescence, a substantial number of established pro DFS players already do daily fantasy full-time and have a decided edge. Beginners should avoid such players whenever possible.

Let's take a look at who's who in the DFS world.

Sharks/Grinders/Pros—These descriptors are fairly interchangeable and those familiar with poker will undoubtedly notice the carryover from that game's lexicon.

Although collectively, sharks and grinders are seen as DFS professionals with experience on their side, there are differences. The sharks are seen as predatory, ready to seize any edge and eager to take advantage of lesser-skilled players, always with an eye for the big score. Grinders are perceived as more self-effacing. They see themselves as hard-working numbers-crunchers wringing out a mathematical advantage from the sheer volume of contests that they play.

The concept of a poker grinder was exemplified in the aforementioned film *Rounders* by actor John Turturro's portrayal of the steady risk-adverse Joey Knish, who scoffed at the Damon character's lofty World Series of Poker dreams thusly: "I'm not playing for the thrill of victory here. I owe rent, alimony, child support. I play for money. My kids eat."

There's not much difference in a DFS grinder. They're the game's Steady Eddies. Sure, they'd love to win one of the giant GPP tournaments sometime and maybe get to one of those live-event finals in a glamorous location for a crack at seven figures. But their bread and butter lies in playing the percentages and playing in volume. The beginning DFS player could aspire to a lot worse than becoming a profitable grinder.

Fish—Truth be told, everyone who plays DFS starts out as a fish. There's no shame in that. It's just the way it is.

Fish make up the volume of players who help fill the huge contests of cash games and tournaments. The best direction for fish to take is to swim with their own kind as much as possible. Unfortunately, that won't always be the case. Just as there's a range of players at a poker table in terms of experience and skill, there's a similar range of DFS participants in most contests.

So, as a fish trying to move up the food chain, how do you avoid becoming lunch for sharks and grinders?

For one thing, stay away from the high-stakes games, meaning just about any cash game that has a buy-in of $10 or more. Avoid those until you can win consistently at the lower levels.

If, as a beginner, you have an appetite and the bankroll for the high-variance GPPs, you can justify splurging for a bigger buy-in, because the massive tournaments designed to attract thousands or even tens of thousands of DFS entrants are populated by plenty of other fish. However, many GPPs are multi-entry contests, which means a single player can submit many entries. Prolific DFS players often flood GPPs with lineups and research has shown that volume pros often win disproportionate shares of big-field tournament prize pools because of the sheer number of entries combined with superior skill and research.

The nature of GPPs also means you're in something of a lottery situation. And even though it's a lottery influenced by skill, you have to resign yourself to the reality that you'll fail far more often than you'll succeed in the GPPs. You need both the psyche and the bankroll to fortify yourself.

Donkeys—Some DFS players simply give their money away or at least mail it in. Sometimes, they're pure gamblers. Many of them are probably a little lazy and don't feel like doing any research. Others are so tied to their favorite teams and players that they let their emotional attachments as fans guide (or misguide) their lineup selections. And some are merely dilettantes, dabbling in this newfangled fantasy thing they've seen the commercials for on TV. They'll deposit $100 or so, lose it, and never return.

None of those characteristics make such folks bad or even wrong, but they are, in the poker lingo, donkeys or donks. And the more of them there are, the better for you.

Donkeys make up DFS' bottom strata. They don't check the weather for baseball and will lose a player or two to a rainout. Or they don't check the list of inactive players before the NFL games kick off and wind up missing the news that a starting running back or wide receiver is out with an injury or for a team infraction.

Even if they make up only 10% of a field, that means in a 50/50 contest, instead of having to beat 50% of the field, effectively you need to beat only 40%, because the donks have, essentially, eliminated themselves.

As a beginning or intermediate player, you probably won't be able to isolate donks, but you do, in turn, want to avoid being isolated by the sharks and grinders. That's why it's advisable to play low-limit 50/50s, rather than even low-limit head-to-head contests.

Which brings us to the pros. Already, some of the most high-profile professionals have become legends within the DFS community (such as Condia). These pros are known mostly by their screen names, which give them an aura of mystery and contribute to their mystique.

Some pros have become wildly prolific, with hundreds, even thousands, of entries in multiple contests. As a result, some DFS websites, such as FanDuel, have imposed restrictions to limit the number of entries one player can submit on a given day.

To give an example of how ubiquitous players like Condia can be on DFS websites, he divulged during a podcast in 2011 that he'd entered as many as 2,000 contests during one NFL weekend. It's safe to say that whenever a beginning DFS player enters any contest with 10 or more players, there's a good chance that one or more pros are in the field.

To avoid overexposing yourself to professionals, it's a good idea to consult the RotoGrinders website's rankings of daily fantasy players, which can serve as a guide to the most prolific of them. (Note that when DFS players are ranked by how much money they've won, the amount is a gross total and doesn't account for entry fees.)

Competition Selection—No summary of the DFS food chain would be complete without an introduction to the concept of competition selection. Competition selection is the DFS equivalent of what's called table selection in poker circles. And while both competition selection in DFS and table selection in poker are sound theories, they're difficult to put into practice in the real world.

In daily fantasy sports, you can choose the competition only to a limited extent. On FanDuel, you can track players by clicking onto their screen names to see how many times they've cashed in various sports. When you see a player with thousands of cashes, you can infer that this is an experienced and formidable competitor.

The problem is that tracking competitors is difficult and time-consuming. The better route is to limit investigating the competition to the people you face in head-to-head contests, and put your time into researching the athletes and assembling your lineups.

Setting Goals

Your approach toward daily fantasy sports and what you hope or expect to get out of it will depend largely on your personality.

When you sit down with a financial advisor for the first time, he'll ask a lot of questions. One reason he does that is to obtain some guidance that will lead to relevant recommendations. Another reason is to hold a mirror up to you, so you can better understand who you are from an investment standpoint.

So, the financial advisor will ask about your goals. Do you hope to buy your own house in the next two or three years? Are you interested in saving for your toddler's college education? Are you concerned about retirement in 25 or 30 years? Depending on your stated priorities, the suggestions will vary, because while all of these goals are reasonable, prudent, financial concerns, they all fall at different points on a client's timeline.

Financial advisors also like to assess a person's tolerance for risk. For instance, will you lose sleep when the stock market gets hammered for a couple of weeks and your investments lose 5% or 10% or 15% of their value?

As a DFS player, it's important that you make the same assessments about yourself. What are your motivations for playing daily fantasy football or baseball or golf? The best guess is twofold: fun and profit. That's why you're reading this book. But now comes the trickier part—the balance between fun and profit.

We've already discussed bankroll management. We haven't talked about what that starting bankroll should be, and with good reason: The decision regarding how much to commit to DFS participation is a highly personal one. But here's a way to help decide that.

Let's reverse engineer the process, beginning with a small-picture question: How much can you afford to lose on a given NFL weekend without putting pressure on the necessities of life—the rent, utilities, groceries, etc.? Yes, the expectation is for a negative outcome. You want to test your tolerance for worst-case scenarios, at least in the short run.

Let's say the answer is you can afford to lose $30 and still pack the kids' lunches, buy the dog some kibble, pay the light bill, and basically be able to sleep soundly at night. Even on an NFL weekend with a terrible result, a DFS player on average should lose no more than 70% of his contests if the investments are spread sufficiently in terms of lineup variation and types of contests played.

Why not? It's a product of the salary-cap lineup-building process. By its very nature, the salary cap has a tendency to narrow the variance between winning and losing outcomes, especially in contests where half the field will cash. Even a DFS player totally lacking in skills—but still expending the entire salary cap—will invariably put together some lineups that are successful.

So let's assume you limit your participation to just 50/50 contests, all at small buy-ins, in this example, 30 cash contests at $2 buy-ins for a total investment of $60. You win just nine of them, for a win rate of 30%.

The gross return is $3.60 for each winning outcome, for a total return of $32.40. Since the original investment was $60 for all 30 contests, the bottom line for the weekend is a loss of $27.60. And although it was a loss, it was within your comfort zone.

If your rule of thumb is to never put more than, say, 10% of your total DFS bankroll in play on a single NFL weekend,

$60 indicates that the bankroll on hand is $600. Spreading only 10% of your bankroll over multiple contests should, even with a horrible NFL season, last from Week 1 through the NFL play-offs. If you choose to be more aggressive, you'll heighten the chances of losing your entire bankroll faster; however, the idea of spreading smaller amounts over more contests will make the swings less dramatic than betting more on fewer contests.

However, doing the reckoning to figure out how much you can afford to lose and still be comfortable is only a part of the self-assessment process. For a growing number of people, participating in DFS has become integral to the way they enjoy spectator sports and if that's the primary reason you're playing DFS, then it's probably wise that your investments remain modest.

As a hobby, DFS is great fun—as long as the expenses are kept within one's comfort zone. But when DFS becomes consistently profitable, well, it's nice to have fun that you can spend! And that's what the next sections of this book are all about.

Tilt

Daily fantasy sports and poker share a number of commonalties, including the danger of going on tilt. "Tilt" refers to an unfortunate state of mind when a player is so irritated, often following a streak of bad luck or a single "bad beat," that he begins playing wildly and taking imprudent risks.

A poker player who goes on tilt can lose a lot of money fast by playing cards that should be folded and tossing money into the pot that should stay stacked in front of him. The same can happen to daily fantasy players, even though the pace of play is more deliberate than poker. After suffering an especially galling DFS loss or a series of defeats, a player can become desperate to get back into action to recoup (or "chase") losses. That's almost always a mistake.

As you're discovering, DFS requires a lot of thought. You have to stick with contests that best suit your skill and experience. But in an agitated state of mind, DFS players can fall into the tilt trap. For example, a $10 or $20 player who gets in a hole for several hundred dollars might buy into a 50/50 for $500, trying to get it all back in one shot. Hey, all you have to do is finish in the top half of the field, right?

Yes, but remember that higher stakes brings tougher competition. If you haven't been winning at a certain level, the smart thing to do is scale back, not try to run with even faster company.

Losing should be cause for reflection, not action. Review your results. If you've been on the bubble and losing by just a few points, then stay the course to see if you've just had a bad swing.

However, if you've been finishing at the bottom of the pack, it's not the time to start chunking it in.

Chapter 4

Floors, Ceilings, and Higher Mathematics

As daily fantasy has become more popular and advertising alliances have been forged, more sports television programming has been devoted to it. Already, the Internet is filled with advice columns and tips for picking daily fantasy lineups. And as daily fantasy TV shows become more common, you'll be hearing the vocabulary of advanced DFS concepts, with words like "floor," "ceiling," "variance," and possibly even "standard deviation" used liberally.

In its current evolution, somewhere in its adolescence, a framework of best practices is accompanying its development. The most serious DFS practitioners are constantly honing their craft as they drill for new data regarding player performance to plug into statistical models and algorithms with which they constantly tinker.

However, certain building-block concepts are essential for both the most avid number-crunchers and daily fantasy novices making their first deposits into a DFS website account. Those core concepts are: first, the couplet notion of floors and ceilings and second, the gambler's age-old nemesis—variance.

In daily fantasy sports, the latter (variance) is one influence on the former (floor and ceiling). In this chapter, I discuss both concepts as they apply to winning DFS contests.

Variance

Due to the occasional imprecision of the English language, the word "variance" can have a host of meanings, depending on the context. Even when understood in the broad context of "probable or expected occurrences," the concept of variance has several applications.

For the purposes of daily fantasy sports and analyzing player performance, it's enough to define variance as "a measure of the range of possibilities that differ from the expected outcome."

For instance, if Running Back A averaged 20 fantasy points per game over five games and his actual results, game by game, were 16, 18, 24, 20, and 22 fantasy points, his variance is quite narrow. The player never failed to gain fewer than 16 fantasy points and never exceeded 24.

Now consider Running Back B, who also averaged 20 fantasy points per game over five games. His actual results, game by game, were 21, 5, 35, 29, and 10. Running Back B's variance would be considered substantially greater. Notice that he had outstanding days of 35 and 29 fantasy points, but also low-production games when he earned just 5 and 10, and only once did his actual game-day performance (21) come close to reflecting the mean of 20 points.

Some experienced participants find it useful to calculate the standard deviation for players, which is a measure of the variance. Given a number of different point totals across a number of games, a player's standard deviation is a kind of average of the differences of these point scores from their mean value.

After doing the math for the two running backs (and I strongly recommend that you use one of the many free standard-deviation calculators available online), the standard deviation for Running Back A is 3.2 (low) and the standard deviation for Running Back B is 12.6 (high).

The usefulness of the concept of the standard deviation is that now, we know that Running Back A, 68% of the time, will score between 16.8 and 23.2 fantasy points (e.g., within one standard deviation). And 95% of the time, Running Back A will score between 13.6 and 26.4 points (e.g. within two standard deviations).

For Running Back B, with the higher standard deviation, he'll score between 7.4 fantasy points and 32.6 fantasy points 68% of the time (e.g., within one standard deviation). Obviously, his production is a lot more volatile.

While the above illustrations are extreme examples and the dispersal of results is obvious just by looking at them, often the difference in player variance is not so easy to see or the statistics take in a greater range of numbers than just the five games in the above instance. That's when it's handy to have a single number, the standard deviation, which helps define the nature of a player's performance.

But what are we being told and how do we use the information in building daily fantasy lineups? That answer comes next.

Floors, Ceiling, and Standard Deviation

The concept of a floor and ceiling for daily fantasy players relates to expected thresholds. In the cash games—the 50/50s, double-ups, and head-to-heads—the optimal strategy is to have players who can be counted on to deliver a certain number of points. That's where the standard-deviation number is helpful.

Standard deviation is one-stop shopping for determining

a player's performance volatility. Low standard deviation indicates that the player typically has a narrow range of dispersal in his fantasy-points output. In simple terms, he's steady. Such players are said to have "high floors," meaning that their fantasy points are, in general, unlikely to sink very far below their average.

In contrast, players with "high ceilings" have the potential to rack up a large number of fantasy points that far exceed their average, but also run the risk of coming up empty. Charting their game-to-game performances will yield a high standard deviation.

Players with high floors are perfect for cash games, because you're simply trying to finish in the top half of the field. In a 100-entrant 50/50 cash game, for example, the top point-getter and the 50th point-getter earn the same amount of money. So your 50/50 lineup should contain players who, for various reasons, are likely to deliver fantasy points within a certain range that you can usually count on.

On the other hand, such players are sometimes less than optimal for large-field GPP tournaments, where you're shooting for a high score, because where they fall on the standard-deviation scale is indicative of the likelihood that they will perform in a predictable way. For the big tournaments where you need to finish in the top 20% just to cash and at the very top of the payout schedule to make big money, you want players who have the potential to light it up, such as the wide receiver who gets two or three fly routes a game. He could go bust for the day, but he could also catch one for an 80-yard TD.

Certainly, some players have the ability to score a ton of points and are also reliable week to week, such as Pittsburgh Steelers wide receiver Antonio Brown in 2014. But All-Pro players cost a fortune in salary-cap bucks, so you can't include too many of those guys in your GPP lineups. That's when you have to look for some cheaper players—such as that deep-threat all-or-nothing wide receiver—to fill out your roster, and they're the ones with a high standard-deviation scores.

Developing a feel for which players have high floors and which potentially have high ceilings is an essential skill for DFS owners.

Bankroll Variance

So far, we've discussed variance as it relates to player performance. Another way that variance is used relates to *your* performance and financial exposure as a daily fantasy participant. It's easiest explained by example.

Let's say a DFS player decides to invest $100 a week in daily fantasy football contests. In one hypothetical, the player uses that $100 to play four GPPs with $25 buy-ins. The chances of even cashing in a GPP, in which 20% of the field gets paid, are 1 in 5. A likely scenario is that the player will whiff on all four. Alternatively, if the player cashes for the minimum in one of those contests, that means a payout of probably a little more than double the buy-in. And the player could have a magical week and hit a five-figure payday. In this case, the player is facing a huge amount of variance with his bankroll—a range from jackpot to total loss.

In an alternate scenario, a DFS player spreads the same $100 among 20 50/50 cash games at $5 apiece. He also uses four or five different lineups, with slight changes in the rosters to hedge against any one or two of the players having a rotten day and substantially impacting all of the lineups. In this case, the great likelihood is that the player will win some and lose some. It will be highly unlikely to lose all 20 contests, so the possibility of a total loss is remote.

Once again, the tactic of playing smaller amounts on more games proves prudent, especially for the beginning DFS player.

Chapter 5

Football

Introduction

Since the inception of daily fantasy sports, football has been king.

The revenue numbers for FanDuel, the market leader through the formative years of DFS, say it all. In FanDuel's second through fifth years of operation, from 2011 through 2014, the company reported total revenue of $77.63 million. Of that amount, $47.23 million, about 60%, was earned in the fourth calendar quarters. In other words, every year, the revenue FanDuel earned in October, November, and December, the heart of the NFL season, exceeded revenue for the first three quarters of the year *combined*.

In 2014, the leap in year-over-year revenue in the fourth quarter for FanDuel was astounding, quadrupling from $8.9 million to $36 million. As for customer participation, so-called "paid actives" (let's just call them customers) nearly doubled, from about 519,000 in the fourth quarter of 2013 to just over 1 million in the same period in 2014.

Daily fantasy sports companies would love to sustain the popularity of all their sports products through all 12 months of the year, but there's no question that America's passion for the NFL is the locomotive hauling the daily fantasy train. Perhaps that'll change, but if the future follows the past, converts to

DFS will be primarily football people.

Even when it comes to season-long fantasy, pro football has outstripped all the other sports, just as the NFL long ago eclipsed Major League Baseball for the distinction of being the true national pastime.

In some ways, the real beginning of the year for Americans isn't when the big ball drops in Times Square and December 31 slides into January 1. The real start of the new year is right after Labor Day as the kids return to school, a new television season debuts, the new-model cars are rolled out, and most significantly, the NFL season kicks off.

Football's lofty status in American culture is a given. Each year, the Super Bowl is the top-rated show on television. In fact, it's probably the only event that can command the nation's total collective attention, plus major international coverage. And as a wagering proposition, football is the longtime number one in Nevada. In 2014 on the Las Vegas Strip, football accounted for 46% of all sports wagering. Basketball was a distant second at 27%, buoyed by college's March Madness, and all the other sports combined made up the remaining 27%.

Furthermore, for fans just starting in daily fantasy sports, pro football is the ideal jumping-off point for several reasons.

Timing—Football gives DFS participants the most time to assemble lineups. This is where football's normal rhythm, being a weekly event, helps novice and intermediate players.

To help explain the benefits of timing when starting out in DFS with football, let's contrast it with the second-most popular daily fantasy sport, baseball. In baseball, you can't even begin to put together a roster until the day of the game; in fact, the websites that monitor MLB starting lineups, such as RotoGrinders.com, don't post the lineups until mid-afternoon, at best. For the west coast night games, lineups aren't available until early evening. So preparation time is greatly compressed. And then there's the weather-watch, keeping track of whether that storm front in Colorado will wipe out those hitters you were counting on at Coors Field.

Baseball, basketball, and hockey are all truly *daily* events, so DFS players must commit their focus beginning several hours before the real games start and remain vigilant until lockdown time. That means either sitting in front of a computer or tracking developments on a mobile device.

The competition is tough enough that if just one of your players is unexpectedly benched and you don't catch it in time to make the adjustment, your lineup and your money are kaput. In baseball and basketball, you often find yourself wrestling with this time commitment during the work week, and that gives the grinders, who do daily fantasy full-time, an advantage over casual players.

Football, on the other hand, has a more forgiving timeline. At the beginning of every week, a full menu of DFS contests for the following weekend's NFL games is posted, as are the salaries for all the players. So early in the week, people with normal lives can begin tinkering with lineups at their leisure. Then you have the rest of the week to monitor injuries and news about who's going to play. In short, you have the luxury of time and that's a benefit to less experienced DFS players.

It's absolutely necessary to do some last-minute checking on the day of the game. There's the list of inactive players that NFL teams report on game day, and you need to be aware of breaking news that could affect your lineups. But because the NFL is a Sunday event, a lot of folks have the time to do that last-minute homework to avoid unpleasant surprises and to take advantage of some opportunities that come up because of late-breaking events.

Lockdown

Lockdown is the deadline after which daily fantasy participants can no longer change their lineups for a contest (some DFS websites refer to this as "editing" a lineup). Overall, lockdown occurs about a minute or so before a real game is scheduled to start—it's something akin to a game going "off the board" minutes before kick-off in a Las Vegas sports book. It's important to note that lockdown rules vary between the two major DFS websites.

On DraftKings, the lockdown times apply to the start of each real game in which a specific athlete is playing. So in a contest in which a participant's lineup has players whose real games start at varying times—say, 1 p.m., 4 p.m., and 8 p.m. EST—the DFS owner can change/edit a particular player up until that player's game begins. Naturally, any newly selected player has to be playing in a game that starts at the same time or later.

On FanDuel, lockdown for a contest occurs when the first real game of *all* the games included in that contest begins. So if a daily fantasy participant has a lineup with players in games that start throughout the day and evening (1 p.m., 4 p.m., 8 p.m.), once the *first* of those games begins at 1 p.m., no substitutions at all are allowed.

Player Turnover—Another reason that the NFL is more suitable for beginners is that, because of free agency, the NFL draft, the relative brevity of NFL careers (especially at DFS-sensitive positions such as running back), and what sometimes seems like the overnight deterioration of player skills, there's a substantial amount of personnel turnover in the NFL.

That churn hurts experienced DFS participants, because

much of the knowledge they've accumulated about a player and how he fits within his team is no longer valid. And usually, whatever hurts the experienced DFS player helps an inexperienced one. That doesn't mean that they're both at square one in terms of understanding the NFL and its players, but it closes the gap a little.

The Stats Attack—Deep drilling into esoteric statistics isn't the hugely defining differentiator in football that it is in baseball and basketball. For instance, the stats are so important in baseball, many DFS experts feel you don't even have to watch the games regularly to be successful at daily fantasy, because the numbers are so predictive of performance. Football is different.

The numbers don't always tell the whole story in the NFL. Many important predictive factors aren't easily found in the numbers. For instance, offensive line play makes or breaks an offense and impacts the performances of skill-position players. But the common measurements available for offensive-line efficacy are largely inferential, sacks allowed being an example.

Another important part of being predictive in football is understanding coaching schemes and how the weekly chess match between two teams will play out.

And the human element in football, especially within a locker room, has an effect on the performance numbers, and some of the dynamics could be the result of internal team politics. Just a few examples are a head coach's or offensive coordinator's trust or lack thereof in a running back at the goal line; the chemistry between a quarterback and receiver; the likelihood of a player getting touches because he was the high draft pick of the current regime, and the like.

So, watching the actual games, closely following the daily soap operas of various football teams, and, in general, developing an appreciation of the game over time narrows the gap between someone who is diligent about being a student of the NFL—otherwise known as a serious fan—and the numbers-crunchers who rely mainly on their algorithms.

Short Season—Finally, the relatively short season of the NFL, 17 weeks plus the playoffs, and how that relates to daily fantasy also take away the edge of the experienced players who rely on stats. In the first several weeks of the regular season, experienced and inexperienced DFS players alike are on more of a level playing field, as the statistics from the early-season games represent a small statistical sample and, by definition, small samples are less predictive and less actionable. By the time the numbers begin to be reliable, the pro football season is half-over. For the entirety of the NFL season, the numbers-crunchers have limited opportunity—perhaps nine or 10 weeks at most—to use their math skills to full advantage.

Take baseball as a contrasting example. Even if it requires half the season for the baseball numbers to be trusted as predictive (and carryover stats from previous seasons are more helpful in baseball than football), experienced DFS baseball participants still have 80 to 90 opportunities to put their sharpened analytics to work and make money.

As the NFL moves into its playoff phase, the three weeks or so when DFS contests are offered will feature smaller and smaller player pools from which to assemble lineups. That's also to an inexperienced participant's advantage: Smaller pools of eligible players reduce the chances for the skilled DFS player to uncover hidden gems that could be huge difference-makers.

Website Differences in Football

Of the many differences among the various daily fantasy sports websites that have proliferated in recent years, those that have mattered most for practical purposes are the ones that distinguish FanDuel and DraftKings.

Through the 2015-16 football season, both major DFS websites require that you fill nine positions. Despite that fundamental similarity, there are plenty of differences and some are substantial. In terms of lineup requirements relative to the real NFL teams, FanDuel requires that you select players from at least three different teams and it prohibits the selection of more than four players from the same team. DraftKings requires that you select players from at least two different NFL teams and your lineup has to have players from at least two different games.

A significant distinction is that FanDuel requires a kicker. DraftKings does not have a spot for a kicker. Instead, its so-called Flex position can be filled with a running back, wide receiver, or tight end.

Some DFS participants, especially pros and grinders, dislike the kicker position, which is unpredictable and volatile—a $5,000 kicker who boots four field goals and a couple of extra points can rack up as many points as an $8,500 running back who is having a decent day. FanDuel made the kicker part of its game, CEO Nigel Eccles has said, because the "mass market" is accustomed to the position being included from season-long fantasy leagues. These are the types of issues that DFS websites will wrestle with in the coming years as they fine-tune their products. But the kicker issue is further evidence that your strategy will be dictated to a degree by the website you play on. Perhaps you understand the dynamics of dome kickers with proven consistency or you're adept at cherry-picking kickers on high-scoring teams. If you seem to have a knack for picking kickers, you probably want to ride that advantage and play on FanDuel. Meanwhile, DraftKings more heavily rewards pass receptions, awarding 1 point for each catch (full PPR or point-per-reception), as opposed to FanDuel that gives 0.5 points per catch (half-PPR).

Or let's say you have an eye for running backs who are also skilled pass catchers and play for coaches who like to use the pass as a modified running play (head coach Andy Reid of the Kansas City Chiefs is a good example). With such criteria, you'll probably find that you're registering superior results on DraftKings. If you find yourself being more successful on one website than another, by all means play where you win.

Still another difference between FanDuel and DraftKings that warrants mention is the relative point significance of quarterbacks. For the top 20 NFL fantasy points leaders for the 2014 regular season on FanDuel, 13 were quarterbacks. Four were running backs and three were wide receivers. For the same season on DraftKings, among the top 20 NFL players, eight were quarterbacks, eight were wide receivers, and four were running backs. The difference was mainly due to the full point-per-reception scoring rules on DraftKings compared to FanDuel's half-point for each catch. Accordingly, you have to weight receivers more heavily on DraftKings.

One takeaway from the scoring difference is that we can assume, in most cases, quarterbacks will make up a slightly larger percentage of a lineup's total scoring on FanDuel when compared to DraftKings. That means quarterback salary-cap spending should be a little more liberal on FanDuel.

To repeat, you have to give serious consideration to the website you're playing on. The overall approach on the two major websites may look almost identical at first blush, but salary structure and scoring rules are important influences on how you go about putting together a roster.

Statistics

Throughout this book, the topic of statistics has been, and will continue to be, discussed. Delving into statistics and trying to be predictive about how games will play out and individual players will perform are a big part of the great fun of daily fantasy sports. Among a number of excellent stops on the Internet for NFL statistics are NFL.com and ESPN.com.

For daily fantasy football-specific numbers that are sortable in a number of ways, RotoGuru, run by former actuary Dave Hall, has proven its worth for years. "I try to bring together as much as I can in terms of stats in a way that is easy to digest," Hall said. "The goal is to organize the numbers and pump out the information so that it's easy to use."

NFLSavant.com and RotoGrinders.com are websites with breakdowns of the important categories, such as red-zone targets and carries.

And for the really ambitious, even pro football beat writers rely on ProFootballFocus.com for numbers that are hard to find elsewhere, such as snap counts and defensive-back performance. Paid subscriptions are sometimes required.

Football Contest Types

The contest types were introduced briefly in Chapters 2 and 3. Here we'll examine each in greater detail with an emphasis on how they apply to football.

Cash Games—Head-to-Head

In the broad category of "cash games," there are head-to-head contests, 50/50s, and double-ups.

In head-to-head contests, you're matched against one other person. The prize is winner-take-all after the website takes its cut. So, to use a basic example, in a $1 H2H contest, each participant puts up $1 for a total prize pool of $2. The website takes its 10% rake (20¢) and the winner of the contest gets $1.80. Pretty simple stuff.

There's a school of thought that sports fans just starting their participation in DFS are best advised to begin with head-to-head contests. The point of view that favors head-to-head for novice players is grounded in arguments that appear to be reasonable. For instance, it's easier to beat just one opponent than a field of many participants where you have to overcome the additional challenge of sheer numbers. And if a beginner plays a bunch of very inexpensive H2H contests, he or she can reduce bankroll variance, as some opponents over many contests will pick bad lineups at some point, so even the beginner's less-than-stellar rosters will pick up some wins.

Unfortunately, the real-world circumstances of DFS make it difficult for novice or intermediate players to consistently find H2H competitions where they won't be at a serious disadvantage, and the problem is exacerbated when trying to compete in as many contests as are needed to make it at all financially worthwhile.

In addition to the argument that you have to beat only one competitor, there's the further rationale that in H2H, you can pick your specific competition, as opposed to larger fields where that certainly isn't the case. But let's take a clear-eyed view of the daily fantasy environment with which you'll deal when you play.

When entering the website lobby and considering playing in H2H contests, a choice has to be made: You can either be the first person to play and essentially invite all comers, or you can accept an existing invitation and become the opponent.

Literature that offers advice on DFS play often strongly recommends that you not be the first person in an H2H contest. And that's excellent advice. The reason should be obvious, but just to make it clear, when you open an H2H contest to all comers, you're inviting a DFS shark who sees you as lunch.

OK, so that limits the universe of acceptable H2Hs, but practically speaking, on any day of the week during any sports season, you can go into the lobbies of the main daily fantasy websites and find H2H contests galore that have already been opened. You'd only have to drop in on those lobbies for a few days and peruse the long lists of H2H contests before realizing something: The screen names become very familiar very quickly. The same DFS players are there every day, waiting for a competitor.

Looking for Condia? There's a good chance you'll find him. How about Csuram88? That dude is probably there, too. And if you want to lock horns with 1ucror, you can probably get that action as well.

Those cryptic screen names have all belonged to enormously prolific and presumably accomplished daily fantasy sports players. Some of those folks are considered legendary in DFS circles.

When you drill into the backgrounds of many of the players who lurk daily in the lobbies looking for H2H action, you'll find players with not just tens of thousands of fantasy cashes (sometimes simply identified as "wins") under their belts. Often, you'll find DFS pros with *hundreds of thousands* of cashes.

If you go through the website lobby, you'll see that these experienced and skillful DFS professionals routinely mix it up with their fellow high-roller sharks for buy-ins at, say, $535 a pop with $1,000 to the winner. But they'll also move down to the kids' table and play fresh-picked beginners for a couple of bucks and take their lunch money, too.

Of course, even the experts who recommend head-to-head contests for beginners strongly advise avoiding these kinds of players. Again, that's very good advice, unless it's for micro-stakes and you're doing it to scout their lineup-selection process. (The ability to see other players' lineups in contests you're not participating in is possible, for example on DraftKings, but limited. Of course, you see the lineups of many of your opponents on the major DFS sites. You can "go to school" cheaply by hawking the top DFS players when you're competing against them for a dollar or two.)

Further advice you'll hear is that a beginner should locate competition with less experienced DFS players who are beatable by scouring the Internet looking for the nicknames of apparently losing players. That would take a huge amount of time—if it's possible at all. Figuring out that players such as Condia and Csuram88 and 1ucror are the Andrew Lucks, Mike Trouts, and Stephen Currys of daily fantasy sports is pretty easy. Trying to figure out who the fish are—that's a lot tougher. My recommendation, instead, is that you spend your research time on the metrics of athletes' performances that you can put your arms around and better understand.

My lack of enthusiasm for H2H contests for beginners doesn't mean that they should be off your menu forever. You can have fun on the major websites, which permit friends to set up contests between each other. Invite your buddies from across town or across the country to play you one-on-one—and have a blast!

Down the road, if you continue to play, you'll become familiar enough with the DFS community that the who's-who research will be much easier. For example, if you take as much note of who consistently finishes *out* of the money as you do who consistently appears at the top of the payout charts, you'll identify more and more DFS players whose constant presence in the lobbies is more indicative of their appetite for action and not so much evidence of their skill and profitability. Those players may be exploitable.

It's also advisable to take a look at the research on DFS participants that *is* fairly easy to find, if only to have a better idea of whom you're dealing with when you jump into any contest. Some of the low-hanging research fruit on your fellow players has been on FanDuel, which, through 2015, ran charts on DFS players listing total wins (cashes), including a breakdown by sport.

For more on DFS-participant results, the RotoGrinders website has seasonal leaderboards. Plus, RotoGrinders has a searchable database of DFS participants by screen name.

Keep in mind that even when you do discover participant-performance information, it's incomplete. The stats are more a reflection of participation volume than a precise accounting of net profit. In other words, you might see that someone has had 2,000 cashes in NFL contests, but what you don't know is if that person entered 3,000 or 10,000 contests to achieve those cashes. Still, it's reasonable to infer that a player with thousands of cashes probably has been profitable; otherwise he would already be out of the daily fantasy business.

Cash Games—50/50s and Double-Ups

So if head-to-head contests aren't the place for beginners to start or intermediates to try out their skills, what is?

The best recommendation is to start in the other cash

games, meaning 50/50s, double-ups, and later, triple-ups. As a reminder, 50/50 and double-up contests are competitions where you can double (or nearly double) your buy-in. A triple-up allows you to triple your buy-in.

There are two rules to follow even in these cash games: Make sure they *don't* allow multiple entries; and enter contests with the largest fields possible without falling afoul of the previous rule (extremely large-field cash games probably allow multiple entries).

There are a number of reasons this type of game is most recommended for beginning and intermediate DFS players. For one thing, it's easier to show up on the plus side of the ledger when you simply have to finish in the top half of the field. In a 50/50, you have to finish in the top 50% and you'll earn an 80% profit on your buy-in. In a double-up, you have to finish in the top 45% of the field and you make a 100% profit on your buy-in. It doesn't matter if you finish at the top of the heap or just inside the cut-off (also known as "the bubble") for cashing; the payoff is the same.

A triple-up, technically a multiplier league or tournament, requires that you finish in the top 30% of the field and your profit is 200% of your buy-in.

To repeat: The strong recommendation is that you pursue non-multiple entry contests and while holding fast to that rule, you also seek the largest field possible. The multiple-entry contests, whether cash games or GPPs, simply afford the DFS pros too great an opportunity to enter many lineups.

Here's an example of how that can play out and the impact on average players.

Let's say in a 50/50 contest with a field of 800 maximum entries (400 places paid), five DFS pros submit just 20 lineups each. That means that only five accomplished competitors account for 12.5% of the entire field; if they're on their game, they have a good chance of taking 25% of the available prizes. Thus, the remaining 795 competitors are vying for 300 prizes. All of sudden, the 50/50 contest doesn't feel much like a 50/50 anymore.

The above example is an oversimplification, but the point is absolutely valid: Grinders take advantage of multiple-entry contests in order to lessen their variance, but average players are competing against a tougher overall field than they may realize, with the pros and grinders having a proportionately greater presence. On the other hand, if the contest forbids multiple entries, a small number of pros cannot dominate the field. As a beginner or intermediate player, you want as diverse a field of competitors as possible and the larger the field, the less impact the most talented DFS players can have on the outcome.

On the practical order, if you follow the above rules, you should find yourself usually playing in cash-game fields from 20 to 100 participants. The contests that allow more than 100 entries often allow multiple entries. Indeed, you'll even find contests of fewer than 100 that allow multiple entries. Unless you've developed considerable skills, you should avoid those small-field multiple-entry contests entirely.

In tackling cash games, remember that your goal is not the best score; it's a score good enough to cash.

Multipliers

Multipliers are contests that reside somewhere between classic cash games and large-field tournaments. Multipliers offer an opportunity to step up in profitability as you sharpen your game.

Take the triple-up multiplier, where you need to finish in the top 30% of the field to cash and if you do so, you triple your money. So in a 40-entry field, you'd have to be among the top 12 finishers in order to make money. And just like in a cash game, you collect the same money if you finish first or 12th. Your approach to multipliers should be similar to 50/50s, double-ups, and head-to-heads. In other words, you're looking for reliable players with high floors. And you should try triple-ups only when you're cashing in the 50/50s a solid 60% of the time and you're making it into the money with some room to spare, not just squeezing into the top half of the field.

Some multipliers, with prizes four, five, and 10 times your buy-in, have a greater risk and higher reward, but the degree of difficulty definitely puts distance between them and cash games. Once you get to the five-times contests, the difficulty of cashing is the same as in a GPP, but the payout schedule is obviously flatter. In a five-times contest, typically 18% of the field gets paid (e.g., the top eight out of 44 entries). By comparison, in many GPPs, the top 20% or so get paid.

The difference is that the return on investment for cashing in the quintuple is five times the buy-in; whether at the top or the bottom of the payout schedule, it's all the same. Meanwhile, a GPP has a huge prize range from top to bottom. For instance, in a $5 GPP that allows 46,000 entries, although 20% of the field gets paid, the top finisher earns $20,000 and those who just barely squeak past the bubble will get $10.

So, even the five-times and 10-times multipliers have a built-in conservative characteristic, in that if you do manage to cash, it's a healthy payday. Of course, if your lineup is good enough to go to the head of the class, you'll be kicking yourself for not entering the higher-upside GPP.

Guaranteed Prize Pools

By 2014, daily fantasy football had gotten so popular that contests were offered routinely with $1 million prizes. In fact, it may have been the seemingly non-stop TV commercials on sports channels touting the opportunity to strike it rich on FanDuel or DraftKings that got you interested in daily fantasy sports to begin with.

Well, that's OK. There's no harm in dreaming big. But if you dream big, you have to play big.

That means forgetting about those safe reliable picks where you're counting on 300 passing yards and a touchdown toss from your quarterback and three or four total touchdowns from your position players. In GPPs, you need your quarterback to light it up, along with the one receiver you've been smart enough to stack with your QB. Plus, your running back needs to get lucky and hit paydirt on a couple of inside-the-3-yard-line carries. And you'll probably need your tight end to get his number called in the red zone and make good on that touchdown opportunity. And almost certainly, you'll need to have a sleeper come through, like wide receiver Eric Decker in the final game of 2014.

In his first year with the New York Jets, Decker had been a non-factor for most of the season and his daily fantasy salary had plummeted to a season-low by the end of the schedule. But in the last game of the season, Decker paid off big with 10 receptions, 221 yards, and a touchdown. That's the kind of sleeper you need to shoot to the top of the leaderboard in a GPP.

For instance, wide receiver Martavis Bryant, who played in the shadow of Pro Bowler Antonio Brown in Pittsburgh, appears to have a penchant for occasionally taking a leap in fantasy points a few times a year. When you're searching for sleepers capable of a breakthrough, you're looking for those wide-receiver speedsters called on only a few times a game to run the deep routes.

The top sleeper pick of 2014 was New England second-string running back Jonas Gray, who rushed for 201 yards and four touchdowns in Week 11 against Indianapolis. The only daily fantasy football players who were likely to have Gray in their lineups were diehard Patriots fans, and, as it turned out, that's exactly who cashed in on the unlikely performance by the rookie.

Two brothers whose mother owns an Italian restaurant, Antico Forno, in Boston's North End entered a bunch of $27 entries in the Millionaire Maker contest on DraftKings in mid-November. Dave and Rob Gomes figured that since all the other Patriot running backs were banged up, Gray, a rookie with just 32 carries in his first year as a back-up, would get the ball most of the day by default. By spending a bargain basement $5,800 on Gray, the Gomes brothers were able to stock up on blue-chippers and stacked their lineup with Green Bay Packers Aaron Rodgers, Jordy Nelson, and Randall Cobb. Usually, even in a GPP, you wouldn't want to stack more than one same-team wide receiver with a quarterback, but the Gomes brothers' unorthodox approach worked out just fine, as the Packers rolled up 53 points and both Nelson and Cobb had more than 100 receiving yards. Of course, Rodgers was throwing the ball and he finished with 341 passing yards and three TDs.

But it was Gray, a player who appeared on less than 1% of the thousands of entries in the Millionaire Maker (0.6% to be exact), who made the difference by racking up a monster 46.9 points on DraftKings. The Gomes brothers also got a surprise boost from their defense, Tampa Bay, which swamped Washington with a defensive touchdown, two interceptions, a fumble recovery, and six sacks.

Selecting Gray and the Tampa Bay defense were examples of a principal ingredient in winning large-field tournaments: Somewhere along the line, you have to be a contrarian. If you select quarterback Peyton Manning and 40% of your competition does the same, you won't get the separation between yourself and the rest of the pack that you need, even if Manning has a great day.

But that also creates a dilemma. If you have a strong hunch that a specific player could earn an enormous amount of fantasy points, you can't dismiss him merely because he'll be a popular selection; if he plays to form, you'll be left in the dust. The Gomes lineup had the right mix of popular players like Rodgers and Nelson, along with longshots like Gray and the Buccaneers defense.

"While all that was happening, I couldn't even enjoy it because I was sick as a dog," Dave Gomes said. "I actually thought I was having a heart attack."

But Gomes' real distress was yet to come. Although the two brothers had racked up an enormous total of 233.74 points in their games on Sunday, they didn't have any players in the Monday night game, featuring Pittsburgh against Tennessee. In that game, Steelers' running back Le'Veon Bell went wild, rushing for 204 yards and a touchdown. As the clock wound down with the Steelers comfortably ahead, Bell ran the ball seven straight times as the Gomes bothers sweated out their fantasy competitors getting closer and closer. Finally, Pittsburgh quarterback Ben Roethlisberger took two kneel-downs to end the game and the celebration broke out in the Gomes restaurant.

"That taught me a lesson to either play Sunday-only contests where you don't have to worry about the Monday night game or make sure you have someone in the Monday night game," Dave Gomes said.

Rob and Dave's Big Adventure

Rob Gomes admits that his 2014 NFL season was a sports-gambler's dream-come-true. Not only did he and his brother, Dave, win a ton of cash, but they did so by putting their faith in—and their money on—their favorite team, the New England Patriots.

The Gomes brothers' saga began before the NFL season started, when Dave visited Las Vegas. Rob couldn't make the trip, but his money did: $10,000, just about all the money he had in the world. "I was just out of college, waiting tables," Rob said, describing his own Hail Mary pass.

In Vegas with the wad, Dave made a futures bet at New York-New York on the Pats to win the Super Bowl.

"We were figuring on getting 10-1 but it was 7-1," Rob said. "So Dave put up a little more money."

With their futures betting tickets in hand, Rob and Dave were also playing daily fantasy football on DraftKings. In November, while collaborating on a $27-entry-fee Draft-Kings Millionaire Maker lineup, the brothers drafted unknown Patriots running back Jonas Gray. Gray's 46.9 points made the relatively obscure running back one of the highest single-week fantasy players of 2014, and along with a list of better-known players on the Gomes' lineup (under the screen name DaveTheChamp), helped catapult the brothers to a $1 million payday.

With their windfall, Rob and Dave Gomes made their way to Super Bowl XLIX in Glendale, Ariz., where the Patriots hung on to beat Seattle, 28-24, by the grace of rookie defensive back Malcolm Butler's interception of a Seahawks pass at the goal line with less than 30 seconds left. The interception sealed the Patriots' fourth Super Bowl win and another jackpot of $78,400 for the brothers.

"You know, while the money was certainly great," Rob Gomes said, "I can honestly say that I was ecstatic for Tom (Brady) that he got his fourth Super Bowl ring."

Meanwhile, Rob was being immortalized in the most recognizable of the dozens of DraftKings ads and is in the process of opening his own DFS website.

And Jonas Gray? After his big day, he gained fewer than 100 total yards the rest of the season and was inactive for the Super Bowl. The following September, he was cut by the Patriots.

Rob and Dave Gomes' winning lineup is displayed here.

LIVE SCORING VIEW H2H   **TEAM:** DaveTheChamp (37)   **RANK:** 1st   **YTP:** 0   **PMR:** 0

POS	NAME	% DRAFT	GAME	SCORING	FPTS
QB	Aaron Rodgers	14.5%	PHI 20 GB 53 Final	3 PaTD, 341 PaYds, 32 RuYds, 1 300+Pass	31.84
RB	Jonas Gray	0.6%	NE 42 IND 20 Final	4 RuTD, 199 RuYds, 1 100+Rush	46.9
RB	Jeremy Hill	24.8%	CIN 27 NO 10 Final	13 RecYds, 152 RuYds, 1 REC, 1 100+Rush	20.5
WR	Randall Cobb	7.5%	PHI 20 GB 53 Final	129 RecYds, 10 REC, 1 100+Rec	25.9
WR	A.J. Green	23.1%	CIN 27 NO 10 Final	1 RecTD, 127 RecYds, 6 REC, 1 100+Rec	27.7
WR	Jordy Nelson	27.4%	PHI 20 GB 53 Final	1 RecTD, 109 RecYds, 4 REC, 1 100+Rec	23.9
TE	Mychal Rivera	7.5%	OAK 6 SD 13 Final	40 RecYds, 3 REC	7
FLEX	Brandon Marshall	5.8%	MIN 13 CHI 21 Final	2 RecTD, 90 RecYds, 7 REC	28
DST	Buccaneers	0.7%	TB 27 WAS 7 Final	6 SACK, 2 INT, 1 DFR, 1 DefTD, 1 7-13 PA	22

TOTAL FANTASY POINTS: 233.74

Satellites/Qualifiers

Satellites and qualifier tournaments hold out the promise of competing in still another tournament where the prizes can be spectacular. In fact, winning a qualifier could include a value-packed bonus prize, such as an expenses-paid trip to the Playboy Mansion, where the bigger tournament is held in a live, rather than virtual, setting. Previously, many of those live events were held in Las Vegas. But Nevada's insistence that DFS websites be licensed in the state has chilled these prospects.

While satellites and qualifiers are generally regarded as low-entry-fee tournaments where participants are making a grab for the brass ring, entry fees can also be considerable if the qualifier structure narrows the chances of winning a berth in the next, bigger tournament. Here's an example.

A DFS website schedules a football (or baseball or basketball) "world-championship" contest to be held near the end of the regular season in some glamorous locale. The winner of the eventual live event earns $1 million, maybe more. Part of the reward for the 100 or so qualifiers is airfare and hotel stays and parties leading up to the live tournament gala.

Those 100 fortunate contestants make it to the extravaganza by winning their way in through satellites and qualifiers. Satellites can cost very little, a couple bucks, but their next-of-kin tournaments, qualifiers, can have hefty buy-ins of a few hundred or even a few thousand dollars.

A satellite with tens of thousands of hopefuls may cost just $5, but the odds of hitting the grand prize are like those of a progressive slot machine. But sometimes dreams come true and lottery-ticket odds produce life-changing money. That's exactly the road that Scott Hanson traveled.

Hanson, a 33-year-old personal trainer, was watching TV

with his wife when a daily fantasy sports commercial popped on the screen and she said something like, "Honey, you know a lot about sports. Why don't you try that?"

So Hanson put a modest $35 into a FanDuel account in the fall of 2014.

"I worked on some lineups and after a few weeks, I decided I liked the GPPs," Hanson said. "In the third week, I spent $5 on a large-field tournament and finished first and that was worth $15,000."

But Hanson was just warming up. "Now, I realized I had to start getting serious about it," he said. "I heard about the FFFC, so I wanted to take a shot at that."

The FFFC is short for FanDuel Fantasy Football Championship, FanDuel's grand football finale, sort of its own Super Bowl. But rather than being in February when the real Super Bowl is held, the FanDuel championship takes place in mid-December, when all 32 NFL teams are still playing and most of the games have relevance. That means fantasy participants can count on all the teams fielding their best players, something you can't be totally certain of in the NFL's Week 17 when teams that have locked up playoff seedings may rest some starters.

Hanson, emboldened by his $15,000 win in a big field, invested $60 in a $2 qualifier to try for a spot in the FFFC—and finished first out of 59,000 entrants. He and wife Danielle were on their way to the Cosmopolitan casino in Las Vegas, where he and 99 other fantasy football hopefuls would vie for the big money. In the end, Hanson, with a game-flow approach (see pg. 144) and a contrarian pick of Cincinnati rookie running back Jeremy Hill, walked away with the $2 million payday. Overall, FanDuel handed out $7 million in prizes that day.

"Actually, the finals were a cakewalk compared to the qualifier," Hanson said. "In the qualifier, there were fifty-nine-thou-

Scott Hanson's Recipe

When Scott Hanson won $2 million in FanDuel's Fantasy Football Championship in 2014, his lineup strategy was a textbook approach to winning the big tournaments: Imagining game flow, being contrarian, and knowing when to save and when to splurge. Here's how he put the pieces together after one of 30 lineups he submitted in a $2 qualifier with 59,000 entries put him in a short field of 100 finalists.

The key to Hanson's strategy in the final was his vision of the unfolding of a specific game: the Cincinnati Bengals playing the Browns in Cleveland. His premise was not that a specific player would do especially well, but rather that one was headed for trouble—Cleveland rookie quarterback Johnny Manziel was the key. The strategy was based on Hanson's belief that Manziel would turn the ball over, allowing Cincinnati to get a lead that it would protect by running the ball in the second half. Having read that Bengals' rookie running back Jeremy Hill would shoulder the rushing duties, Scott drafted him.

Manziel had a horrendous debut as the Browns made just five first downs all day. Meanwhile, Hill scored two early touchdowns and finished with 148 rushing yards as Cincinnati turned to the running game after building a big lead. Of the 100 DFS lineups assembled, Hanson's was the only one to include Hill, who racked up 27.7 FanDuel points.

The bargain $7,100 salary-cap price on Hill allowed Hanson to splurge on some high-salaried players, such as running back Le'Veon Bell ($9,600), and wide receivers Odell Beckham Jr. ($8,500) and Demaryius Thomas ($9,000), all of whom performed as expected, earning 26.4, 36.3, and 21.3 points, respectively.

Other key selections Hanson made are also instructive. At quarterback, he went with backup-turned-starter Derek Anderson for $5,000, who figured to put up solid, if not spectacular, numbers against a weak Tampa Bay. Anderson earned 16.48 points. Hanson also selected the Kansas City Chiefs defense/special teams playing against a hapless Oakland Raiders group that was an 11-point underdog. The Chiefs scored on a punt return, recovered a fumble, and had four sacks. Finally, Hanson settled on the high-scoring Denver Broncos kicker Connor Barth, who tallied five field goals and an extra point.

Scott Hanson's winning lineup is displayed here.

POS	escot4			SCORE
1	0 Quarters Remaining			176.58
QB	**Derek Anderson** TB 17 @ CAR 19 FINAL 14 RuY, 277 PaY, 1 PaTD	$5000 SALARY	47% OWNED	16.48
RB	**Le'Veon Bell** PIT 27 @ ATL 20 FINAL 47 RuY, 2 RuTD, 5 Re, 72 ReY	$9600 SALARY	47% OWNED	26.4
RB	**Jeremy Hill** CIN 30 @ CLE 0 FINAL 148 RuY, 2 RuTD, 1 Re, 4 ReY	$7100 SALARY	1% OWNED	27.7
WR	**Demaryius Thomas** DEN 22 @ SD 10 FINAL 6 Re, 123 ReY, 1 ReTD	$9000 SALARY	13% OWNED	21.3
WR	**Odell Beckham Jr.** WAS 13 @ NYG 24 FINAL 12 Re, 143 ReY, 3 ReTD, 1 FL	$8500 SALARY	61% OWNED	36.3
WR	**Donte Moncrief** HOU 10 @ IND 17 FINAL	$5700 SALARY	14% OWNED	0
TE	**Antonio Gates** DEN 22 @ SD 10 FINAL 6 Re, 54 ReY, 1 ReTD	$5500 SALARY	22% OWNED	14.4
K	**Connor Barth** DEN 22 @ SD 10 FINAL 2 FGu20, 1 FGu30, 2 FGu50, 1 XP	$4700 SALARY	19% OWNED	18
D	**Kansas City Chiefs** OAK 13 @ KC 31 FINAL 4 S, 1 FR, 1 RTD, 1 PA7-13	$4900 SALARY	16% OWNED	16

sand entries. In Vegas, I just had to deal with ninety-nine other people." In the process, Hanson became the winner of the single largest daily fantasy sports prize to that point.

"I try to imagine how the game might go and which players will benefit if it goes the way I'm thinking," Hanson said. "That time, it worked out pretty good."

When it was all over, Hanson and his wife flew back home in a private jet. So, yes, it worked out pretty good.

While Hanson's experience was a fantasy sports dream come true, satellites and qualifiers need to be viewed in practical terms. To be sure, they're enormously popular, because they can lead to endings just like the one Hanson experienced. However, the reality of multi-tiered satellites and qualifiers is that usually, you have to prevail against long odds—not just once, but multiple times, to get to the big contest.

If you're a beginner or even an intermediate DFS participant, satellites should make up just a small fraction of your regular play. With respect to building your bankroll, they have to be considered as before-the-fact losses. If a satellite comes through, it's gravy. But until you've amassed a sizable war chest, play satellites the way you'd buy lottery tickets—sparingly (see "Baseball Contest Types," pg. 183, for more on satellites and qualifiers).

The Vegas Numbers

The starting point for *all* fantasy sports lineups comes from the Las Vegas oddsmakers. In subsequent chapters, you'll learn how the official odds also provide the first steps in assembling lineups in other sports. For football, the process is methodical.

To begin, go through the list of NFL games and note the over-under (O/U) number for each game. The O/U, often referred to as the "total," poses a wagering proposition that involves whether the two teams combined will score a total number of points that's over or under the posted figure. For example, the Chicago Bears are playing the Detroit Lions and the game has a total of 45. Bettors who wager on the over win their bet if the Bears and Lions score a combined total of 46 or more points; under bettors collect on 44 points or less. (While it doesn't have relevance in discussing daily fantasy sports, if the two teams score exactly 45 points, the bet is a tie, also called a "push.")

From the over-under number, you learn how the line makers, using their own sharp vision of sports outcomes, view the complexion of the game: Is it likely to be high-scoring? Low-scoring? About average?

For a frame of reference, the average total for NFL games in 2014 was 45.2 points. Of course, you have to consider each NFL week separately and judge within the context of all the games whether each game is forecast to be higher- or lower-scoring relative to the others. And for the purposes of daily fantasy football, you'll prefer players in higher-scoring contests (except when you're trying to select a defense).

But the Vegas odds don't end with the over-under numbers. Next, consider the pointspreads. Combining the pointspreads with the totals gives you an approximation of the final score.

Continuing to use the hypothetical Chicago-Detroit game with a 45-point total, let's say that the oddsmakers make Detroit a 3-point favorite. For the game to go exactly as the oddsmakers project it, the final score will be Detroit 24, Chicago 21.

Of course, it probably won't go exactly as indicated by the line, but in doing this simple calculation, you get an idea of how the gambling experts see the contest unfolding. Armed with a projected final score, you can then formulate some informed opinions about how much offense to expect out of the two teams.

In a game ending Detroit 24, Chicago 21, it would be a fairly even distribution of offense and, consequently, fantasy points. Now let's change the example a bit. Again, we have a 45-point total. But this time, Detroit is a heavy 11-point favorite for a projected final score of Detroit 28, Chicago 17. In this case, the Vegas odds tell you that the Lions are likely to have more offensive production than the Bears. So now you have some guidance that Lions players may be better choices for daily fantasy lineups than Bears players.

And that's not all. If a game is projected to be high-scoring *and* close, that's an indication that both teams will be throwing the ball until the last minute. As a result, you should consider that players involved in both teams' passing games, especially the quarterbacks, are being forecast to have big fantasy-points days.

Now let's say that the oddsmakers set a pointspread where one team is a huge 17-point favorite. If you think about the likely flow of a blowout, the projected scenario suggests that the winning team will build a big lead, then protect its scoreboard advantage by running the ball, especially later in the game, to burn time off the clock. If the game takes that shape, the running back on the favored team is a candidate for a bunch of fantasy points, thanks to an increased workload in the second half.

In terms of defense, it seems an obvious call to go with a low O/U and a low pointspread. However, don't overlook the defense of a relatively high-scoring game where one team is a big favorite. The frequent scenario here usually features several turnovers by the losing team—interceptions and lost fumbles—and a bunch of sacks on the quarterback. In DFS football, defense is rewarded heavily for turnovers, plus those turnovers present excellent chances for defensive scores.

So when an NFL team is heavily favored, it's not only an indication that position players on that team are poised for a windfall of fantasy points. A gaping pointspread might be saying the same thing about the defense.

Projections and Value Quotients

Projecting point production and calculating value quotients in assembling DFS lineups are part of the weekly routine for experienced daily fantasy grinders. Here's how to think of these two concepts:

- Player projection is exactly what it sounds like: coming up with a forecast of how many fantasy points a player will accrue in his next game.
- Player-value quotients are a measure of an athlete's value relative to the amount of salary-cap money being spent on him.

To be candid, it may be an unrealistic expectation for you—a beginning or intermediate DFS participant—to go through the statistical research and mathematical rigors to calculate projections for every player you consider selecting. And with websites available that do the research and arithmetic for you, such as RotoGrinders (in several sports) or Steamer Projections or FanGraphs (baseball), there might not be much advantage in trying to do it yourself. After all, there's a point of diminishing returns, both for research and calculation, and each person has to decide when he or she reaches that point.

You might determine that your DFS preparation time during the NFL season is better spent following team developments reported by the local beat writers, keeping track of depth-chart changes, or monitoring the day-to-day injury updates, rather than trying to fill in the blanks in algebraic equations.

Plus, while player projections can be a useful tool in succeeding at daily fantasy sports, they're not perfect by any means. That's because the statistics used in building a projection can be the product of a certain amount of randomness and "luck," and that alone undermines the predictive nature of the projections.

The math wizards in the DFS community will object, and with reason—a daily fantasy professional armed with even somewhat imperfect player projections is likely to be more precise in assembling lineups than the daily fantasy novice who's just winging it. But for most beginners, using the pre-packaged numbers from a credible website is as good as (or better than) trying to create your own.

Whether or not you go through the exercise of calculating projections yourself or take the shortcut and consult the projection advice available online, it's helpful to understand the concepts of player projections and value quotients. In other words, although we all use calculators these days to balance our checkbooks, it's still good to be able to do simple arithmetic with a paper and pencil.

So here goes.

For most DFS participants, my suggestion is to wait until three or four games into the regular season before getting too invested in player projections. Up to that point, simply use the player's average fantasy points per game (FPPG) as the baseline for projections, without regard for the quality of the past opposition, because usually the past-opponent-quality issue will even out to a neutral factor or close enough to it.

To arrive at a more accurate projection, it's necessary to consider the *next* opponent's defensive performance against other players at that same position and adjust accordingly.

Here's a step-by-step example:

1. We're considering a running back who has produced an average of 20 fantasy points per game.

2. We look at his next opponent and calculate that the opposing team has yielded an average of 18 FPPG to running backs.

3. We calculate the league-wide average for defenses against running backs and find that it's 22 FPPG.

4. The strength of the upcoming opponent against running backs can be expressed as the FPPG yielded divided by the league average of FPPG yielded. In this case, 18/22 = .82.

5. To adjust our running back's projected fantasy point output versus this upcoming opponent, multiply his FPPG average times the upcoming opponent's strength factor (20 x .82) and come up with a projection of 16.4 points for the upcoming game.

There are far more complex ways of calculating player fantasy point projections. For example, the player's base FPPG can be initially recalibrated by calculating a defensive strength factor for *each* of his past opponents (also known as "strength of schedule"), then taking the average of those opponents and dividing that number into his FPPG even before adjusting for the upcoming opponent. (Applying this more complicated approach with the same hypothetical example used above yields a projection of 18.3, indicating that the simpler method undervalued this player by about 10%.) And for an even *more* complex refinement, each component of the running back's fantasy point total, meaning running and receiving, can be broken down relative to past and future opponents by using the same basic principles as in the simpler calculation.

But in the end, a process is only useful if people can conveniently implement it. If you do your own projections, the step-by-step method just presented will give you what you need to be effective with a minimal amount of effort.

Remember, if you're careful about what contests you choose and don't tangle with the pros in head-to-heads, applying these concepts and strategies, even at preliminary levels of implementation, should render you far more sophisticated than your opposition.

Once armed with a player projection, you can move on to calculating your own player-value quotient. Value quotients are expressed in two ways that tell the same story. In some instances, you'll see player values expressed as dollars per points ($/PT) and at other times, you'll see them as points per $1,000 (PT/$m). In both cases, the resultant number quantifies what kind of "value" a player has been or is projected to be.

When looking at $/PT value, the *lower* the number the better, because it means you're paying less in salary-cap money for each fantasy point. When looking at a PT/$m value, the *higher* the number the better; because you're getting more fantasy points for each salary-cap dollar spent (expressed in $1,000). These two expressions convey the same conceptual results in inverse fashion.

I'll give examples, first using the dollars-per-point method, then the same thing in points-per-$1,000.

In deciding between two players at the same position, one way to make your choice is to first calculate the points projections for the two players, then divide those numbers into their daily fantasy salaries. The player who has the lower number in the $/PT method is the better value. Example:

Travis Benjamin has a projection to score 20 fantasy points and a salary of $8,000, while Eric Decker has a projection to score 16 fantasy points and a salary of $5,500. The $/PT method divides the salary by the projected points to come up with the value quotient.

Dollars-Per-Point ($/PT)			
	Projected Points	Salary	Value Quotient
Travis Benjamin	20	$8,000	400
Eric Decker	16	$5,500	343.75

In this example, Travis Benjamin's value quotient is $400 ($8,000/20). So, you're paying $400 for each point he's expected to score. Eric Decker's value quotient is about $344 ($5,500/16). So, you're paying $344 for each point he's expected to score. The lower number is better, so Decker is the better "value." You pay fewer dollars for each projected point.

Even if the player with the better value quotient has a slightly lower projected points total (Decker), the salary-cap money you save can be used at other positions to select players projected to produce high point totals for your lineup.

In the points-per-$1,000 method, the projected points are divided by the salary.

Points-Per-$1,000 (PT/$m)			
	Projected Points	Salary	Value Quotient
Travis Benjamin	20	$8,000	2.5
Eric Decker	16	$5,500	2.9

The calculation indicates that Travis Benjamin has a value quotient of 2.50, or 2.5 points for every $1,000 of salary spent. Eric Decker's value quotient is 2.90, or 2.9 points for every

$1,000 of salary spent. In this method, the higher of the numbers being compared is best, again indicating that Decker is the better value.

A handy place to look up player values is RotoGuru, where the value is expressed in points per $1,000. Remember, in that case, the higher value is more desirable.

Player Correlations

The game flow of real-life sports events produces statistical results that are often predictable and, as a result, are actionable. In short, if we're fairly certain something is likely to happen, we can do something about it.

In daily fantasy sports, if we have an understanding of what one athlete is likely to do, we're in a position to deduce the likely impact on other players in the same game.

Here are some obvious examples of player correlations in two sports, baseball and football:

- Let's say Washington Nationals slugger Bryce Harper typically bats third or fourth in his team's lineup. It's a reasonable assumption that the players who bat immediately before Harper will score more runs than they would than if they batted after.
- In years when Green Bay quarterback Aaron Rodgers has played a full season, he's averaged about 35 passing touchdowns, which has ranked him in the top 11% among NFL quarterbacks. With a reasonable assumption that Rodgers' production remains consistent, we can expect his top receivers, whoever they may be, to catch more TDs passes than the average receiver.

The above examples illustrate correlations between certain

players and their teammates. Though such correlations appear obvious, surprisingly, the concept is lost on many daily fantasy participants. And some who do understand the obvious positive correlations can miss more subtle ones, in which the fantasy points relationship between players is negative and need to be avoided.

Many sports have player correlations and corollary situations that are useful to daily fantasy participants, but football has more than most, or least more that are actionable.

The correlation that's most often discussed in DFS advice literature is between quarterbacks and receivers. It's considered almost a given that to succeed in large-field guaranteed-prize-pool tournaments (GPPs), you need to "stack" same-team quarterbacks and receivers, usually a wide receiver, but in some cases, a stud tight end.

If the quarterback hits his receiver for a 60-yard touchdown pass and you have both in a lineup, you receive a double bonus of fantasy points credited to the QB (passing yards and the passing TD) and to the receiver (receptions, receiving yards, and the touchdown) for the one big play. And in GPP tournaments where you need a big point total to cash and a gigantic point total to make big money, you need that type of play.

In cash games, on the other hand, the lineup strategy should be different. Here, the goal isn't to score the most points as possible to climb the payout ladder; it's to score *enough* points to make the money. In this case, stacking is dangerous.

Let's say you stack a QB and a WR and the quarterback fails to throw a touchdown that day. Not only does your quarterback earn mediocre fantasy points, but because you paired him with one of his wide receivers, you'll struggle at that position as well. So in cash games where you want players who have reliable high floors (you're counting on them for a predictable number of points), you don't want to put all your eggs in one team's passing-game basket. Instead, it's wiser to select dependable players from different teams.

Other player correlations involve avoiding certain players in the same lineup, whether it's a cash game or a GPP.

A Baseball Aside

Stacking isn't nearly as risky in baseball cash games as in football, because the adverse correlation involving teammates isn't as impactful in terms of fantasy points.

For instance, if Packers quarterback Aaron Rodgers fails to throw a touchdown pass during a game, his receivers will also be shut out from scoring (barring a rushing touchdown). So there's the jeopardy of that double hit to the lineup that stacks Rodgers and a Green Bay receiver.

But in the stacked baseball lineup involving Washington's Bryce Harper and his teammates, if Harper doesn't hit well, that doesn't preclude the batter in front of him from having a big game on his own and producing a bunch of points. Of course, there are still some potential adverse consequences, such as the batter after Harper in the Nationals' lineup missing out on some RBI opportunities. But clearly, the fantasy points dependency among baseball players isn't as closely linked as between a quarterback and receiver.

The conventional thinking is that it's unadvisable to include a quarterback and a running back from the same team, due to the inherent bifurcation of offensive production between the passing and running games. And it's a good general rule. But there are (admittedly) rare occasions when the QB-RB pairing does work. In 2014, Chicago running back Matt Forte had an NFL-record 102 receptions and having Bears quarterback Jay Cutler paired with Forte in fantasy lineups was just fine.

Even when the Bears trailed in games, which was often during their 5-11 campaign that season, Forte was in the back-field and catching passes as part of the comeback effort. But re-member, Forte had a record-breaking year and 29 more catches than the next NFL running back, so the Bears' situation was extreme.

Having a same-team running back and wide receiver in a fantasy lineup also poses risks. And in cash games, it seems to be an unnecessary risk, unless you're counting on that team to score an extraordinary number of touchdowns or gain an exceptional amount of yardage. In 2014, the average number of touchdowns per game per team was about 2.3. The highest-scoring team in the league, the Denver Broncos, averaged 3.4 touchdowns per game. So, if you pick a running back, hoping to get a TD from him, and he succeeds (making you a happy daily fantasy foot-ball owner), it correspondingly means the chances with your receiver from the same team are diminished (detracting your happy-camperhood), considering that logic and statistics indi-cate a limited number of scoring opportunities.

The exception is when a high-octane offense is projected to light up the scoreboard and dominate the stat sheets. In that case, teammates who appear to be vying for offensive pro-duction, from a fantasy points perspective, could turn out to be complementary. After all, if a receiver catches a pass for a first down, it gives his running-back teammate an opportunity for more touches. If your view of the game flow convincingly presents such a scenario—and you're right—having a running back and wide receiver or tight end from the same team in your lineup can be beneficial. However, in general, avoid situations where the success of one of your players works against the success of another, and having three offensive players from the same team is almost always a bad idea.

It should be obvious, but to point it out anyway, you should also avoid selecting the defense that's playing against your quarterback. A defense accumulates fantasy points and a quarterback loses points for interceptions. There's little overall value to your lineup if a positive play by one of your roster positions results in a negative outcome at another position. Not to mention that it creates a very conflicted rooting situation.

Corollary Circumstances

Apart from player correlations, both in creating and avoiding certain combinations, corollary circumstances can create big fantasy points opportunities. A corollary circumstance is one in which we can reasonably infer a certain outcome that results from an antecedent occurrence. Understanding these types of situations can be particularly beneficial to new and intermediate DFS participants, because they present opportunities to gain an advantage that stands apart from the edge enjoyed by more experienced numbers-crunching DFS grinders. Here's how corollaries work.

Player salaries are determined by the daily fantasy websites early in the week, usually on Monday, and *they don't change.* So if a starting running back is listed at a relatively high salary of, say, $8,000 and he gets hurt in practice, the salary will stay at that number. Meanwhile, the injured player's backup might have started the week at $5,000 and although he's in line for 20 or 25 carries as a fill-in who just got promoted, his low salary remains the same.

For an extreme example, I have to return to New England

running back Jonas Gray who, when pressed into service in Week 11 of the 2014 season because of injury to a teammate, responded with a 201-yard four-touchdown game against the Indianapolis Colts. Gray's salary that week on DraftKings was a bargain-basement $3,300. To put that into perspective, the most expensive RB on DraftKings that week was Matt Forte at $10,100, more than three times Gray's number.

Because NFL offensive schemes often remain the same regardless of the starters, an injury to a front-line player can mean a bonanza from a backup player. And such situations are opportunities to pick up starter-caliber fantasy points for a backup salary.

While news regarding injuries and backups being promoted to an unexpected start is available to everyone participating in DFS contests, it's amazing how many of your competitors won't pick up on important developments. Going back to the Jonas Gray example, remember that when the Gomes brothers won the DraftKings Millionaire Maker with Gray as their sleeper pick, less than 1% of all lineups in that contest included Gray—even though he had that dirt-cheap salary and the Patriots had been known to run the ball successfully against the Colts in the past. The genius in selecting Gray didn't come from any complicated algebraic equations. It was simply a result of understanding football.

An often-overlooked corollary situation early in NFL seasons is the impact that free agency has on daily fantasy. Because the websites' salary numbers cannot always reflect football realities, an understanding of what offseason personnel moves may mean presents an opportunity for DFS participants who understand this dynamic.

A 2014 case in point was wide receiver Emmanuel Sanders leaving Pittsburgh and signing with the Denver Broncos in the offseason as a free agent. While the Broncos were adding Sanders to an offense led by one of the NFL's all-time top passers, Peyton Manning, Denver lost wide receiver Eric Decker in free agency, and another Broncos receiver, Wes Welker, wound up being suspended for the first few games of the 2014 season. As an unknown quantity in the Denver offense, Sanders' salary on DraftKings was $4,800 in Week 1 and over his first seven games, it stayed at bargain levels averaging $5,700. During that time, Sanders averaged a healthy 20.6 fantasy points per game.

As a comparison on DraftKings, Dallas wide receiver Dez Bryant, who enjoyed a Pro Bowl-caliber season, had an average salary in his first seven games of $7,400, nearly 30% higher than Sanders. During that time, he averaged 19.5 fantasy points per game, or about 1 point fewer than Sanders.

The failure of the website to quickly adjust to the evolving situation in Denver resulted in an inefficiency in Sanders' pricing. Of course, by Game 8, Sanders' salary shot up to $8,000 and it stayed in the $7,000 to $8,000 range for the rest of the season, but the example illustrates that the website salaries can be imperfect as Sanders was available at a discount for nearly half the season. Observant NFL fans who understood the corollary circumstances involving Sanders and the Broncos early in the season were able to take advantage.

Quarterbacks

In assembling winning football lineups, you start as if you were putting together a real NFL team—with a quarterback. The most consistently important position in terms of fantasy points, the quarterback is the keystone of a DFS roster. That's not to say that quarterback is routinely the position that produces the most points for your team. In fact, if you're making the right roster calls, the guy who spikes in your lineup should be a wide receiver or a running back, especially in GPPs.

The mathematical quirk you need to appreciate is that although quarterbacks, as a group, represent the highest-scoring position in daily fantasy football, wide receivers and running backs have higher variance, the swings up and down from their fantasy points average. So as an owner, you certainly hope to pick wide receivers and running backs who perform on the high side of variance.

Still, you have to put quarterbacks on your teams who unfailingly are among your top four scorers if you hope to be a consistent winner (especially in cash games), exactly because they occupy the position that has the least variance and, consequently, the most predictability.

What is a good quarterback fantasy points total? It varies among websites, but as a guide, on FanDuel, the average for the 30 NFL quarterbacks with at least nine games during the 2014 regular season was 16.5 points per game. On DraftKings, the average for the same 30 quarterbacks was 17.5 points.

Of course, "value" is relative to what you pay for the player. So by that measure, you'd have done a solid job selecting QBs if they gave you 2.10-2.15 points for every $1,000 you spent on FanDuel. On DraftKings, where the basic salary constructs and rules for points are slightly different, a good return would have been about 2.60-2.65 points per $1,000.

Just as pitching is the position where you can't afford to miss in baseball, quarterback is the position in football where you need to get a reliable result. Quarterback in football is not nearly as critical as pitcher in baseball, but it's still a foundational position for putting together consistent money-winning lineups.

The scoring differences between the major DFS websites for quarterback aren't as significant as they are at other positions. On FanDuel, a QB earns 4 points for a passing TD, .04 points for a passing yard (i.e., 1 point for 25 passing yards), and 2 points for a 2-point conversion pass. On the negative side, quarterbacks take a hit of -1 point for an interception and -2 points for a lost fumble. They accumulate the normal statistics of 0.1 points for a rushing yard (i.e., 1 point for 10 rushing yards), 6 points for a rushing TD, and 2 points for a rushing 2-point conversion. Quarterbacks also earn receiving stats in the rare instance of a quarterback reception. The points are the same on DraftKings, with the notable exception that a QB gets 3-point bonuses for a 300-yard passing game and a 100-yard rushing game, and a lost fumble is just -1 point.

This bonus is a real differentiator for scoring, as prolific passers who routinely throw for 300 yards have a bit more value compared to QBs in offenses that are less pass-dominated. For this reason primarily, quarterbacks on FanDuel score slightly fewer points than on DraftKings. But relative to the other offensive skill positions, quarterbacks on FanDuel tend to score a greater proportion of a team's overall points. That's due, in part, to fewer points awarded for pass receptions made by wide receivers, tight ends, and running backs on FanDuel compared to DraftKings.

While quarterbacks and pitchers share the DFS commonality of being the starting-point position for assembling lineups, there's considerable difference on whether you should elect to use a sizable chunk of your salary cap on the position. In baseball, especially in cash games, it's almost always a good idea to spend whatever it takes to get an outstanding pitcher. However, in football, because player point production is tied to weekly matchups, coaching schemes, and likely game flow, you can sometimes save on the quarterback and use that saved cap salary elsewhere.

Here are two examples where game flow was a dominant factor and fantasy owners would have been better off with the cheaper QB.

Frequently, a high-scoring team—such as the Denver Broncos in 2013 and '14—create a dynamic in which the *opposing* quarterback has an opportunity to outperform his own passing averages, yet he'll still be a bargain in salary cap pricing. This happens for two reasons. For one, the quarterback facing the Broncos (with Peyton Manning as their quarterback in those seasons) had to score a ton of points to keep up with Denver's high-octane offense. So that QB's offensive coordinator was forced to call more passing plays. Second, when the Broncos did build a big lead, their pass defense was relatively soft to avoid giving up big plays. That scenario often resulted in more offensive stats for the opposing quarterback.

In 2013, in a 51-to-48 losing effort against Denver, Dallas quarterback Tony Romo threw for more than 500 yards and five touchdowns for a season-high 41 fantasy points on FanDuel. Romo's FanDuel salary was just $8,200 that day. In contrast, Manning, while also having a good game and racking up 36 fantasy points, cost quite a bit more, $10,400.

In 2014, Miami QB Ryan Tannehill had an $8,100 price tag on FanDuel when he was slated to play against Denver. The Dolphins lost, but Tannehill's fantasy owners got 27 points out of him as he was forced to keep up with the Bronco's scoring. Again, the losing QB was the bargain. Manning had one more fantasy point in that game, but he cost $1,800 more than Tannehill.

Here's one more important observation concerning quarterbacks. While on-field efficiency is certainly a good thing, simply being prolific can be even better. The coach of a real NFL team would certainly prefer that his quarterback throw three touchdowns and zero interceptions compared to four TDs and three interceptions, because turnovers are so devastating on the scoreboard. But in daily fantasy scoring, those three TD passes and zero interceptions equal 12 fantasy points, while the four TD passes and three interceptions are a slightly better outcome of 13 fantasy points. So in DFS, it's OK if you have a quarterback without a conscience who keeps airing it out.

In selecting quarterbacks, fantasy owners should consider the following factors:

1. Type of contest entered
2. Opponent match-up
3. Offensive scheme
4. Cost, including $/point
5. Anticipated game flow
6. Weather/Stadium

The priority of the above factors could change, depending on circumstances.

Here's a closer look at the factors that influence quarterback selection:

Type of Contest—In cash games, you should heavily favor quarterbacks with high floors. This point is made repeatedly in any DFS-advice literature and it applies to most positions. It's particularly important with quarterbacks, whose production is more consistent, thereby more predictable, than other positions. It's more justifiable to splurge on quarterbacks (also known as "paying up") in cash games than in GPPs.

Match-up—In NFL football, matchups can be predictive of individual performance. Systemic strengths and weaknesses on NFL teams tend to carry over from week to week, because there's little time in practice to correct deficiencies. As a football beat writer, I learned that once a season begins, the opportunity for coaches to fundamentally alter performance among individual players is severely limited; most of the prep time is spent dealing with the game plan for the next opponent. So in selecting quarterbacks, examination of the upcoming opposing pass defense is important. Barring injuries, the matchup has predictable results.

Offensive Scheme—In no sport are team performance and playing style more reflective of the head coach than in football. In picking quarterbacks, you have to keep this in mind, although a QB's stats and DFS salary probably already reflect whether a coach is prone to throwing the ball more frequently. An example of a coach having an extraordinary impact on scheme and, as a result, statistical output is Chip Kelly, who became the head coach of the Philadelphia Eagles in 2013. Kelly attempts to run 20% to 30% more offensive plays than the NFL average. When Kelly's offense is clicking, his offensive players (including the quarterback) are the beneficiaries of increased statistical production. That's precisely the type of situation of which a DFS owner needs to be continuously aware.

Cost, including $/point—Of course, cost is an important factor in choosing players at any position. In selecting quarterbacks, it becomes more a function of the type of contest you're entering. In cash games, be willing to spend more for a quarterback you can trust to play according to form, thereby delivering DFS points close to his projection. That means one with a low standard deviation. In large-field GPPs, you'll have to take a gamble to save on the quarterback, so you have more money to spend on the high-upside positions, particularly wide receiver.

Anticipated Game Flow—One of the things that makes the NFL so appealing is that the combination of factors already discussed, such as match-ups and coaching schemes, make imagining the ebb and flow a fun exercise. In this book, I call the anticipated story line of a game "game flow." Others who offer DFS advice call it "game script." Regardless of what it's called, it's an important factor to take into consideration when choosing a quarterback. An NFL game on a blustery day in early December in the Northeast that features two outstanding defenses is more likely to have coaches playing a field-position chess match. That's not a great opportunity for terrific quarterback numbers, so you should avoid the quarterbacks in that game. On the other hand, a game played in a dome with two Pro Bowl quarterbacks that figures to be close is the perfect setting for great passing stats.

Weather/Stadium—The impact of severely inclement weather on DFS contests is much more pronounced in baseball than in any other sport: The games are simply called off. And if you have players from that game in your lineup, you're out of luck; you get goose eggs for any players you have in that game.

In football, games don't get called off, even when the weather is ferocious. For quarterbacks, the biggest concern is wind. Extraordinary wind affects accuracy, particularly long passes. On the other hand, we've all seen a pass get held up in the wind and, because the receiver has his eyes toward the line of scrimmage (as opposed to the defensive back, who's marking the receiver), the offensive player comes back to the ball for the catch.

But you're not counting on freak plays to win your DFS contests. In picking QBs, it's usually best to avoid high-wind game conditions. Conversely, climate-controlled domed stadiums, as pointed out above, are excellent for passing games, not just for the quarterback, but for the receivers who can be more secure in making their moves.

Finally, quarterbacks appear to put up slightly better stats at home. Jonathan Bales, in *Fantasy Football for Smart People*, calculated that over an eight-year sample period, quarterbacks playing at home threw for nearly 3% more yards per attempt. Bales theorized that part of that statistic derived from the presumption that underdog teams are less conservative at home and throw the ball more often earlier in the game. Given the increase in yards per attempt, the average total gain seems to be between five and ten yards at home. Another way to factor home-field QB advantage is team by team. It was no secret that, for a long time, when the New Orleans Saints and their quarterback Drew Brees played in the Superdome, they fared far better than on the road. The Saints were 47-25 at home from 2006 through 2014 in the regular season and 40-32 on the road. If history is a barometer, you want Saints in your lineup when they're home.

A handy way to sort quarterbacks for DFS evaluation is to divide them into three categories, as will be explained.

Premier Quarterbacks

Every year, six to eight quarterbacks in the NFL are likely to have Pro Bowl-caliber seasons. In prior eras, we'd be talking about passers like Johnny Unitas, Joe Montana, and Brett Favre. More recently, quarterbacks in the premier category have included Aaron Rodgers, Peyton Manning, Andrew Luck, Drew Brees, Tom Brady, and Russell Wilson.

Premier quarterbacks, week after week, are some of the most expensive players on any daily fantasy website and put quite a dent in your salary-cap budget if you pick one. In 2014, Rodgers' average cap salary on FanDuel was $10,000. Considering the total cap is $60,000 and you have to fill eight other positions, taking Rodgers for $10,000 leaves an average of $6,250 per position. Even though you could save some money on a kicker and a defense, taking Rodgers meant you'd still be bargain hunting at running back, wide receiver, and tight end.

In baseball, occasionally on FanDuel, a pitcher will score as much as half the total points for your team, so it's worth paying whatever it takes to have a good one in your lineup. That will never happen with a quarterback in football. A quarterback having a good day could wind up contributing 20% of the total points for a lineup that makes it into the money in a cash game. You have to consider whether it's worth paying $10,000 for a QB from whom you expect to get 22 points, compared to $8,000 for a QB's 17 or 18 points.

The circumstances when it's most advisable to take top-tier quarterbacks is in cash games—50/50s, double-ups, and head-to-heads (when you can find a reasonable match-up).

The expression in daily fantasy for spending big on a player is "paying up." To pay up means you're investing a large percentage of salary-cap money in that player, because you know you'll get a quality performance.

Premier quarterbacks can usually be counted on to deliver a high floor and that's what you need in cash games. (As a reminder, a high floor means that a player performs consistently enough to earn a reliable minimum number of points.) Of course, it doesn't always work that way, but you're playing the percentages.

For example, in 2014, Andrew Luck was incredibly consistent. Through the first 10 games of the season, he operated within a 10-point range with a floor of about 20 and a ceiling in the low 30s. He cost, on average, about 16% of salary cap (about $9,900 of $60,000 in FanDuel) and delivered an estimated average of 20% of the points typically needed to make it into the money in cash games. In the final six games of 2014, Luck hit his season-high of 33 fantasy points, but also recorded his four lowest fantasy points games of the season.

To further illustrate the importance of identifying premier quarterbacks and relying on them in cash games, let's look at Drew Brees during the 2014 season. Brees exhibited remarkable DFS reliability, even though his New Orleans Saints struggled in the regular season to a 7-9 finish and Brees himself made some key blunders that cost his team dearly. But Brees had 10 games in which he scored 19 or more points, rendering him a reasonably reliable cash-game player. The drawback to Brees was that his points-per-dollar spent was only average or slightly better than average, though that didn't disqualify him from being a reasonable cash-game QB selection on any given Sunday.

Value Quarterbacks

Value quarterbacks can come from a broad spectrum of passers. They can range from starters who are good enough to get a team to the playoffs (but are not perennial Pro Bowl candidates) to backups handed the reins in a situation that could produce a big statistical day. Value opportunities present themselves when a first-string quarterback is unable to start and the backup is summoned to take control and has a hugely discounted salary.

Throughout his NFL career, Mark Sanchez has never demonstrated that he's anything more than a mediocre starter and a better-than-average backup. But on Thanksgiving Day 2014, he made his first start for the Eagles following an injury to Nick Foles. On FanDuel, Sanchez was a measly $6,600 for his start against Dallas, which meant he had the potential to be a bargain. Playing in Eagles head coach Chip Kelly's hurry-up offense, Sanchez scored 21 FanDuel points for a dollars-per-point quotient of $314, which was a big bang for the buck.

Compare that to Andrew Luck—the top points QB on Fan-Duel for 2014—who had a season-long $/points quotient of about $432 (remember, lower is better here).

So for a single game, Sanchez was the right guy in the right place, and DFS owners who took him could have used their extra salary-cap dollars on top players at other positions that weekend, such as Pittsburgh running back Le'Veon Bell who cost a rich $9,200 on FanDuel, but produced 35 points that week. Those are the kinds of opportunities that present themselves in GPPs when a value quarterback comes through, as Sanchez did in week 13.

The DFS owner who goes the value-QB route is certainly taking a chance, but the payoff can be big. To place high in big-field guaranteed-prize-pool tournaments, you have to take some calculated risks with your roster.

Running Quarterbacks

Because of the way daily fantasy scoring rewards rushing yardage, you have to give special consideration to running quarterbacks in your weekly evaluations. Cam Newton is an example of a quarterback whose running ability helps both his GPP potential and stabilizes his floor value week in and week out. Consider this: One 30-yard TD run by a QB like Newton translates to 9 fantasy points. A non-running quarterback has to throw for 225 passing yards to earn those same 9 fantasy points. So a big running day from Newton means that he'll boost a GPP lineup into contention. And on occasions when the called running plays for Newton are held in check, he still has a chance to pick up 20 or 30 yards as he scrambles to avoid the pass rush. That gives Newton a bump of 2 or 3 fantasy points that a conventional pocket quarterback doesn't get.

In 2014, Newton had a solid fantasy year as his Carolina Panthers limped into the playoffs with a 7-8-1 regular-season record and he made 14 starts. Newton tied for seventh among quarterbacks in average fantasy points per game for QBs on FanDuel (18.64 FP/G) and ninth in the same category on DraftKings (19.43). Using FanDuel as a reference website, Newton's two blockbuster weeks were games in which he racked up about 35 fantasy points in each—the kinds of totals you need to send you to the top of a large-field tournament. In both cases, his point total was bolstered by a rushing touchdown. Removing the two top-end outlier performances, in his remaining 12 starts, Newton averaged 15.8 fantasy points per game, substantially helped by rushing yardage of about 29 yards per game or almost 3 fantasy points (nearly 20% of his total).

In other words, Newton's legs propelled him to huge point totals in his best weeks and were the difference between having acceptable weeks as a cash-game player as opposed to what would have been substandard or outright stinkers. But be careful with running quarterbacks. You have to remain mindful of the erosion of their running abilities. A running quarterback's fantasy value is highly dependent on that facet of his game.

For example, in his first 85 games in the NFL, former Pro Bowl quarterback Donovan McNabb averaged about 29 yards per game rushing. Over the final 82 games, that average dropped to 12.2 yards a game. Yet McNabb continued to be thought of as a running quarterback long after he stopped sprinting for yardage.

Daily fantasy owners must constantly re-evaluate players and subject their own perceptions to reality checks. More than any other daily fantasy sport, in football you need to trust your eyes over the numbers. When you begin seeing a running quarterback get caught from behind or failing to outrun outside linebackers to the edge, you might not want to count those automatic 3 to 6 extra points you thought his running ability would contribute to your lineup.

Yet DFS owners will latch onto a player such as a running quarterback week after week, thinking he'll revert to the form that they have fixed in their minds of him running for 50 and 60 yards and a TD, and it simply never happens again. As former wide receiver Michael Irvin noted nearly a decade ago of an aging Brett Favre, "Father time is undefeated."

Running Backs

Your two running backs are the heart of your fantasy football lineup in cash games, and the specialization that is so much a part of the modern NFL poses some challenge in filling the position. On the major DFS websites, you're required to fill two running-back spots. When a Flex position is part of the lineup, you can pick a third running back to use in that spot as well.

As is the case with all positions when entering cash games, you want running backs with high floors. And in GPPs, you'll seek running backs with higher potential ceilings. Since running backs tend to produce fantasy points in a narrower range than wide receivers and tight ends, it's easier to find the ideal running back for your cash-game lineups than for the big-field GPPs. And therein lies the good news about running backs for beginning DFS players—their production, week to week, is relatively predictable, at least compared to wide receivers.

Chris Raybon, a daily fantasy expert and writer, calculates that among the three major positions, quarterbacks represent the least volatility, wide receivers and tight ends have the most volatility, and running backs are in between. According to Raybon's research, quarterbacks have a potential volatility of 45% (either positively or negatively), running backs potentially have a 55% volatility, wide receivers 65%, and tight ends 67%. That means that if a running back has a projected total of 18 fantasy points, his likely range is about 8 to 28 points. To figure the top-end projection, the calculation is 18 + (18 x .55). For the low end, it's 18 - (18 x .55).

Evaluating running backs is all about opportunity. In other words, how much are they on the field (snap counts) and how many touches do they get (carries and receptions)? Apart from the most obvious correlating statistics of yards gained and touchdowns scored, snaps and touches have a closer correlation to fantasy point production than any other stats, Raybon says. But although he can crunch numbers, he's a fan of giving players the eyeball test.

According to Raybon, "Even if you have all the mathematical research in the world available to you, what you learn from that only makes you able to predict about 45% or 50% of what a player is going to do. That's because of the inherent volatility of the game itself. So to be as accurate as possible, you have to watch the games and use your own intelligence to learn what you can."

Raybon subscribes to NFL.com's Game Pass (formerly Game Rewind), which provides condensed versions of every game with the dead time wrung out of them, and it even gives a so-called Coaches' Film perspective that provides a wide-field view of all 22 players. Raybon also claims to watch every NFL game, again because he believes a DFS player can't rely on the numbers alone.

"There's an ongoing debate on Twitter between the data people and the film people," Raybon says. "I think you have to use both, data and film. If a player scores a sixty-yard touchdown, it may be because a defensive player fell down, and it's not the type of thing that's likely to occur again. But if a running back or a wide receiver has a big day like that, the stats might be reflected in his pricing the next week and you'll want to avoid him, because the jump in salary isn't warranted. When I watch film, I'm looking for things that are repeatable."

Here are factors to consider when selecting running backs.

Scheme—If there are constants week to week in the NFL, one is overall coaching philosophy. If it's a coach's philosophy to hand the ball to the running backs 25 or 30 times a game (Gary Kubiak), that won't change. If it's to throw short passes to the backs (Andy Reid), that won't change. It was no accident that Ravens running back Justin Forsett flourished as a between-the-tackles rusher when Kubiak was the offensive coordinator in Baltimore. Nor was it any coincidence that Kansas City running back Jamaal Charles saw his targets and receptions double in Reid's first year as head coach of the Chiefs. So coaching schemes become a predictor for DFS players who pay attention.

Opportunity—If you do only one bit of statistical research to pick your running backs, examine touches—both carries and receptions, as well as snap counts. Obviously, snaps and touches are correlated numbers. And don't forget the most important touches of all, carries in the red zone.

The Vegas Numbers—Running backs on winning teams put up bigger numbers than running backs on losing teams. Of course, that's related to game flow. When a team is ahead, it runs the ball more. When a team is behind, the running back is picking up blitzes if he's even in the game at all. Remember, the Vegas line combined with the over/under total suggests not only a final score, but a flow. If a team is a 14-point underdog, its running back should not be in your lineup.

DFS in the Sports Books

Up to now, the legal sports books in Nevada have refrained from jumping into full daily fantasy mode. But there have been forays.

In March 2012, Cantor Gaming (now CG Technologies)—at the time an up-and-coming bookmaking group with roots in Internet gambling that was making a play in Nevada—received approval to launch a new betting option called the "Cantor Five." Few understood it at the time, but it was a DFS-style model for the NBA, by which bettors selected a 5-man roster that could be matched against one of two Cantor computer-generated rosters. No salaries were involved and players could bet on or against their own teams, with Cantor's computer spitting out take and lay prices designed to retain a profit regardless of which way players bet.

Cantor Five got a chilly reception, but that didn't derail the introduction of "Cantor6" in August 2012, the baseball version of Cantor Five. And only a few months later, "Cantor 7" (yes, the formats of the names were all different), the football version, was introduced. Cantor6 allowed for baseball rosters that comprised a pitcher, two outfielders, and three infielders. Cantor 7 had one quarterback, two running backs, two receivers, a kicker, and a defense.

Unfortunately for the casinos, most of the players were sports-betting pros who did what pros do: exploit vulnerabilities in embryonic systems. Since Cantor didn't make its money from a rake, it needed square action (unsophisticated players) to participate, but the squares didn't understand the game and stayed away. Since Cantor discontinued the 5/6/7 series, there've been a few weak efforts to mimic DFS, with nothing catching on.

DFS author Jonathan Bales researched the Vegas line as it applies to rushing results and his findings indicated that teams that had a projected score of 30 or more points averaged about 14% more yards on the ground than teams that the line indicated would score 21 to 23 points (the NFL average in 2014). Naturally, the disparity was even greater for teams projected to score fewer than 21 points.

Receptions—This is huge, especially under full PPR (point-per-receptions) rules, such as on DraftKings. A running back who carries the football for a nice 10-yard gain on first down earns his team a first down and his DFS owners 1 fantasy point (0.1 point per rushing yard). In PPR rules, a running back who catches a swing pass on first down and gains just one yard puts his team at second-and-9 and earns his fantasy owners 1.1 fantasy points (0.1 point per receiving yard and 1 point for the reception). If it doesn't seem fair, well, daily fantasy, like life, isn't always fair. But you still need to understand how to make the rules work in your favor.

Running backs who can catch the ball have an extra fantasy dimension, plus they may even be in the game when their teams are behind, because they're important to the passing attack.

In the short history of DFS, pass-catching running backs like Danny Woodhead, Shane Vereen, and Darren Sproles have become daily fantasy stars, thanks to a potent one-two punch: their potential to put up big numbers and bargain salary-cap pricing.

Right Guy for the Right Contest—Actually, selecting running backs for cash games is one of the easier decisions in daily fantasy football. Because you're looking for reliable production, the prudent move is to go with the backs getting a decent number of touches, both carries and receptions, and balance their projected fantasy points with your salary constraints. If

Above: Nigel Eccles started FanDuel in Scotland in 2009 before moving operations to the United States.

Left: U.S. Representative (R-Iowa) Jim Leach sponsored the Unlawful Internet Gambling Enforcement Act of 2006 that contained the important fantasy sports carve-out.

Below: Paul Liberman (L), Jason Robins (C), and Matt Kalish (R) started DraftKings in Boston out of Liberman's spare bedroom.

Scott Hanson, pictured with his wife Danielle, emerged from a FanDuel satellite with 59,000 entrants and beat 99 other finalists in the championship to win what was the biggest DFS prize to date.

Dave (L) and Rob (R) Gomes cashed in big on the Patriots, first riding little-known New England running back Jonas Gray to a $1 million payday at DraftKings, then winning futures bets for another $78K when the Pats beat the Seahawks in Super Bowl 49.

facing page: The "giant check" is a staple of DraftKings promotion and TV advertising.

Bill Winkenbach helped codify the rules for fantasy football and hosted the first draft (draft sheet pictured below) in his Oakland, Calif., home in 1963. George Blanda was the first pick.

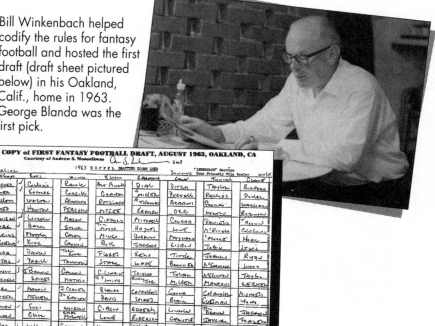

Long before the Internet, this is what fantasy football drafts looked like in the GOPPPL circa 1963. (Courtesy Andy Mousalimas)

Dan Okrent is credited with inventing Rotisserie Baseball, a staple of traditional fantasy, which led to daily fantasy.

facing page: (top) Paul Charchian, an early fantasy strategy guru, became president of the Fantasy Sports Trade Association; (center) Adam Krejcik of Eilers Research projects that daily fantasy sports revenues will hit $1.4 billion by 2020; (bottom) "It's inevitable … increasingly, fans are going to identify with players more than teams," says NY radio personality Anita Marks, whose favorite fantasy baseball pitcher is the Mets' Matt Harvey.

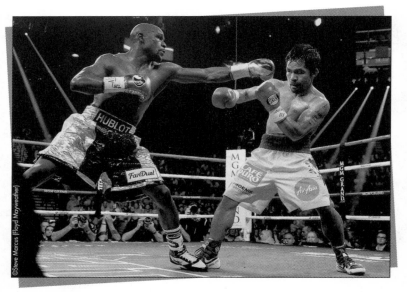

DFS' promotional tentacles have spread throughout the sporting world. The FanDuel logo was prominent on the trunks of Floyd Mayweather Jr. during his mega-fight against Manny Pacquiao, while a DraftKings logo adorned the saddle blanket of American Pharoah at the Belmont when he won the Triple Crown.

DraftKings' branding was everywhere during the 2015 World Series of Poker in Las Vegas, as Max Steinberg rode a $27 DFS qualifier to place fourth in the WSOP's Main Event.

you come up with two backs in that category, your production from that position should have you on pace to make the money in cash games.

Picking running backs for GPPs is trickier. For instance, Justin Forsett of the Ravens had his coaches beaming in a game against Tampa Bay in 2014 when he gained 111 yards on 14 carries (a gaudy 7.9 yards-per-carry average). But he failed to get a touchdown and finished with a so-so 14.1 points on DraftKings. That would be OK (but not great) in most cash games, but it would be absolutely no help in a GPP where you need points in bunches.

In the big tournaments, you want touchdown scorers and you have to get them relatively cheap, because you have to pay up for wide receivers. So GPPs are the places for those cheap, part-time, but pass-catching running backs like Darren Sproles, who had seven catches for 152 yards and a rushing TD in a 2014 game. Nothing inflates a running-back's fantasy-points total like six or seven short passes with a couple turning into big gainers. Or you could rummage in the bargain bin for a touchdown vulture like Matt Asiata, who scored three TDs in one game for Minnesota in 2014—despite gaining a total of just 26 yards. Touchdown vultures are backs who get their numbers called on the goal line to punch home the TD after their teammates have done all the work to put the ball deep in the red zone.

When you put together your running-back combinations, it's normally better to avoid a corollary circumstance: picking running backs from opposing teams. It has to be judged case by case, but game flow dictates that running backs on winning teams have better production than those on losing teams. So here, the risk you take is that success by one of your players, if the game unfolds in typical NFL fashion, will mean that your other running back will be adversely impacted.

The exception is the running back on a trailing team who is routinely part of the passing game, because he'll also be part of the comeback effort and that would be good for your lineup (think Matt Forte).

So while taking opposing running backs isn't always a mistake, you have to give it some thought and only make the move if you're convinced one of the backs is available at an enormous salary discount, or if you believe the back on the projected losing team can overcome the challenge of the anticipated game flow.

Wide Receivers/Tight Ends

Any NFL fan knows that pro football has evolved into a passing game, and there are a number of reasons why the game has taken to the air. Those who steer the NFL's course with rule changes long ago figured out fans like scoring. As a result, a number of modifications over the last few decades (limiting contact with receivers downfield is one) have helped offenses light up the scoreboards.

More recently, though, far more serious motives have influenced how the game is played. It's no secret that the NFL has been dealing with a long-simmering crisis related to concussions and brain trauma. Medical investigation has discovered that long-term cognitive disorders are the result of the pounding players' heads endure over the course of a career.

Not so long ago, a player knocked woozy from a collision was referred to with the almost comical observation of, "He just got his bell rung." However, medical science has told the NFL lately that those seemingly minor episodes are hardly inconsequential, and the league has responded by trying to take some of the violence out of the game. In the process, rules designed to help protect players have further disadvantaged defensive play. Vicious blows that were once a standard tactic among defensive backs to intimidate receivers now prompt penalties. As a result, offenses operate more easily in today's NFL than they used to.

Many of the changes, whether to make the game more entertaining or safer, have meant greater emphasis on throwing the ball and it's easier than ever to be successful doing that. As a daily fantasy player, you have to account for that by placing the appropriate emphasis on the wide-receiver position.

As the point has been made several times already, the decision about how to allocate salary cap resources to various positions—chiefly, quarterback, running back, and wide receiver—is a function of whether you're in a cash game or a GPP tournament.

In determining how much cap salary to use on wide receivers, keep two things in mind:

- Wide receivers, because of their volatility, are more significant in GPPs than in cash games (although they're important in both).
- Wide receivers have more impact relative to other positions under full-point-per-reception rules (DraftKings) than half-point (FanDuel).

In this section, I discuss both wide receivers and tight ends, since the bulk of the daily fantasy points they accumulate are earned in the same fashion: by catching the football.

Looking back at the 2014 NFL season, eight of the top 20 overall point-getters on DraftKings were wide receivers. On FanDuel they were just three of the top 20. That difference was mostly a reflection of the different point allocations. However, it would be a mistake to underestimate the overall importance receivers represent even under half-point rules. As evidence of that, among FanDuel's fantasy point leaders from numbers 21 through 40 were nine receivers and one tight end. Obviously, you do better earning full points from receivers, but guys who catch the ball are important to your success regardless of which website you're playing on.

Let's start with some overall factors in evaluating wide receivers.

Targets—The most important criterion in selecting pass catchers, whether wide receivers or tight ends, is the statistic known as "targets." In daily fantasy sports, a key factor is *opportunity*. An athlete can't generate fantasy points for your team unless he has the opportunity to do so.

So in choosing wide receivers and tight ends, the first number to look at is the one that tells how many times during a game the quarterback throws the ball in a particular receiver's direction, i.e. makes that receiver the "target" of the pass.

Lots of variables dictate an offensive game plan and those affect how many times a particular receiver is a target on any given Sunday. But as a rule, targets are the bellwether statistic for WRs and TEs.

While circumstances change plenty from season to season for individual players in the NFL, targets is one statistic that has some consistency year over year for elite receivers, assuming the basic personnel in a passing game remain the same. However, like everything in sports, and especially in the NFL, you have to constantly revisit the statistics to see if new trends are emerging.

Finding the statistics for targets is relatively easy. It has become a common stat in NFL box scores. Among the places to find targets, both cumulative and trending, is on ESPN.com.

If you're looking for correlation between targets and fantasy points, you don't have to search too hard. The top wide receiver in targets in 2014 was Denver's Demaryius Thomas

(184 targets) and he was the No. 2 wide receiver in daily fantasy football points on both FanDuel and DraftKings. The wide receiver with the second-most targets, Pittsburgh's Antonio Brown (182), was the number-one fantasy points WR on both websites.

Similar correlations are evident in the list of the top 20 receivers in fantasy points. With just a few exceptions, if a player was among the top 20 in targets, he was probably in the top 20 in fantasy points. The issue of targets is especially important in DFS lineup building once you get beyond the elite wide receivers and start sorting through the second tier of receivers.

On FanDuel and DraftKings, you have to select three wide receivers among the nine positions. On DraftKings, the Flex position can be drawn from the pool of wide receivers, running backs, and tight ends. Because DraftKings uses full PPR rules, it's essential to choose a Flex player who catches passes. While the best Flex option is usually a wide receiver, at times tight ends and pass-catching running backs offer more value.

Remember, when making the tough calls on lower-salaried wide receivers, targets is often the starting point.

Red Zone Targets—Picking receivers who catch a lot of passes is good. Picking receivers who catch a lot of touchdowns is better. Just as identifying receivers who get a lot of targets helps inform your choices for wide receivers in general, going a step further and researching which receivers are targeted in the red zone (from the opposition's 20-yard line to the end zone) gives you an edge on those who don't. Most touchdowns are the result of plays that start in the red zone. Among websites that track red-zone targets, and a wealth of additional information, is NFLSavant.com.

When making your own evaluations about the likelihood of a receiver getting red-zone looks from the quarterback, a key factor to take into consideration is size. Quarterbacks prefer big targets in the end zone for the obvious reason: Bigger receivers can outmuscle smaller defensive backs on their pass routes into the end zone; taller ones can out-jump the defender on contested balls.

DFS author Jonathan Bales quantified the correlation between wide-receiver size, both height and weight, and touchdown efficiency in the red zone as a result of extensive research that covered a 14-year period. Conclusions that football coaches reach through observation, Bales was able to establish empirically.

Receivers 6-foot-3 or taller were 20% more likely to convert a red-zone target into a TD than receivers 6 feet and shorter, Bales' research indicated. And weight appeared to be an even more significant contributor. Receivers who weighed 217 or more converted 35% more of their red-zone targets into touchdowns than receivers who weighed 196 or less.

"With height, that's certainly an advantage but it's an advantage mainly on one route, the fade route," Bales said referring to the pass route that features a receiver running toward the back corner of the end zone and the quarterback lofting the ball in his direction.

"But a wide receiver who has height *and* weight can fend off a defender in what is a fairly small space," Bales continued. "And that's what it's all about down there in the end zone— giving the quarterback just a little bit more room to squeeze the ball in. You'll see [Dallas receiver] Dez Bryant [6-foot-2, 220 pounds] do it all the time where he runs right into the cornerback, turns around, and [Cowboys quarterback] Tony Romo lets the ball go."

Although Bales' research looked at wide receivers, the correlation between size and red-zone efficiency helps explain why nearly 30% of receivers who had at least 16 red-zone targets in 2014 were tight ends who always have a size advantage against defensive backs and often even against linebackers.

Of course, every rule has its exceptions and the most elite receivers, regardless of height and bulk, will put up their stats no matter where the play starts on the field. For example, Antonio Brown—the most productive NFL receiver in 2014 with 129 receptions, 1,698 yards, and 13 touchdowns—is just 5-foot-10 and 186 pounds.

But in daily fantasy, you're looking for reliable predictors and Bales' work cements the anecdotal observation that with receivers near the end zone, bigger is usually better.

Wideout or Slot—A factor in choosing wide receivers getting more attention in daily fantasy analysis is where within an offensive alignment the receiver plays. Some receivers typically line up to the far outside of the formation ("wideouts"). Other wide receivers generally play from the so-called "slot," between the interior linemen and another receiver who's closer to the sideline.

The practical difference between the wideout and slot is that the wideout's pass routes tend to take him deeper down the field, while the slot receiver works between the hash marks. As a result, the wideout is often the player on the receiving end of the quarterback's long arching home-run throws, while the slot receiver catches the tough passes in the middle of the field to make first downs and keep drives alive.

For DFS owners, the differences are significant. Slot receivers produce fantasy points with more reliability. In the language of mathematical probability, slot receivers have a lower standard deviation. In contrast, wideouts produce huge fantasy point days when they haul in those long bombs from the QB. But when they don't, their output can be disappointing. As a result, wideouts can have high standard deviations.

So putting that understanding together with using players with high floors in cash games and potentially high ceilings in GPP tournaments, slot receivers are better suited for cash games and wideouts are more appropriate for the big-field tournaments.

Of course, as always, no rule is hard and fast. If you believe that a Pro Bowl wide receiver has a favorable matchup and he fits into your salary cap, you should consider selecting him regardless of where he lines up. But when you get down to your second and third WRs, or have to make a decision on the Flex position, understanding the predictive math related to a WR's position helps you make your decision.

A real-world contrast between two star wide receivers who happened to play on the same team in 2014 involves Green Bay's Jordy Nelson and Randall Cobb. Nelson, the wideout, averaged 21.8 fantasy points per game on DraftKings. Cobb, the slot receiver, was close to his teammate's production, averaging 19.4 fantasy points per game. However, Nelson's game-to-game production was filled with peaks and valleys. He had four games of 30 points or more, seven games of 15 points or fewer, and just five games between 15 and 30 points. Cobb, the slot, had a much more even production: just one game with more than 30 points, four with fewer than 15 points, and 11 where he delivered between 15 and 30 points. Not surprisingly, Nelson's standard deviation was relatively high at 11.08, while Cobbs' was low for wide receivers in general (although about average for a slot) at 7.71.

This chart provides a graphic depiction of this effect. Note how Nelson's weekly output varied from very high to relatively low, while Cobb's results were concentrated predominantly in the middle area.

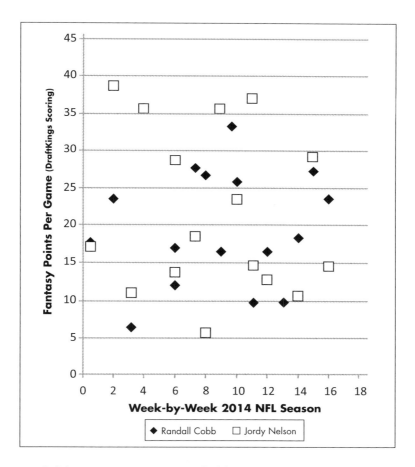

Of the two star receivers, Cobb was the guy you wanted in your cash games, because he had the higher floor, while Nelson was the choice for those shoot-the-moon GPP tournaments, because of his potential to have a mega-points game.

Matchups—Because of the nature of football, the wide receiver position entails a classic man-to-man confrontation with a defender, usually a cornerback. Certainly, sophisticated NFL defenses employ a range of schemes to thwart opposing wide receivers with all types of zone coverages. But when a defense has a so-called "shutdown" cornerback, the defensive coordinator tends to assign that super-skilled pass defender to the offense's top receiver man-to-man to take that weapon away from the quarterback.

In recent years, cornerbacks such as Darrelle Revis, Richard Sherman, and Patrick Peterson achieved NFL stardom as elite shutdown corners.

From season to season, shutdown cornerbacks change, but whoever those players are, it behooves DFS owners to get it figured out and avoid taking wide receivers likely to be shadowed by that type of defender. Quarterbacks avoid throwing in the direction of a shutdown corner.

In terms of corollary circumstances, a school of thought believes that when the opposing defense has a shutdown corner who will take away an offense's top receiver, there may be merit in giving greater consideration to the offense's number-two receiver. Since the quarterback will avoid throwing in the direction of his normal number one, the number two will get more targets than usual and his salary-cap pricing might not reflect his increased opportunities.

While that may be true, such thinking can be an oversimplification and dangerous if you don't take it to the next level. If the defensive coordinator can get away with single coverage on the number-one wide receiver because of the shutdown corner, the number two WR could get saddled with double coverage.

As mentioned previously, some daily fantasy websites have built analysis tools into their player-selection pages, so customers will have a convenient shortcut in their research, including matchup comparisons. For example, the DFS websites may tell you that Chicago is the 30th-ranked defense (out of 32 teams) against wide receivers. So, that may be helpful information when considering wide receivers playing against the Bears. Be sure to take advantage of the handy research tools, but also remember to do a little of your own legwork to go beyond the easy information that's available to everyone.

For instance, if you spot an occasion when a particularly tall wide receiver will be working against much shorter cornerbacks, that's an actionable situation that might not be reflected in matchup rankings based mainly on statistics. That's the type of circumstance where someone who understands the game can get an edge on fantasy owners going strictly with the numbers.

Deep-pass Targets—This statistic is one of the many advanced metrics available on analytics websites. As the name implies, it measures the frequency with which receivers are targeted with pass attempts of 20 yards or more. The metrics associated with deep-pass attempts and success rates are helpful in selecting GPP receivers, as long as you understand that big plays are rare occurrences.

Tight Ends—Tight ends aren't generally counted as being among the stars of a daily fantasy team. Exceptions have included New England's Rob Gronkowski, a threat to score fantasy points in bunches as long as he's healthy, and Jimmy Graham and Julius Thomas, who both changed teams after the 2014 season, leaving behind prolific passers Drew Brees and Peyton Manning, respectively.

Tight ends are helpful in cash games if they get a reliable number of targets (especially in the red zone). But because their receptions are for relatively short yardage, tight ends have more impact under the full PPR rules in place at DraftKings.

Still, you're required to find a tight end to fill your roster, so what should you do?

Daily fantasy owners should look at targets, red-zone targets, snap counts, and the defensive matchup. Tight ends are covered by linebackers and safeties, so especially fast linebackers and particularly larger and physical safeties give a TE the most trouble in the passing game.

In recent years, tight ends have been sorted into receiving or blocking tight ends. Since the websites don't hand out points for blocks that spring a long run, you're looking for the receiving tight ends. This is where knowledge of the game comes into play as you try to judge a player's abilities and the offensive scheme in which he plays.

However, one of the most important factors to consider in deciding on a tight end is the chemistry he has with his quarterback. The tight end can be the quarterback's security blanket in the passing game, meaning he's the guy the quarterback looks for downfield when he absolutely needs a first down or is in a tight spot. For instance, consider the chemistry between Dallas QB Tony Romo and TE Jason Witten or San Diego QB Philip Rivers and TE Antonio Gates. However, at times, you don't have many good tight end options and that's when you have to "fade" the position.

The term fade in DFS means to avoid a specific player or de-emphasize an entire position. There are two primary reasons for fading.

In a large-field GPP, you might want to fade an especially popular player who'll be on an overwhelming number of teams. This is a contrarian play that creates variance, which is what you want to do in GPPs. If the popular player has a bad day and you fade him, it hurts enough opponents that it's almost as strong as making a good pick for yourself. For example, a player like Steelers WR Antonio Brown—who was the leading fantasy points player in 2014 on DraftKings and the leading non-quarterback on FanDuel—is a natural pick for many players in the enormous-field GPPs. To win a GPP you have to break away from the pack, so if you draft Brown, even if you're correct and he has a big day, you'll be right with a whole bunch of other players and you won't get separation. By fading Brown, you have a chance for the swing against the field and save a huge chunk of salary. Remember, to knock it out of the park in a GPP, you have to go against the grain somewhere along the line.

Fading also comes into play when all the players available at a given position are projected to produce points in a very narrow range, regardless of their salary pricing. This concept is more applicable to baseball, but it also has some application to football, especially with regard to tight ends. If one who presents an obvious advantage isn't available, the best move is to pay as little as possible for an acceptable starter and spend the salary-cap dollars on some other position where you think there's more potential for points.

In 2015, there were three tight ends of note: Rob Gronkowski, Jimmy Graham, and Greg Olsen. If those three are way overpriced, you have 29 remaining starting TEs who figure to accrue fantasy points in a fairly narrow range. A reasonable strategy is to identify one of those who is cheap, but also has a good chance of performing at least in that range where the bulk of tight ends are likely to perform. Fading situations are also common for kicker (in FanDuel only, since there is no kicker in DraftKings) and defense/special teams.

This is also a strategy that you can come back to. Say you've picked a tight end and later decide that you need someone in another spot, but don't have the cap space. You can go back and dial the TE spot down to recoup the needed buying power.

Kickers, Defense/Special Teams

Placekickers are the Rodney Dangerfields of daily fantasy sports—they get no respect! It's so bad, DraftKings doesn't even include kickers in its contests. That's a heck of way to treat a bunch of guys who represented the NFL's top 24 scorers in 2014.

FanDuel does include kickers in its contests, though that's not without controversy. The more accomplished DFS players often complain that kicker is a totally unpredictable and hopelessly incalculable wild-card position that can blow up the best laid plans of mice and algorithms.

At least through 2015, FanDuel wasn't persuaded to jettison kickers. It's kept kickers, mainly because they're a familiar part of the NFL and have been a fixture in season-long fantasy contests. With FanDuel contending that it wants to appeal to the casual fan—and, presumably, casual fans include the more than 50 million or so folks who participate in traditional fantasy sports—its kicker position might be around for a while longer.

In terms of salary-cap pricing, kickers typically have been priced in a very narrow range on FanDuel, often in the $5,000s, and are much cheaper than other position players. Reliable kickers on high-scoring teams, such as New England's Stephen Gostkowski who led the NFL with 156 points in 2014, are priced several hundred dollars more than the least expensive kickers.

Many DFS experts suggest merely "punting" the position, no pun intended there.

In the parlance of DFS regulars, to punt a position is to pay as little as possible for a player to fill it. Some grinders rationalize that the position is unpredictable and the difference in fantasy points between the highest and lowest kickers is narrow. But the numbers may be saying otherwise.

The difference between the most and least productive kickers who played in 16 games in 2014 was nearly five points per game. Taking into account the 28 kickers who played in at least 15 games, Gostkowski (10.63 fantasy points per game) averaged 2.38 points more than the middle-of-the-pack guy, Arizona's Graham Gano (8.25 FPG) who was number 14. Considering the razor-thin margin that decides DFS contests, those are not insignificant numbers.

Yes, you want to squeeze as much value as you can out of the position, and there will be days when someone like Josh Brown of the New York Giants will trot out and unexpectedly put up 21 fantasy points, to carry a handful of lineups past a bunch of carefully crafted rosters.

However, it's not true that the position is entirely unpredictable. When selecting kickers, consider the following.

Team Scoring—In 2014, Eagles rookie Cody Parkey was the number-two fantasy points kicker in the NFL, as head coach Chip Kelly's hurry-up offense provided lots of yardage and field-goal scoring opportunities. Some DFS players try to get cute and pick kickers on teams whose offenses have trouble scoring TDs in the red zone. Don't overthink the process. Just go with offenses that move the ball.

Efficiency—The gold standard for kickers is field-goal percentage, a metric that can usually be counted on from season to season. In 2014, 41-year old Adam Vinatieri of Indianapolis led the NFL with a field goal percentage of 97%. Eventually, kickers do lose distance and accuracy, but their skills remain intact longer than many other positions.

Long-Distance Attempts—On FanDuel, kickers are awarded extra points for longer field goals. Field goals of 40-49 yards are worth 4 fantasy points. Field goals of 50 yards or more are worth 5 points. So look for a kicker whose coach trusts him to make those longer kicks. In 2014, Atlanta's Matt Bryant led the NFL with attempts over 50 yards with 10; he made seven of them. He was 8-for-8 on kicks of 40 yards or more.

Domes—Kickers love domes for two reasons: no bad weather and a smooth surface from which to launch kicks. So make an enclosed venue part of your calculation.

Defense/Special Teams (D/ST)

On both FanDuel and DraftKings, players are required to pick a defense/special-teams combination (referred to as D/ST) from a single NFL team, and the fantasy points derived from eligible statistics for both units are combined.

On FanDuel, special-team stats that go into the calculation are kickoff and punt-return touchdowns and blocked kicks. A partial list of defensive stats that add fantasy points are touchdowns (interceptions/fumble recoveries), sacks, opponent fumbles recovered, interceptions, safeties, and a scale based on how many points the opposing offense scores. DraftKings awards points based on many of the same categories.

However, of absolutely no relevance are the yards a team gives up on defense. Curiously, yards-allowed is the statistic the NFL uses to rank defenses throughout the season. But in DFS, that number is completely irrelevant. In truth, points-allowed isn't the statistic a DFS owner should worry about when picking a defense. And here's why.

This is how both FanDuel and DraftKings awarded points for defense based on points-allowed for 2014:

0 Points Allowed = (10)
1-6 Points Allowed = (7)
7-13 Points Allowed = (4)
14-20 Points Allowed = (1)
21-27 Points Allowed = (0)
28-34 Points Allowed = (-1)
35+ Points Allowed = (-4)

Frankly, the fantasy points scale is ludicrous. Once a defense gives up its first TD and extra point, its fantasy points drop from 10 points to 4. Give up a second touchdown and it goes to a measly 1 point.

So an NFL defense could be having a stellar game stifling the other side by giving up very few yards, throttling third-down conversions, helping the offense build, say, a 31-7 lead, and giving up a meaningless TD in garbage time—and a DFS player's reward for being shrewd enough to pick that defense is 1 point. OK, no one ever said that daily fantasy sports was for purists.

So what does get rewarded on defense? Mainly turnovers and to a lesser degree sacks. But the big points come on defensive TDs, usually off of interceptions and less frequently from fumble recoveries.

In 2014, the best-scoring daily fantasy defense/special-teams combination was not the Seattle Seahawks whose defensive prowess took that team to its second straight Super Bowl. Nope, instead it was the Philadelphia Eagles, a team that gave up 25 points a game (more than nine more per game than league-best Seattle's 15.9 PPG). How did that happen?

Remember, this is a combination of defense and special teams and in 2014, the Eagles had 11 return touchdowns of various types, the third-highest total in NFL history. In one game (which the Eagles lost!), they scored all three of their touchdowns on some kind of return: a kickoff, punt, and blocked punt.

Here's the point. Unless, the team you're selecting has a return guy with the explosiveness of a Deion Sanders or a Devin Hester when they were at their peak and there was a chance for a TD any time they touched the ball, special-teams touchdowns are rare. So the decision on the defense/special-teams combination is best made on the strength of defense.

Two things to consider when deciding on a defensive team are the pressure a defense can apply on the quarterback and the impotence of certain teams' offenses.

Pass-rush pressure is good for accumulating defensive points directly through sacks (a rewarded category on both FanDuel and DraftKings) and because it causes the opposing quarterback to make mistakes, either with fumbles or throwing interceptions. So the stats to be analyzed are sacks and hurries. For example, the Houston Texans were one of the top defense/special-teams fantasy points teams in 2014, despite being in the middle of the pack in most official defensive categories, due to its one-man wrecking crew in J.J. Watt. Watt not only put consistent pressure on opposing quarterbacks, he also scored twice on defensive returns. Because of Watt, the Texans had 77 hurries, which had them tied for fifth in the league.

However, one of the best ways to select a high-scoring defense in daily fantasy sports is to find a wretched offense and select whatever defense has the luxury of playing against it.

The Jacksonville Jaguars were consistently predictable foils for whatever defense they happened to play against in 2014, with its anemic offense giving up about twice as many fantasy points to opposing defenses than the NFL average. In some cases, futility is more predictable than success.

In cases where the type of ineptness that the Jaguars displayed in 2014 isn't immediately apparent, look for substitute quarterbacks pressed into service when the starter is hurt. In those cases, you can actually land a promising D/ST at a bargain price, because the personnel move might not be announced until mid-week and there will be a pricing inefficiency in salary for the defense.

Injuries/Weather

Making sense of the NFL's traditional injury report requires a lot of reading between the lines. Toward the end of each week during the season, the NFL requires teams to list the status of injured players using four categories:

- Probable
- Questionable
- Doubtful
- Out

To start with the easiest one, Out definitely means not playing in the next game.

Probable and Doubtful are also fairly definitive. In 2011, the *Wall Street Journal* reported results of an examination of players listed in the various pre-game injury categories from the 2010 season. It found that of players listed as Doubtful, less than 1% actually played. So, one can assume, for the purposes of DFS lineups, that Doubtful is almost as certain as Out.

Of the players listed as Probable, 94% did play. So Probable is a green light in the vast majority of cases. In fact, one of the more humorous instances of what could be called "overuse of the injury designation" was from 2009 through 2010 when New England quarterback Tom Brady was on the Patriots injury report for 34 straight games (32 as Probable and two as Questionable) and he didn't miss a one.

The Questionable category is where the guesswork starts. A player listed as Questionable suited up 57% of the time in 2010, the *Wall Street Journal* reported. So while a player listed as Questionable is probably more likely to play than not, it's still a close call for DFS owners who can't afford to get a zero from a lineup position. So that's where you have to do some homework if you're considering rostering a player who is listed as Doubtful.

Near the end of the practice week, teams release the practice-participation reports—full, limited, or not at all—of many players, including those who are hurt. However, you have to be careful what to infer from practice participation. Some veteran players are held out of practices later in the season to save wear and tear on their bodies, and being held out of practice is certainly not an indication that someone won't play.

The NFL has become much more sensitive to injury issues in recent years, especially regarding concussions, and that's a very good thing for player safety. However, the challenge for daily fantasy owners is that because teams are more careful about sending injured players onto the field, the decision about playing or not playing is often made at game time or very close to it. So if you can't be in front of a computer or on a mobile device checking last-minute injury status reports before kickoff, the safest thing to do is simply not roster players who are Questionable. And that goes double if the injury that makes the player Questionable is a concussion.

As the 1 p.m. Eastern Time kickoffs approach, it's a good idea to check the inactive list for every game that's available. Unfortunately, the later NFL games often don't have their inactive lists posted by the early lockdown deadlines. But to the extent that the inactive lists are available, be sure to check them out.

NFL rosters include 53 players eligible to appear in games and approximately 90 minutes before kickoff, teams must identify seven players who won't suit up ("inactive"). To locate the lists, just type "NFL inactive list" into a search engine an hour or so before kickoff and they'll pop up.

Several times a season, key starters unexpectedly show up as inactive at the last minute. Maybe a player missed a team meeting on Saturday and he's being disciplined, or perhaps one fell ill and had to be rushed to the hospital. You just don't want to get caught by surprise if you can help it.

The best way to track injuries is through the beat reporters who cover the NFL teams, or through ESPN's Injury Wire. Will Carroll, a sportswriter who's specialized in injuries and medical issues, is considered a knowledgeable source for injury information on the Internet.

Some injuries seem to be more incapacitating than others. For instance, players are perhaps most afraid of hamstring injuries. So-called "hammies" are a killer; while they can feel sort of OK, they're easily aggravated and if that happens, a player can be out for an extended time. They're especially problematic for wide receivers who have to put it in high gear sprinting downfield. Accordingly, if a player has a fresh hamstring injury and he's a Doubtful, he probably won't play. Ankle injuries can also be a big problem, especially for running backs (who need to change direction quickly). A player may try to tough it out on a bad ankle, but there's a good chance he won't finish the game. Still another seemingly minor condition that will slow down a running back is a serious toe injury.

Injuries are so much a part of pro football, it's impossible to make intelligent lineup decisions without staying on top of them, and it's not just important in order to fade starting someone who'll sit or play only part-time. It's also important to take advantage of salary inefficiencies on backup players. Or if the injury is to a defensive player in the secondary, it might be an opportunity to latch onto a receiver who's more likely to have a big day. Or if the injury is to the left offensive tackle who has to protect the quarterback's blind side, that could mean the quarterback is in for a rough time. In so many ways, reading the tea leaves on injuries is another way for serious football fans to close the gap between themselves and DFS grinders who rely on metrics and algorithms.

Weather—The elements aren't nearly the factor in football that they are in baseball. If you roster players in a baseball game that gets rained out, you've just wasted those salary-cap dollars. In football, inclement weather may affect the game statistically, but you can be fairly sure the game will go on.

Weather doesn't begin to pose a threat in football until the second half of the season, and even then only on rare occasions. Plus, a number of NFL teams play in climate-controlled domes.

The biggest problem with weather is wind, and the positions most affected are quarterback (and by extension, receivers) and kicker. High wind keeps passes shorter and definitely influences a coach's decision on whether to try longer field goals. For kickers, wind isn't the only adverse factor; cold hard footballs don't travel as fair and slick surfaces affect a kicker's plant leg—all of which are reasons to stick with kickers in domes or who are kicking in dry milder conditions.

Typically, snow doesn't influence how an offense attacks the defense. Rain is more of an influence and while wet conditions suggest that offenses will run the ball more, it's also true that wide receivers have an advantage on slippery surfaces; they know the route they're running and defensive backs have to change direction unexpectedly. Plus, the consequences are vastly different for the two sides. If a receiver slips and falls on a rain-slicked surface, the result is probably an incomplete pass (although sometimes an interception does result). If a defensive back falls on a slippery field, the result could be a touchdown.

A website that keeps track of weather is NFLWeather.com.

Chapter 6

Baseball

For nearly a decade, I wrote a syndicated travel column on casinos—and that meant writing quite a bit about Las Vegas. Naturally, everyone who was headed to Las Vegas always asked me for my best advice, expecting to hear where the casinos stash all those slot machines that pay off big, or which buffet serves king crab legs for under $10, or how to skip the long lines to get into the sexiest nightclub. I told everyone the same thing: The most important thing to know when you go to Las Vegas … drumroll, please … is to wear comfortable shoes.

The advice seekers were usually sorely disappointed, especially the women who had planned on taking several pairs of high heels. But it was the soundest advice I could give anyone. I elaborated by explaining that the distance from hotel rooms to the front door of casinos is often about a half-mile, maybe more. I also told them that just walking to the casino next door on the Strip, even though it might look close, is another half-mile, maybe more. And then there's the subtle but harsh truth regarding walking in Las Vegas, whether indoors or outdoors. It's simply impossible to walk in a straight line anywhere. Whether it's blackjack tables or other tourists, there's always something in the way that adds steps to any trip. I concluded by saying that everyone who tries hoofing it in Las Vegas learns the hard way.

I would say it over and over: Wear comfortable shoes.

Which brings us to daily fantasy baseball. Like my advice about Vegas, it might sound obvious to say the following: To succeed at daily fantasy baseball, it helps to be a big baseball fan. It can't be over-emphasized. You want to play? You better be a big fan. And if you're not, at least be committed to immersing yourself in the numbers of the game.

Certainly, you have to be an enthusiastic football fan if you want to play daily fantasy football and compete with the smart money, but the substantial difference between football and baseball is time commitment. It's that old business about a 16-game season versus a 162-game season. Tracking the arc of an NFL season is much more manageable than staying in step with the daily rhythm of a MLB season. And you have to keep track of half the number of basketball games compared to baseball, with fewer relevant players league-wide.

Having said that, if ever a sport were tailored to daily fantasy sports, it's baseball. For starters, baseball gives a DFS participant the opportunity to play *literally* daily. While that, too, may be an obvious point, it's an important feature about baseball to embrace. It means you have more opportunity to evolve as a competent practitioner of DFS in general.

Baseball is also a great fit for fan competition, because it's so quantifiable. Yes, there are a lot of games to consider, but you really never have to watch a game to understand and handicap the teams and players. If you watch a lot of games, all the better, but you don't have to watch to compete. That can't be said of football. Many aspects of the game, such as offensive line play, aren't so neatly charted in a statistical way. And the statistics that are qualitative about some of those important facets of football are indirect.

In baseball, just about every on-field outcome is charted

and, as a result, can be parsed, evaluated, and used in the aggregate to make educated predictions. That's a good thing, because unlike pro football, unless you're a rabid baseball fan, trying to watch enough games to hone your expertise is quite difficult, not to mention mind-numbing. But baseball is the quintessential numbers game and if you commit to following the numbers and persevere in staying on top of a sport that plays the bulk of its games mid-week, DFS baseball is beatable. Why? Because we're talking about a peer-to-peer competition and most of the fans who pursue DFS casually don't have the discipline and concentration to commit themselves to the stoic analysis needed to win consistently.

So let's get started.

DFS Baseball Rules

As I've already pointed out, there are considerable differences between the two major DFS websites, FanDuel and DraftKings, and even among the dozens of smaller competitors in the DFS universe. Major differences that separate the two big guys are in scoring, salary ranges, and the composition of rosters. Thus, building rosters is influenced to a certain degree by which website you play on. The sound advice is to try at least the two major websites and even a couple of smaller ones to see where your style of analysis is more conducive to winning.

On FanDuel, you pick a standard National League-style lineup, meaning eight position players, one at each fielding position and one starting pitcher. The pitcher's hitting stats won't count and in the unlikely event any of your position players winds up on the mound, those pitching numbers won't count.

To give you a heads-up on what you should observe, notice how simplified FanDuel scoring is compared to DraftKings.

For pitchers, the scoring is: win 4 points, strikeouts 1, inning pitched 1 (including fractions), shutouts 1, earned run -1. There are no deductions for hits allowed or walks.

For hitters: single 1 point, double 2, triple 3, home run 4, RBI 1, run scored 1, walk 1, stolen base 2, hit by pitch 1. Outs are scored as -0.25 each, with outs defined as the number of at-bats less the number of hits. An 0-for-4 night is therefore worth -1. As a result of this definition, sacrifice outs incur no penalty.

The salary cap is $35,000 for nine players.

Because pitchers account for a disproportionate share of a roster's total points, pitcher salaries typically spread from a high in the $12,000s to lows in the $5,000s. Position players range from the $5,000s to the $2,000s.

On DraftKings, the scoring is much more complex, especially for pitchers. You pick an extra starter for a total of two pitchers, along with the eight position players, one at each field position.

For pitchers: win 4 points, inning pitched 2.25 (plus fractions), strike out 2, earned run -2, hit against -0.6, walks -0.6, hit by pitch -0.6, complete game 2.5, complete game shutout 2.5, no-hitter 5.

For hitters: single 3 points, double 5, triple 8, home run 10, RBI 2, run scored 2, walk 2, hit by pitch 2, steal 5, caught stealing -2.

Unlike FanDuel, there is no penalty for an at-bat that doesn't result in a hit.

Salary cap is $50,000, which allows for the extra starting pitcher. Pitchers range from the $14,000s to the $4,000s. Hitters range from the $5,000s to $2,000.

Weighing the Differences

The scoring rules and pricing ranges on both websites illustrate the huge premium placed on pitching, and that's as it should be. The premium placed on strikeouts for pitchers cannot be overlooked. Also, more points are awarded for racking up innings, so pitchers who eat innings are a big plus.

In short, it's impossible to overemphasize the importance of pitching in daily fantasy. Frequently, a pitcher will account for between 25% and 50% of the scoring on a nine-player roster that winds up cashing. On FanDuel, for instance, 35-40 fantasy points often puts a DFS owner in the hunt to cash in a 50/50 contest (although those target totals will vary day-to-day). Consider that a starting pitcher who has a relatively strong outing of seven full innings, giving up three earned runs, striking out seven, and earning the win will earn 15 points in FanDuel, and assuming a benchmark of 35-40 points to make it to the money in a 50/50 in FanDuel, it's plain to see how important it is to get the pitching right. Conversely, get it wrong and you'll need some monster performances from your hitters, which is tough. Predicting hitters is far trickier than picking the right pitcher; even a great hitter can go 0-for-4 often, but a great pitcher is far more likely to perform consistently. So, when it comes to spending salary-cap money, don't scrimp on pitching.

On the hitting side, the emphasis is on power hitting and, surprisingly, stolen bases. But in the stolen-base category, note that DraftKings rewards base-stealing efficiency by punishing runners who are caught. FanDuel imposes no such penalty.

On both websites, the home run is paramount. Between the two majors, FanDuel proportionately rewards home runs even more than DraftKings.

A daily fantasy owner might feel like a genius for picking a player who goes 4-for-4 with four singles. But where it counts in fantasy points, those four singles can't match a humble solo home run.

On FanDuel, four singles, at one point each, add up to 4 points for fantasy owners. Meanwhile, the solo home run earns 6 fantasy points (4 for the homer, 1 for a run scored, and 1 for an RBI). So, the solo homer yields 50% more points compared to four singles. It's reasonable to argue that the singles could potentially produce more points if they result in either RBIs or runs scored, but on their own merits, the four singles pale compared to one home run.

Turning to DraftKings, the four singles (3 points each) are worth 12 points and the solo home run is worth 14 points (10 points for the HR, 2 points for one RBI, and 2 points for one run scored). In this case, the solo homer is 17% more valuable than the four singles. Of course, the same disclaimer about the potential points for the singles also applies, meaning the potential for RBIs and runs scored.

Given the naked comparison of singles to home runs, it's clear that power is richly rewarded.

One significant difference between the two major DFS websites in baseball is that FanDuel has fixed positions, while DraftKings has flexible positions, also known as multi-positional eligibility. Translation: On FanDuel, a player is assigned one position and he can be used only in that position. On DraftKings, a player capable of generally playing more than one position can be used at any of the positions assigned to him by DraftKings and he'll earn fantasy points regardless of where he actually plays in a specific game.

Example: On FanDuel, power-hitting Chris Davis is listed as a first baseman, and that's the only position where he can be used in a FanDuel lineup. But on DraftKings, Chris Davis has been listed as a first baseman-third baseman, so a fantasy player can list Davis as a third baseman in a DraftKings lineup even if he goes on to play first base in the actual game. The DFS owner is credited with Davis' offensive stats no matter where he actually plays, even if it's as a designated hitter. Another important difference between the two major websites is that DraftKings allows for late substitutions, while FanDuel does not.

Let's say that you're selecting baseball players for a 50/50 contest from a slate of games with some scheduled for normal evening starts on the east and west coasts. Midway through the east coast games, you discover that one of your starting players in a west coast game—which begins three hours after the east coast game—has been benched. On DraftKings, you can edit your lineup as long as the games involving the players that require a substitution haven't started. However, the ability to edit lineups on FanDuel is locked once the first pitch is thrown in the first game for the entire contest.

It remains to be seen whether that will change on FanDuel.

Baseball Contest Types

On the major websites, the range of contests available in daily fantasy baseball parallels those in football; the distinctions that separate the various contests are also comparable. If you've been through the football section, some of this will be familiar, but it's important enough that reinforcement, like chicken soup, couldn't hurt.

Baseball contests are broadly divided into two categories: cash games and tournaments. Within those two broad categories are subsets.

Under cash games fall head-to-head (H2H) contests,

50/50s, and double-ups. These are contests in which, if you're successful, you'll double or nearly double your money, and half or nearly half the total entrants earn a profit. In both cases, the websites take about the same rake, roughly 10%.

Tournaments are mainly distinguished by their payout structures. A smaller percentage of entrants earn a profit—say, 15% to 20%—but the payouts in tournaments are usually higher than in cash games and the finishers at the top of the leaderboard are rewarded with prizes many times their original investments. The top prizes can reach jackpot-sized proportions.

DFS players often refer to tournaments generically as GPPs, an abbreviation that stands for "guaranteed prize pools." That means the host website guarantees that a certain amount of money will be awarded, regardless of how many (or how few) entrants actually contribute to the prize pool. It's in these contests that valuable overlays can materialize.

In a multiplier, all entrants who finish high enough to earn a prize receive the same amount. That's certainly a characteristic of cash games, but multipliers are different, because when paying out higher multiples, in order for the DFS websites to make a profit, a smaller percentage of the field gets paid.

In a 10-times multiplier with 100 entrants, for example, typically only nine entrants (9%) will qualify for a 10-times payout.

It's reasonable to consider triple-up multipliers as being closer to a cash game and for multipliers higher than that to be viewed similar to tournaments. The rationale for categorizing multipliers in this way is that lineup building for triple-ups should more closely follow the guidelines for cash games. Conversely, rosters for the higher-multiplier contests need to lean toward tournament-style strategies.

Another type of daily fantasy sports contest includes "satellites" and "qualifiers." This same category also includes "step" and "survivor" tournaments.

In brief, these are contests—for a relatively small buy-in, but occasionally for substantial amounts—that qualify a successful participant to enter another tournament where a cash prize or some other award of significant value is at stake.

For instance, a $1 satellite with 22 entrants might award the winner an entry into a $20-buy-in tournament. In turn, that $20 tournament may itself be a qualifier that sends its top finishers to still another tournament where the buy-in is normally $200 and where the top prize is worth tens of thousands of dollars.

The point is that satellites and also some qualifiers are the DFS equivalent of lottery tickets. As already pointed out, to win the satellite in the above example is a 4.5% shot. Now let's assume the subsequent $20 qualifier rewards the top 9% of entrants who advance to the major $200-buy-in contest.

The odds of initially finishing in first place in the satellite, then finishing in the top 9% of the qualifier tournament, are less than one-half of 1%. And if you do make it, that only puts you in a field of entrants for the major $200-buy-in tournament.

Of course, the odds of getting through the satellite *and* a qualifier *and* cashing in the main event are extremely long. Such things do happen, though, and so do slot-machine jackpots and $1 million lottery scratch-offs.

Which Contests Are for You?

As has been pointed out, the answer to this question lies in a DFS player's tolerance for risk relative to the reward he aspires to achieve. But here's a guideline that should serve as sound advice across the board, and especially for beginners. It's smarter to invest about 70% of the total money being committed in a day or a weekend of daily fantasy play in the cash games.

The ambitions are modest in cash games, and that's OK. In the beginning, DFS play should be about learning the game without putting a dent in your wallet. Here, you're simply trying to do better than half the players in the field, whether it consists of just two entrants in a H2H contest or 2,000 in a 50/50.

For beginners, larger-field 50/50s for smaller buy-in amounts are the safest way to travel, because you're not vulnerable to being singled out by sharper players who are trying to isolate less experienced opponents in head-to-head match-ups. And the smaller buy-in/single-entry contests are often not worth the time to professional-level DFS players.

In baseball, as in other sports, some DFS contests allow multiple entries; one player can have more than one lineup in a particular contest. In fact, better DFS players make a habit of doing just that.

Some DFS contests may accept 5,000 entrants at a buy-in of $10 each. That totals a gross entry amount of $50,000. If the rake is 10%, the prize pool that's distributed to the players will be $45,000. Depending on the payout structure, the first-place prize may be about $4,500, and with 15% to 20% of the field getting paid, the lowest prize may be about $25.

If the above tournament is multi-entry, professional DFS players or those who simply think they're pretty good might enter five or ten or many more teams, depending on website limits for entries. Those experienced players are banking on enough of their teams finishing high enough to produce a tidy profit, along with the equity in their chances of hitting the big one.

Completely shying away from lower-priced big-field tournaments, solely because they allow for multiple entries (and might attract sharper players), is probably too inhibited, but it's still good to be aware of how top DFS players approach their craft.

Where To Start

Just like in daily fantasy football, the starting point for determining how to build your baseball roster is that shining city in the Mojave Desert: Las Vegas, Nevada. Or to be more precise, start with those old reliable sports books and the odds they post regarding that day's menu of baseball games.

The first numbers to scan are the over-unders for the day. Those will tell you which games are projected to be low- and high-scoring. For your position players, you want to focus on games that have higher totals, because the forecasts are for more offense. (For those unfamiliar with sports wagering, the over/under, or O/U number, is the total amount of points in football or runs in baseball that both teams, combined, are expected to score.)

In baseball, most games will range from a total of 5½-6 runs on the low end to 8-9 runs on the high side. On rare occasions (usually games played at hitter-friendly Coors Field in Denver), the O/U can go as high as 10 or 11.

Next, check the odds for the favorites and underdogs.

Baseball odds can be confusing to fans whose familiarity with sports betting is limited to NFL pointspreads. Baseball wagering doesn't use pointspreads. It uses money lines. The favorites are listed with a minus number and the underdogs have a plus number. It looks something like this: L.A. Dodgers -155, Philadelphia Phillies +140. For sports bettors, that means if you want to bet on Los Angeles, the favorite in this case, you have to risk $155 to win $100. If you want Philly, the underdog, you risk $100 to win $140.

LA -155

PHIL +140

The daily fantasy participant, however, is looking at the money line for somewhat different reasons. For starters, if the over/under is a high number and the money line tilts heavily toward the favorite, you should target the hitters on the favored team. If there's an extraordinarily high over/under and without an overwhelming favorite indicated by the money line, then hitters on either team should be considered.

In cases where one team is a big favorite—say, at -150 or more—the favored team's starting pitcher has to be considered almost regardless of what his salary-cap number is, because of the way both FanDuel and DraftKings reward pitching wins so heavily. When competing on FanDuel in particular, daily fantasy players have to be willing to pay up for pitching, especially in games where the money line is lopsided. On DraftKings, because two pitchers will be in the lineup, it's reasonable to pass up the most expensive pitcher of the day and grab a pair from the top four to six to more prudently allocate cap dollars.

As a shortcut, DFS players can use the projected-runs-scored numbers for each team found on RotoGrinders.com where the starting MLB lineups are listed.

Targeting games where the O/U is 8.5 runs or more and where one team is heavily favored should tell you that the pitcher on the underdog team could be in for a rough day. Stay away from those guys, no matter how cheap their salary number. To capitalize on such a situation, instead, DFS players should load up on as many hitters as possible from the favored team. And when it comes down to making some tough lineup decisions when you're running low on cap salary, consider low-priced players on the favored team with the thought that they'll be batting against a struggling pitcher and getting into the opposing bullpen early in the game.

Alphabet Soup—
The Statistical Building Blocks

As mentioned, baseball is the most quantified sport in America. Just about every outcome on the field winds up in the box score. And this gave rise to a set of statistics that were the gold standard for baseball analysis and comparisons for decades. Among the most familiar of those stats are batting average, hits, RBIs, runs scored, stolen bases, strikeouts, walks, earned run average, and slugging percentage. But if you think that those are still the end-all for baseball statistics in the 21st century, get ready to sharpen your game.

A new crop of statistical categories, such as OPS, wOBA, and WHIP, the products of what's known as sabermetrics, are considered to be much more accurate measures of a baseball player's efficiency and overall performance. The name sabermetrics is derived from the Society of American Baseball Research (SABR), whose high priest was Bill James. James' *Baseball Abstracts* in the 1980s blazed new trails for the analysis of the National Pastime.

Sabermetrics gained increased legitimacy when some forward-thinking baseball executives, such as Oakland A's general manager Billy Beane, employed those principles in the actual building of Major League Baseball teams. The approach enjoyed a little mythologizing in the book and subsequent Brad

Pitt film *Moneyball*. In addition, Nate Silver, a sabermetric devotee, applied similar mathematical approaches to politics and famously predicted the outcome of the 2012 presidential election correctly in every state. Silver went on to supervise the highly respected data-driven news website FiveThirtyEight.

So what does all of this have to do with you and winning money playing daily fantasy baseball?

Plenty.

Batting averages and earned run averages are fine, but you'll need to get acquainted with more sophisticated statistics to stay competitive. For hitters, some of those stats are OPS (on-base plus slugging percentage), wOBA (weighted on-base average), and ISO (isolated power, or extra-base hit frequency).

Weighted on-base average (wOBA) is especially applicable to daily fantasy, because it applies a *weight* to several ways of reaching base—singles, doubles, triples, home runs, unintentional walks, and hit-by-pitches—and divides that by a multi-factor denominator. The components that make up the denominator are at bats, walks (excluding intentional walks), sacrifice flies, and hit-by-pitches. If it sounds complicated, it's actually fairly simple when examined closely, and it's ingenious in how it summarizes hitting performance in a single number.

So what's a good wOBA and what's a bad one?

Many baseball fans understand that a hitter with a .200 batting average isn't so hot, while one with a .300 batting average is All Star material. And a guy batting .250 to .270 is sort of average.

However, the new-age sabermetrics, which are more relevant to daily fantasy baseball handicapping, may not be so easy to figure out even for avid baseball fans. So here's a primer.

Let's start with a baseline. The average wOBA is .340, according to the advanced baseball metrics website FanGraphs.

FanGraphs ranks wOBA this way:

Excellent	.400
Great	.370
Above Average	.340
Average	.320
Below Average	.310
Poor	.300
Awful	.290

To take the comparative metrics a step further, consider that certain positions are more likely to have higher wOBA averages. That's not surprising; most fans know that the better hitters play first base, third base, the outfield and, of course, designated hitter.

Slugging is especially rewarded in daily fantasy sports. As we've seen, doubles, triples, and home runs not only accrue more fantasy points in and of themselves, but they can produce fantasy points, immediately or subsequently, for other categories. For instance, a home run is worth 4 points on FanDuel, plus an immediate reward of at least 1 point for an RBI (and possibly more) and another 1 point for a run scored. A double is worth two points and, if runners are on base, there's potential for an RBI or two or even three. Plus, it puts the batter who hit the double in a position to potentially score a run himself. Obviously, extra-base hits, and the power hitters who account for them, play a big role in determining daily fantasy outcomes.

On the playing field, the player who does all those old-timey team-oriented things, such as bunt or hit to the right side of the infield to advance runners, are great for the manager in the dugout, but they do exactly nothing for a DFS owner.

The shortest statistical route to determining the hitters who do a DFS owner the most good is wOBA. Remember, that's weighted on-base average.

Other revealing stats are OPS (on-base percentage plus slugging average) and ISO (isolated power). Like wOBA, OPS measures overall batting and an average OPS is .700 to .770. Good is .800 and excellent is .900.

For DFS players, ISO is relevant for GPPs, where long-ball potential (to produce bigger fantasy point totals) is preferred. ISO is simply slugging percentage with batting average subtracted. The average is .140 and an ISO of .170 is desirable.

For pitchers, because of the emphasis on strikeouts, the K/9 (strikeouts per nine innings) is a huge stat, as is innings per outing. Given the choice between similarly priced pitchers, it's wise to lean toward the pitcher more apt to rack up strikeouts, followed closely by innings per start. In regard to the latter, you need to look at American League pitchers over National League pitchers; NL pitchers get pulled for pinch-hitters, as opposed to AL pitchers whose innings-per-outing stat is helped by the presence of a designated hitter.

In 2014, the top four pitchers in the majors in innings pitched were American Leaguers at the time—David Price, Cory Kluber, Max Scherzer, and Felix Hernandez. Don't over-emphasize the league difference, because managers and pitching coaches have become fanatical about pitch counts. In recent years, once a pitcher hits the 100-pitch mark, he's out of the game, but the designated-hitter factor can keep AL pitchers on the mound just a bit longer.

Another sabermetric stat that can be important to DFS participants regarding pitchers is WHIP: walks plus hits per inning. That's especially true in DraftKings, where pitchers are penalized for issuing bases on balls and for yielding hits.

In FanDuel, where the penalty is assessed for earned runs,

the time-honored stat of ERA (earned run average) is more relevant.

And then there are less important sabermetric numbers. Baseball junkies swear by a statistic called WAR (wins over replacement) that measures how many more wins a team gains with Player A in the lineup as opposed to his replacements. That's a fine statistic for baseball fanatics who want to settle a debate over who's more valuable to their respective team, Mike Trout or Troy Tulowitski. But in daily fantasy, WAR means little for position players because, in their cases, team wins are of no consequence in daily fantasy results. However, for pitchers, WAR has some DFS relevance, because pitchers are rewarded with fantasy points if they earn the team win.

Another sophisticated stat that may be of interest to DFS players is BABIP, or batting average on balls in play. It measures how often a ball put in play falls for a hit. The number, relevant to both pitchers and hitters, should be around .300 on average and for individual players, BABIP should be relatively the same over time. Note that an exceptionally high or exceptionally low BABIP is an indication of luck at play.

A pitcher cursed with a high BABIP at the beginning of a season relative to his historical numbers may be ready to regress. In other words, he may experience a return to his more typical performance statistics. A batter who has raised his average, with no change in BABIP, may have actually changed his approach at the plate.

Because a high BABIP is frequently viewed as more a reflection of luck than ability, even many skilled and experienced participants ignore the stat. Some DFS pros find it useful in evaluating baseball players whose other metrics, such as OPS and wOBA and even batting average, might not reflect that specific hitter's real abilities and, consequently, indicate an inevitable regression to the mean. In simple English, for an athlete, regression to the mean is returning to typical performance.

So for the especially canny DFS participant, detecting unusually high or low BABIP statistics may well call out players who are better or worse hitters than their metrics indicate and are likely to experience an increase or decrease in production as their bad or good luck evens out over time. Every once in a while, that can mean finding a pitcher or a hitter at a value price.

To be honest, some may consider that to be post-graduate-level DFS analysis and not worth the time for whatever edge may be gained. But as you progress in this game, it's helpful to sort through the more sophisticated metrics. Fact is, your best competition is already doing it.

So where does a DFS participant round up the valuable and useful statistics, such as wOBA?

A favorite website is the aforementioned FanGraphs, an Arlington, Virginia-based company founded by David Appelman that uses data from a variety of primary statistics sources. Savvy daily fantasy baseball players have come to rely on FanGraphs, which saves them time in researching sophisticated metrics. And it includes independent DFS analysis columns.

Other websites that furnish sortable statistics are ESPN.com and MLB.com.

Projections

Speaking of FanGraphs, it's also a convenient site for finding another valuable player-performance forecast tool—projections.

Experienced DFS players attempt to determine projections on a daily basis, admittedly something that is much easier for an entire season than for a single game. After all, baseball is a game of extraordinary volatility day to day. A batter hits two homers on one day, then goes 0-for-4 the next. It happens all the time. But it still helps to have at hand mathematically sound projections—even if they are for an extended time frame—to serve as a guide.

Some of the most sophisticated projections have been developed by Steamer Projections, the product of work done by a high-school math and science teacher, Jared Cross, and two of his former students. Steamer Projections started in 2008, mainly intended to help two of Cross' students win their own traditional fantasy baseball league.

The class project that Cross kiddingly says "went way too far" evolved into a mathematically deduced projection that creates a forecast for each major league player's entire season. These projections are must-reading for the most serious DFS players and they're tweaked daily to adjust each player's figures for the rest of the season.

The Steamer Projection formula includes a player's performance over the last several seasons, weighting the most recent seasons more heavily. The formula accounts for a regression to the league mean and for the assumed effects of a player's age. In some cases, age is a good thing, as it reflects a likely maturation of a player's skills and performance. Other times, added age means the opposite, a diminution of skills and performance.

In applying the sophisticated calculations of Steamer Projections to the task of selecting a daily fantasy lineup, there are still challenges. A DFS participant can take a player such as Miguel Cabrera and see that his projection is to score, say, 4 points per game on FanDuel over the course of the remaining games. But then there must be an accounting for more immediate factors. Some of the more important ones are the daily pitching matchup, the ballpark, the weather, even where a player is hitting in his own real lineup.

Still, measuring past performance and adjusting for the arc of a player's career to understand current talent level have become a science that produces relatively reliable projections. And while no one would contend such projections are flawless, when daily fantasy contests are routinely determined by a point or two, meaning a single base hit or a strikeout, having that kind of knowledge will certainly add up over a long baseball season.

Regression/Reversion

In the discussion of statistics such as BABIP, the concept of regression to the mean (also known as reversion to the mean) was mentioned. Regression, a statistical concept the daily fantasy player has to always be aware of, can be helpful in predicting a downturn or upswing in a player's statistical performance for the remainder of the season. Of course, no one has a crystal ball, but we can be reasonably certain that statistical averages have their own gravitational pull.

For instance, in Major League Baseball, the batting average for all hitters for a full season from 2010 through 2014 ranged from .252 to .257. In the decade before that, the range was .261 to .270.

Based on the downward drift of long-term averages in big samples (hundreds of thousands of at-bats), one has to assume underlying fundamentals at work—the trend to play "shift" defenses with three infielders on one side of the diamond, generally faster pitching velocities, more use of relief pitchers, and perhaps most significantly, a crackdown on performance-enhancing drugs—that have led to lower batting averages. As a result, the new normal in MLB has meant mean batting averages in the .250s, down from the .260s.

So in the absence of any changes in the fundamentals of the game, if a league-wide April batting average were, say, a surprising .275, one could reasonably expect lower batting averages from May through September as they experience a regression to the mean of somewhere in the .250s.

For individual players, the same principles apply, though of course with less predictability. If a career .270 hitter begins a season batting .400 in his first 100 at-bats, you can reasonably expect a lower batting average during the rest of the season.

However, regression to the mean doesn't imply that the player will perform *far* worse than his previous mean, in order that he averages out to the mean. A slightly above-average offensive player who has hit safely in 40 of the first 100 at bats (our .400 hitter) is likely to see the next 100 at-bats produce fewer hits. But it's more reasonable to assume a number closer to that average—say, 25 hits in the next 100 at bats—rather than something like the 10 hits that would smooth out the first 200 at bats altogether.

And if the unexpected extremes keep occurring—say, 15 hits in the next 50 at-bats (.300) and 18 hits in the 50 at-bats after that (.360)—it's time to adjust the expected mean for that player, because quite possibly something fundamental in his game has changed.

Ballpark Factor

In football and basketball, the home-field advantage is usually about fan support, and the differences in playing surfaces are relatively minor, because the dimensions are specified by the rules. Baseball is different. In baseball, ballparks can vary widely. And the idiosyncrasies of each ballpark can influence the tone of the game and scoring.

Just as certain golf courses favor certain golfers, certain ballparks favor certain hitters or pitchers. But even without trying to figure out which specific players might profit from a certain ballpark's dimension, it's absolutely key to be aware of which ballparks favor hitters and disadvantage pitchers and which favor pitchers and dampen offense.

This is actually one of the easier statistics to sort and use. Most ballparks fall in the middle range of runs scored and they can vary from year to year, depending on the offense or the pitching of the teams that call them home. But on the extreme ends of the offensive spectrum, some ballparks stand out as either hitters' parks or pitchers' parks.

The most offense-friendly ballpark in the Major Leagues is Coors Field in Colorado. The thin air of mile-high Denver lets those balls fly out of that ballpark. From 2010 through 2014, Coors Field was at the top of the list four times in offense and in second place once. Some other parks that have been generous to hitters over the 2010-2014 stretch are Globe Life Park, home to the Texas Rangers; Chase Field in Phoenix; venerable Fenway Park in Boston; U.S. Cellular Field, home to the White Sox; and Rogers Centre in Toronto.

At the other end of the scale, Safeco Field in Seattle and Petco Park in San Diego are well-known as places where pitchers flourish and hitters languish. Petco Park was so notorious, in fact, that after the 2012 season, some stadium fences were drawn in and others lowered. The modifications probably helped hitters a bit, but Petco Park is still extremely hospitable to pitchers. Meanwhile, Seattle—where some believe humidity is a factor—is particularly tough on home-run hitters.

So you need some very good reasons to pick any pitcher

with the unenviable task of starting a game in Colorado, or picking hitters at Petco Park or Safeco Field.

Good statistics regarding ballpark tendencies can be found on ESPN.com and RotoGrinders.com.

Handedness

Of all the pitcher/hitter-matchup considerations in daily fantasy baseball, the one that's most predictive is called "handedness." This refers to the circumstance that, in general, left-handed pitchers do better against left-handed batters and right-handed pitchers do better against right-handed batters.

The phenomenon is most pronounced in the lefty-against-lefty duel. For starters, there's the numerical issue that, since left-handedness is less common than right-handedness, batters of all stripes see fewer left-handers. Beyond that, batters generally are able to get good wood on pitches on the inside half as opposed to the outside edge of the plate. Also, they get a better look at pitches coming toward them (inside) as opposed to heading away from them (outside).

When left-hand pitchers deliver fastballs, the pitch tends to drift left to right, or away from the left-handed batter. When left-handers throw breaking balls, the pitch's movement away from a left-handed hitter is even more pronounced. When a left-handed hitter faces a right-handed pitcher, the opposite occurs. A right-hander's breaking pitches move toward the left-handed hitter and fastballs make their way across the plate directionally toward the left-handed hitter. The takeaway here is that when assembling daily fantasy lineups, you should look for opportunities to match left-handed hitters against right-handed pitchers and right-handed batters against left-handed pitchers.

Before exploring that strategy further, other matchup theories need to be discarded.

The first is that certain hitters "own" specific pitchers. Most sabermetricians have concluded that trying to divine what specific batters will do against specific pitchers, predicated on past performances, is an entirely futile exercise for some fundamental reasons. For starters, the sample sizes are far too small to be reliable. Also, the changing current circumstances of a pitcher alter the one-on-one dynamic so dramatically that what happened in the past two or three seasons tells you little about what will happen in the immediate future.

Almost as unreliable, again because of the ephemeral complexion of teams and players, is matching entire teams against a pitcher, meaning the notion that a team that dominated or failed offensively against a certain pitcher in the past will continue that trend in the future. Even if there were substantial reasons for that success or failure, it's unlikely that they'll remain constant in the future.

Yet, if one is disposed to drilling for that information, it's certainly available on MLB.com where you can research, say, how Joey Votto has hit against Adam Wainwright over the last few years, to your heart's content.

Handedness is much more important. A study done by Jonathan Bales, who authored *Fantasy Baseball for Smart People* and is a writer for DraftKings, mined data for the 150 top hitters since 2000. Bales found that in more than a decade of righty-lefty comparisons, left-handed hitters had an OPS (on-base plus slugging percentage) of .738 against left-handed pitching and .846 against right-handed pitching. That's an improvement of more than 14%, and illustrates why lefty hitters against lefty pitchers is a situation to be avoided.

When it comes to long-ball hitting, an important element

in DFS baseball, Bales found the contrast even more striking—left-handed batters hit home runs at a rate of once every 32.2 at-bats against lefties, but improved to once every 22.2 at-bats against righties.

However, the statistical weight of offensive advantage falls on the side of the right-handed hitters against left-handed pitchers. In Bales' study, right-handed hitters had a .811 OPS against right-handed pitchers, but it soared to .894 against left-handed pitchers. Plus, right-handed batters had more consistent power—hitting a home run once every 22.7 at bats against righties and once every 20.5 against lefties.

Righty-lefty splits for both the current season, and historically for individual batters, are available on MLB.com.

Of course, one way to avoid the righty-lefty dilemma is to use switch-hitters in your lineup as much as possible. Even switch-hitters will probably fare better against a certain handed pitcher, but you're protecting your lineup against having your player lifted for a pinch-hitter of the opposite handedness in the late innings, as the manager plays his own game of matchup.

There's one more favorable thing about switch-hitters. In cash games, they're likely to have higher floors, because of their more even batting stats against starting and relief pitchers of the opposite handedness.

Weather

Weather is more important in baseball than football. In football, certain conditions may hamper offensive stats. But in baseball, a rainout will make scoring, in a word, impossible. Thus, it's extremely important to check weather forecasts to look for any chance that your players might be scratched due to a rainout.

As is the case in any peer-to-peer competition, you'll profit from your opponents' mistakes. It's astounding how many DFS participants will choose baseball players in games where a rainout is imminent. Don't be one of those people who give their money away by ignoring obvious and easy-to-access information.

Other weather factors aren't as total in their effect, but can still help you get an edge in putting together your roster. One of these is wind. Wind can make the difference between fly balls staying in the park (good for pitchers, especially those with lower percentages of ground balls) and leaving the park (helping hitters and hurting those same pitchers).

Another effect is humidity. High humidity effectively makes baseballs heavier and reduces home runs.

A good website for finding weather information for ballgames is DailyBaseballData.com. It maintains a specific weather page that gives information on conditions for each city hosting a game, including the chance for rain, the relative humidity, and the wind speed and direction, depicted clearly against the orientation of the baseball diamond.

Keep in mind that sports books and professional bettors have known about these factors for some time, so the weather effects are incorporated into the run totals for games. As mentioned numerous times in this book, the over/under lines tell you a lot about what to expect from the offense, but that's just for starters. More in-depth information about the weather, for example knowing that the wind is blowing in on a humid day at a particular park, might help seal the decision between two players with similar stats and salaries.

Starting Lineups

It's not just a rainout that can cause a player to put up a big fat goose egg. Baseball managers often change starting lineups, and not just due to injury. Favorable matchups (lefty-vs.-righty), the need to give players a day of rest over a long season, hunches (the desire to play the "hot hand"), and even trade intrigue can result in players starting or sitting.

Before any contest, when possible, you should check to confirm that your players will be in the starting lineup. Final lineup cards are due only a few minutes before a game, but generally, big-league managers release starting lineups several hours before. This can make a difference if you enter contests with games that span afternoon starts on the east coast to west coast games with the first pitch at 10 p.m. Eastern Time.

Not only is this something that you need to be aware of before game time for making sure everyone on your roster is starting, but examining starting lineups also presents opportunities for finding bargain position players.

Daily fantasy sites make contests available relatively far in advance of the games on which they're based—often the evening before in baseball. Player salaries are set according to their perceived value at the time the contests are first posted, long before starting lineups are made public. Bench players, who don't often start games, are usually discounted substantially. However, when such players get the nod to start a game, they offer value. Often, the player is on the bench because he doesn't have the best statistics. But it might also be because he's relatively ineffective against right-handed pitching; with a left-hander on the mound, a manager might call his number to play for the matchup. The danger there is he might be removed from the game after a pitching change, but generally he'll get three plate appearances. And that may be enough for a low salary to deliver value.

A convenient website for checking MLB starting lineups is RotoGrinders.com; you'll also see the handedness of the hitters and pitchers, weather, a projection of runs scored for each team, and salary prices for players for the top DFS websites. The lineup page even has convenient filters by position, so you can isolate players and check for handedness against opposing pitching. Finally, it's handy for checking a player's lineup position within a batting order. Which brings us to the next consideration.

Batting Order

The lineup not only tells you the players in the game, but also their batting order. In general, the higher in the order a player gets to hit, the more at-bats he's likely to receive and therefore the more chances at scoring points.

As a rule, managers tend to cluster their best on-base-percentage players at the one and two positions, the best hitters at two and three, and power bats in the cleanup or fourth position. The age-old theory is to get players on base, move them into scoring position, then bring them home.

Generally, this all gets incorporated into statistics and, in turn, the salary price for players. But some managers (Joe Maddon, recently of the Chicago Cubs, comes to mind) tinker with lineups, batting order in particular. That can mean a surprise player batting in the first or second spot of the lineup and a chance to pick up some fractional edges for scoring.

Remember that leadoff hitters, as well as hitters in the two though four spots, are tactically important for DFS, often collecting extra plate appearances. The average plate appearances per team per game for the majors in 2014 was 37 to 38. Considering nine batting positions, that means each player in the lineup getting at least four plate appearances, with the first and second positions getting a fifth plate appearance on average. This metric puts a bit of a premium on top-of-the-order hitters who have some power, such as José Altuve, Brett Gardner, and Charlie Blackmon. That extra at-bat with extra-base potential can win some close DFS contests.

OTHER FACTORS

Umpires

As the judges of the strike zone, home-plate umpires can have a huge impact on a game. Calling strikes generously aids pitchers, while so-called "squeezing" the strike zone leads to more favorable conditions for hitters.

This effect is well-known among gamblers; like weather, an umpire's proclivities are factored into the run total for a game. Nevertheless, if you need a deciding factor between one pitcher and another, you could do worse than checking to see who's calling the games behind home plate and what their tendencies are. The website Covers.com, which provides a broad range of news, commentary, and statistics regarding sports wagering, offers information on what the over/under totals are like for all umpires. It also lists the home-plate umpire for each game.

Team K%

I stated previously that evaluating hitter-versus-pitcher matchups, individually or team-wise, doesn't help much in putting together winning daily fantasy lineups. The problem is one of sample size, which is too small in this area to draw any reliable conclusions. Besides, when looking at a pitcher versus an opposing team, the composition of that team can change drastically from season to season, even from one start to another, for the pitcher you're trying to evaluate.

However, a team's offensive strikeout rate, or K%—defined as the number of strikeouts divided by the total number of plate appearances—can be very helpful when looking for strikeout pitchers. Remember, in daily fantasy, pitchers are rewarded for strikeouts, so if a hurler is going against a free-swinging bunch that chases pitches, it should boost that pitcher's DFS numbers for the day.

To be sure, K% is a composite stat based on players who can change game to game, but it might also reflect the philosophy of the manager and hitting coach (whether or not they want players to swing away freely). This is a statistic that's perhaps best employed once the baseball season has delivered a reasonable sample of games, say 40 to 50. The roster turnover from one game to another is nowhere near as significant as from one season to the next.

Steals

Sabermetrics has charts for run expectancy given various game states (the number of outs and which bases have runners). For instance, at the start of any inning, with no one on and no one out, we expect 0.461 runs. Now, get the leadoff hitter to first base and that number moves to 0.831. Get the leadoff guy to second with no outs and the run expectancy rises to 1.068.

So a steal of second, in the best of circumstances (with no one out), is worth about one fourth of one run. But as we've seen, daily fantasy scores it much higher—at two whole points on FanDuel, for example.

Steals are relatively rare (among scoring events for offense, only hit-by-pitch and triples are rarer) and they don't factor in as much for actual run expectancy, so this is one event where the impact for DFS outweighs the impact on the real game. It's similar to strikeouts for pitchers: They're as good as any other out in the game for the pitcher, but they're worth more for daily fantasy results. Thus, the steal is worth a little extra look.

Just as you should be aware of the K% for strikeouts, for steals it's worth noting which pitchers allow a large number of stolen bases and at what rate. For instance, Tommy Hanson, through only 15 games pitching for the Angels in 2013, allowed 21 steals on 24 attempts in 73 innings. That's an average of 2.59 steals per 9 innings. But is this an edge people are thinking about? Probably not, and maybe with good reason. After all, steals are relatively few and far between and might not be significant from a statistical standpoint. If, however, you can find a position player with a high OBP and a fair number of steal attempts facing a pitcher who seems unable to hold runners on base, there may be value above what you might garner just from the run total.

Before we leave the topic, it's also noteworthy that some DFS websites penalize failed steal attempts, i.e., caught stealing (CS). FanDuel doesn't, but DraftKings does. On FanDuel, a steal is worth 2 points with no takeaway for CS. On Draft-Kings, the successful steal is worth 5 points and the CS is -2 points.

Of course, steals allowed is something of a team effort involving pitcher and catcher, so sometimes something can be gleaned from looking at a team's defensive CS% (percentage of steals allowed). The Major League average for CS% in 2014 was about 27%. So when considering picking a player based on his stealing ability and weighing that offensive factor against the defensive opposition, a CS% lower than 27% for the opposition means your speedster is possibly going against weaker opposition and certainly may be more inclined to run.

Teams with a poor CS% tend to make improvements in that category during the offseason, so it's best to get a representative sample of the current season before relying on it too heavily.

Cash-Game Contests

It's often been said that baseball is a game of failure. Ted Williams, arguably the greatest pure hitter of all time, put it best when he said, "Baseball is the only field of endeavor where a man can succeed three times out of ten and be considered a good performer." Of course, Teddy Ballgame was referring to the fact that even the best hitters in the game—the ones who hit .300—fail to achieve their objective on seven out of 10 attempts.

You have to reconcile yourself to the fact that when you assemble eight position players to accumulate offensive numbers for your team, typically only three to five of them will earn significant points for you. Still, sometimes, when just four or five of the eight produce good, even if not great, numbers, it will be enough for you to make it into the money in cash games—as long as you've also latched onto solid pitching, and pitching is far more predictable than hitting.

The theory for succeeding in cash games is the same as it is for football: Select players who have high floors. You won't be able to do that for every position in your lineup, but you don't have to, either. You do need to be consistent in your pitching selections and that can be as simple as committing the proper amount of resources to that position.

Race and sports bettors often resist going with "the chalk," meaning the favorite, in just about any wager, because the return is so low. For instance, in horse racing, betting the chalk may mean winning a return of as little as, say, 40¢ on a $2 bet. But in daily fantasy baseball, chalk pitching (and I'll use that term to refer to the three or four highest-priced pitchers) is often the safest pick you can make and usually the surest points in your lineup.

How much of your budget should you pour into pitching?

On DraftKings, since you're picking a total of 10 players and two of them are pitchers, the absolute proportional distribution is 20%. But if you do that, you'll burn through your bankroll by the All Star break—because you won't be cashing very often.

Some surveys of winning lineups indicate that cash games that hit the money on DraftKings invest a little more than 25% of the salary cap on the two pitchers combined. However, even that may be too low. An investment of closer to 30% in pitching is not exorbitant. Invest in pitchers. They're the foundation of your fantasy team.

How many points do you need to cash in a 50/50 game? It depends.

On DraftKings, a reasonable target to make the money in cash games is 90 to 110 points. On FanDuel, it's 35 to 40. But those ranges vary day to day, depending on how the large-percentage players perform.

For a 30-entrant field in a 50/50 contest, it doesn't matter if you finish with the number-one score or the number-15 score; you get the same money. You don't need to over-reach. You just have to put together a lineup with a floor that allows you to hit the threshold for cashing in the contest. Once again, playing in cash games calls for choosing players with high floors.

But if your best hitter takes an 0-fer, his floor is zero on DraftKings and in negative territory on FanDuel. Remember what Mr. Williams said, even the best hitters fail seven out of 10 times, so a few of your hitters will likely flame out.

But back to pitchers, they get points for innings pitched and strikeouts—two highly predictable statistics. In a cash game, you're trying to rack up at least a third of your total points from the guy on the hill.

Pay attention to the fundamentals on pitchers.

- Check the Vegas odds and lean on the pitchers in heavily favored games.
- Take note of the over/under and try to stick with pitchers in games forecast for a 7.5 or lower O/U.
- The ballpark and even the wind are generally factored into the O/U, but check anyway. If the wind is blowing out at Wrigley Field, stay off the pitchers in that game.
- Favor pitchers with a high strikeouts-per-nine-innings figure. There's a reason why guys like Clayton Kershaw, Felix Hernandez, and Max Scherzer are among the highest-priced pitchers in daily fantasy. That's the cost of consistency. And it's usually worth paying.
- Favor pitchers who eat innings. They collect points for innings pitched. Also, if they remain effective, they'll collect more points for strikeouts (of course, if they run out of gas, they can also lose points for yielding additional earned runs, hits, and walks). Plus, pitchers who stick around longer have a bet-

ter chance of getting the pitching win, and that's a points bonus.

- If you go for a cheaper pitcher (usually as a number two on DraftKings), look for opportunities against weak offensive teams with high strikeout tendencies and low wOBA and OPS.

When the final totals are tallied for cash games on FanDuel, you'd like to get 14-16 points from your pitcher and 22-25 points from your hitters. If you get that kind of production, you'll make the money in a lot of cash games.

Meanwhile, you don't need spectacular performances up and down the lineup (although a 3-for-4 with a home run and three RBIs always helps), but one or two hitters have to deliver a homer and three or four other position players have to have solid games for you to get a payout.

As already mentioned, home runs are handsomely rewarded—6 points for a bases-empty tater on FanDuel and 14 points on DraftKings. In both cases, a single swing of the bat can often produce 20% to 25% of the offensive points needed to make it into the money in a cash game.

GPP Contests

Tournaments or guaranteed-prize-pool baseball contests follow the same arc as in football.

DFS participants hope to leverage a fairly modest buy-in into a jackpot. As a rule, 15%-20% of all entrants cash. However, a sizable percentage of the prize money is squeezed at the top of the payoff structure. So it's not uncommon for the top three finishers to take down 25% of the entire prize pool in a contest where, say, 150 entrants make it to the money out of a total field of about 760 players. Put another way, about 0.4% of the original field of 760 would share 25% of the prize money. Which is why I stress that GPPs share similarities with lottery tickets.

To be sure, DFS and the lottery also have significant differences. The former involves a considerable amount of skill in order to consistently be competitive; the latter merely requires buying the ticket. And let's not forget that 15% to 20% of a GPP field will win *something*. But it's also true that only a tiny fraction of all players in the field will make serious money and that a certain amount of luck has to complement the skill for that to happen.

As is the case in other daily fantasy sports, hitting it big in big-field tournaments requires playing the contrarian. Instead of selecting a lineup full of players with high floors as you would in cash games, in GPPs you have the challenge of selecting players with high ceilings, even if their downside risk is evident. Think slugger Ryan Howard, who can go 0-for-4 with three strikeouts for a string of games, then hit a homer, a double, draw a walk, drive in five runs, and score twice the next game.

Also, being the contrarian avoids the problem of having players in your lineup that your competitors are also likely to have conscripted. In GPPs, you want to break away from the pack, not run with it.

One way to approach GPPs that's become a trend among savvy DFS players is to heavily stack a baseball lineup with players from the same team. This is similar to stacking in football with same-team quarterbacks and wide receivers.

In baseball, the application is more extreme. Here, you try to identify a baseball team you think is poised to score a bunch of runs and select as many players as possible from that team, often batters hitting consecutively.

If the GPP contest allows multiple entries, you can do the

same with three or four lineups, each stacked with hitters from several MLB teams you think could have a huge night, or you might assemble lineups with several hitters from teams going against horrible pitching.

Regardless of the reasons, a fantasy lineup stacked with players from the same team could enjoy the synergy of members of a hot club knocking each other home and racking up the kind of big points necessary to reach the very top of a GPP payoff structure.

On the other hand, there are player combinations to avoid. For example, you should always be aware of one directly oppositional statistical relationship, baseball's most obvious duel between pitcher and batter. As a DFS owner, you want to avoid a situation where the success of one of your players leads to the failure of another. Never select hitters playing against your pitcher. Not only is it statistically contradictory, it's also emotionally conflicting.

Finally, as in football, consider "wheel" players in whom you have a lot of confidence in several contests.

Wheeling is a concept familiar to horse-race handicappers. They do it with exotic bets, such as exactas (picking the first two horses in order). It's a difficult thing to do successfully, but it can pay off handsomely. When horse players feel extremely confident about the horse they believe will win the race, they'll play all the other horses in the field to place second. It's called wheeling because of the metaphor of a hub (the winning horse) and spokes (all the others) in a wheel.

In DFS, wheeling involves selecting a key player, usually a pitcher, you're confident will produce a healthy share of points as your hub and assembling several lineups around him. Assuming you're right about your ace player, your teams will be contenders in all your contests and you'll have achieved less volatility in your overall outcomes, hopefully winning more contests than you lose. If you're wrong, of course, the faltering key player drags down all of your entries.

Final Thoughts for Beginners

Tackling daily fantasy contests can be a little like playing golf. You try to remember so many things—grip, stance, left arm straight, head down, rotate hips—that you don't get anything right, as evidenced by the errant tee shot slicing out of bounds.

In the beginning, DFS baseball newbies should concentrate on just a few things—strikeouts for pitchers and wOBA for hitters are good starts. You can take it a little further by concentrating on lefty-righty situations, especially right-handed hitters against left-handed pitchers. If you're a beginner, I suggest you play cash games at lower price points to get a feel for the game, for example, five $1 contests a day for a couple of weeks.

Try to get in the habit of checking for surprises in the 30 minutes or so before the players in your contests are about to start their games. Look for last-minute scratches from your lineups or even for bad weather moving in. Nothing kills a DFS lineup like having players in a game that gets postponed by rain.

Finally, frequent websites where the DFS pros go to get a feel for advanced baseball metrics that, in the future, may be a key to a big payday. Websites such as FanGraphs provide statistics and research tools to help their readers make sense of the daily matchups. That's certainly helped close the gap, at least a little, between casual players who don't do much research and grinders who sort through esoteric statistics and apply sophisticated analysis to get an edge.

Chapter 7

Basketball

Pro basketball has become one of the favored sports of DFS grinders and that alone should give newcomers and even intermediate players pause before jumping into the NBA contests. As already pointed out, grinders are making a living (or trying very hard to) from DFS contests, or they at least aspire to it by investing substantial time, effort, and resources into playing the games.

The special affection that the regulars have for NBA contests is due to the sport's predictability, as least in terms of player statistical outcomes. In other words, there's less variance in NBA statistics than in other sports, where unpredictable events can create surprise fantasy outcomes.

For instance, in baseball, you could wind up selecting an inexpensive shortstop for your lineup, merely because that infielder happened to fit under your salary cap after you'd already picked all your other players. Lo and behold, the bargain-priced shortstop hits a double and a home run and collects a fistful of RBIs, resulting in a mother lode of fantasy points. At the same time, the power-hitting first baseman you grabbed for a sizable chunk of your cap dollars takes a horse collar and gives you zero points. That's the sort of unpredictability that drives DFS regulars crazy, and it doesn't happen nearly as often in basketball as it does in other sports.

Why not? Basically, an NBA starter, who is not being rested for the evening and barring injury, will routinely yield a predictable number of fantasy points. Obviously, it won't be exactly the same night after night, but the ups and downs will be more like hills and swales, rather than peaks and valleys.

Here's an example comparing two players from baseball and basketball: Los Angeles Angels outfielder Mike Trout and Golden State Warriors point guard Stephen Curry.

In 2014, Trout was the unanimous selection as the American League's Most Valuable Player, hitting .287 with 36 home runs, 111 RBIs, and 115 runs scored. In the 2014-15 NBA season, Curry led the Warriors to the NBA championship, averaging 23.8 points, 7.7 assists, 4.3 rebounds, and 2 steals per game, and he was named the league's MVP.

Now let's look at these two extraordinary athletes through the lens of daily fantasy points production.

The vagaries of baseball, being what they are, meant that Trout had his good days and his bad days at the plate in 2014. Using DraftKings scoring, Trout averaged a little more than 10 fantasy points per game over the entire year. However, when his day-to-day DFS production is reviewed, Trout delivered less than half his mean fantasy points (5 or fewer) in about 38% of his games (60 of 160), including *absolutely zero* fantasy points in 15% of his games (24). Offsetting those especially low fantasy point days, Trout registered 43 games when his fantasy points total was at least 50% greater than his mean (15 fantasy points).

Now, let's look at the Warriors' stellar point guard. Curry participated in 101 regular-season and playoff games during the 2014-15 NBA season and he averaged a little over 46 fantasy points per game. In 75% of his 101 games, Curry's fantasy points output was in a range from 25% below to 25% above (35-58 fantasy points) his per-game mean.

The point is simple. NBA player production is more consistent and, as a result, more predictable than baseball. That's simply a reflection of the statistical realities of the two sports. A baseball player can hit two home runs and drive in six runs one day and go hitless the next two days. But a basketball player won't pour in 50 points one night and go scoreless the next two games. As a result, the statistical steadiness that's more prevalent in NBA play than in other sports makes it more attractive to daily fantasy players who lean on math and algorithms to set their lineups.

Another circumstance that makes NBA a game that tilts toward DFS regulars is the last-minute nature of lineup changes. The grind of the NBA season means that head coaches decide at the last minute to rest a starter or sit him down due to a nagging injury. In the NBA, these things happen just before tip-off. You don't have all week to sort through injury situations like in NFL fantasy contests. Just having one NBA player in a fantasy lineup who doesn't answer the bell will basically kill that roster's chances of cashing.

Even if DFS owners are paying attention, sometimes they'll get blindsided, because coaches can be devious. In the NBA championship series, Golden State coach Steve Kerr admitted to lying about his starting lineup, in part to avoid speculation on social media. Kerr said that center Andrew Bogut would start in Game 4 of the NBA Finals against Cleveland. Instead, when the starting lineups were announced just before the game started, André Iguodala replaced Bogut. Iguodala played 39 of 48 minutes and scored 22 points.

"I have two press conferences on the day of the game, so I'm asked a lot of strategic questions," Kerr explained. "If I tell the truth, it's the equivalent of me knocking on [the opposing coach's] door and saying, 'Hey, this is what we're going to do.'

I could evade the question, which would start this Twitter phenomenon, 'Who is going to start for the Warriors?' Or I could lie. So I lied. Sorry."

If a DFS owner had been paying attention to the news reports the day of the game, he would have been misled like everyone else. The lesson is that in daily fantasy basketball, participants have to be at their computers or on their mobile devices right up until game time to verify starting lineups. That's a commitment DFS grinders are willing to make, because for them *it's a job*, but it puts casual fans at a disadvantage.

DFS beginners should understand that basketball poses special challenges that can only be overcome by diligently drilling into the stats to assemble the puzzle of their fantasy lineups, *as well as* by getting into the rhythm of following the NBA schedule, in which last-minute changes (although not quite as newsworthy as the one foisted by Kerr) are fairly normal.

Scoring Lineups and Rules

Here are the scoring and lineup rules for FanDuel and DraftKings.

FanDuel Lineup (9 players)—2 point guards, 2 shooting guards, 2 small forwards, 2 power forwards, 1 center. The website determines what players are available to play each position and FanDuel restricts lineups to a maximum of four players from one NBA team; because of that, at least three real NBA teams need to be represented in a FanDuel lineup.

FanDuel Scoring—3-point field goal 3, 2-point field goal 2, free throw 1, rebound 1.2, assist 1.5, block 2, steal 2, turnover -1.

DraftKings Lineup (8 players)—Point guard, shooting

guard, small forward, power forward, center, guard (any), forward (any), utility (any). The website determines what players are available to play each position; lineup players must be from at least two NBA teams and must represent at least two different NBA games.

DraftKings Scoring—Point 1, made three-point shot 0.5, rebound 1.25, assist 1.5, steal 2, block 2, turnover -0.5. Bonus points: double-double (1.5 points, maximum one per player), triple-double (3 points, maximum one per player). Bonuses are determined by points, rebounds, assists, blocks, and steals.

A look at the basketball scoring rules on FanDuel and DraftKings indicates less difference between the two major websites than in any other sport. The main differentiator is in the lineups. FanDuel requires nine player positions to DraftKings' eight. And in keeping with FanDuel rules in other sports, the assigned positions have strict designations. DraftKings offers more latitude in assembling rosters; certainly one of the more interesting lineup decisions is in how the utility position is handled. Depending on the circumstances, point guards and centers are generally the prime candidates to fill that wildcard spot.

Online Tools

In tackling any daily fantasy sport, it's advisable to become familiar with the online tools that can give you guidance. In basketball, *advisable* should be changed to *essential*. It's almost impossible to compete in daily fantasy basketball without the expert tools available online.

In daily fantasy parlance, a tool can be a program that performs calculations and analysis. More frequently, it's a chart containing useful statistical information; these often provide filters to make managing the information easier. Many DFS pros use the RotoGrinders website, thanks to its array of these resources.

An example on RotoGrinders is the Team Stats tool that records the fantasy points and stats for each NBA team in all the pertinent categories, such as points scored, three-point field goals, rebounds, assists, blocks, steals, and so on. A toggle function shows fantasy points earned by a team or that opponents earned against that team. Also, a filter shows the same information by position (point guard, center, power forward, etc.). Finally, the Team Stats tool can be set to measure fantasy points under different website rules. Clearly, this isn't the type of numbers crunching the average fan can do with paper, pencil, and a hand calculator.

Another analysis tool looks at individual player statistics. Still another measures consistency in terms of floor and ceiling for guidance on whether players are suitable selections for cash games or tournaments.

Charts such as these are often sortable, meaning you can analyze players in certain categories, such as minutes played, and filters allow you to look at player performance over various periods of time, such as for the season to date or just the last few weeks.

If this is beginning to sound like a dizzying array of data to wade through, well, you're getting the right impression. And hopefully, a message is coming through that the enormous volume of facts and figures available in basketball is a huge advantage to DFS pros who know their way around spreadsheets that yield actionable forecasts.

Key Points to DFS Basketball

Newcomers should tread lightly when heading into DFS basketball territory. This is the place to remind beginner and intermediate participants that football, for all the reasons described in that chapter, provides the most level playing field.

On the other hand, many people love the NBA game and daily fantasy is a great way to intensify their engagement. And perhaps even as beginners, their feel for the game will allow them to hold their own as they sharpen their analytical skills and become more facile using online analysis resources.

Here are some keys that everyone, from beginners to pros, need to examine.

Participation—Everyone knows the old saw about real estate: location, location, location. In daily fantasy basketball, it's minutes, minutes, minutes. That's not overstating it! Whether you're considering a big-name superstar or a non-star starter or a guy coming off the bench to make an occasional start, the primary consideration has to be the minutes he's expected to play *that night*.

In daily fantasy basketball circles, the concept is often referred to as "opportunity." Opportunity leads to fantasy points. Assuming there are no changes in the status of a starter you're considering to include on your roster, minutes played is not only a highly predictable number; that also makes the other important stats—the ones that translate to fantasy points—reasonably foreseeable. But the player has to get his normal minutes. So, when you use the online tools to start putting together a basketball lineup, one of the stats you have to consider is— let's say it again!—minutes. When a starter is injured or being rested and you understand exactly what backup will be getting those minutes, that's an opportunity to grab starter-caliber fantasy points at backup-salary cap prices.

Injuries—In the world of DFS basketball, injuries are extremely important. Why? Because injuries have an impact on minutes! In the NBA, players miss games all the time because of nagging injuries.

The way injuries to basketball players are treated in terms of public notice is a lot different than in football or baseball. In football, injuries often occur in a way that most fans who are paying attention will know about them, and because there's so much time between games, significant injuries are discussed in the media. There's also a formal way in which information about football injuries is disseminated. In the football section of this book, I discussed how the NFL requires teams to report on a player's practice status throughout the week; as game-time approaches, injury categories, while not completely illuminating, at least put the public on notice about the general status of injured players.

That's not how it works in the NBA.

Sometimes, a player finishes a game and it's not apparent that he's hurting. The NBA season is a grind and players just don't have the time to heal between games. So, in 48 or 72 hours when the next game rolls around, a starter might not be able to go. And because 82 regular-season games are played in the NBA, as opposed to just 16 in the NFL, there's a bit less urgency to have a basketball player take the court when he's hurting. Thus, unfortunately for DFS participants, the drumbeat of news concerning most NBA players' injuries isn't quite as loud as in other sports; a guy sitting out a night isn't so unusual. But if you have that guy in your DFS basketball lineup and he doesn't get out of his sweats, your night is over before it even begins.

The solution is simple, if inconvenient. Daily fantasy basketball owners have to monitor player participation 15 minutes before tip-off. Any DFS participant who can't do that is in for some unpleasant surprises. Even if the injury isn't to one of your players, it presents an opportunity for the daily fantasy regulars to take advantage of a bargain-priced backup who's now starting—and that can lead to a wholesale lineup switch as the grinder loads up with a star or two. DFS owners can change their lineups ("edit" in DFS parlance) until the real games begin and in accordance with the daily fantasy website's rules.

DFS players have several online sources for NBA player news, two of which are RotoGrinders and RotoWorld. In some cases, websites may have special requirements, such as registration and/or a paid subscription, for receiving certain types of information.

Vegas Line—Thank goodness for the guys working the sports books in Las Vegas, who provide a starting point that DFS beginners and intermediates can wrap their minds around without a lot of complicated data mining. NBA odds are expressed in pointspreads along with an over-under number. Even if a DFS player isn't interested in delving too deeply into stats, the Vegas line tells a story that starts with who's favored and by how much (the pointspread) and the anticipated pace of the game (the total).

If an NBA game features a wide pointspread with a high total, that's an indication that some players in the game will probably earn some big fantasy points. Even then, it's not so simple to assemble a lineup. If the favored team builds up a 25-point lead midway through the third period, the coach is likely to begin resting his starters and those guys won't wind up with the windfall of fantasy points for which they were on track.

The better situation is one where both teams are evenly matched (low pointspread) with a high O/U number, and the game script goes just as the oddsmakers thought it would. In that case, the DFS player simply has to use the data available to pick the players most likely to benefit from the scoring shootout.

On the other hand, if Vegas predicts a low total, that's certainly an indication to a DFS player to be wary of selecting players in that game.

Can a DFS newbie expect a money-making result by picking players with no more research than looking at the daily Vegas odds? Probably not. But without using the Vegas odds as a starting point, a beginner will almost certainly be lost.

Defense vs. Position—In all the daily fantasy sports, a key challenge in assembling lineups is trying to determine whether your potential players are facing a favorable matchup or one that could give them trouble. Defense versus Position (DvP) is the most convenient and probably most widely used matchup metric for DFS basketball.

Defense-vs.-Position tools chart how a specific team performs against each position on the court, meaning point guard, shooting guard, small forward, power forward, and center. For instance, by using the DvP tool, you'd discover that, for the 2014-15 season, the average fantasy points yielded to centers (using DraftKings scoring) was a little over 47 per game. But the Utah Jazz—with 7-foot-2 defensive phenom Rudy Gobert—gave up only about 40 fantasy points to centers, which was a league best. So, by using that tool, a DFS player would be advised that it's probably not a good idea to play a center against the Jazz if the tall guy from France is in the lineup. The categories measured include points, three-pointers, rebounds, assists, steals—the works. There are also filters for timelines, such as the full season or the last three weeks or the last game. RotoGrinders.com carries the DvP analysis tool.

Correlation/Stacking—As we've seen, in other DFS team sports, it's occasionally advisable to stack players (include multiple players from the same real sports team in your lineup) to varying degrees, because they can have a positive fantasy-points impact on one another. Broadly, this is a DFS concept referred to as "correlation."

When to Stack

Player correlation—also known as "player stacking," which is including multiple players from the same team in you daily fantasy lineup—is more effective in some sports than others, and it's more necessary in some types of contests than others. Here's a quick breakdown.

Heavy Stacking:
Hockey. Especially members of the same line (center and wingers) in both cash games and GPPs.

Moderate to Heavy Stacking:
Baseball. Consider moderate stacking (two or occasionally three position players) in cash games if the scoring projection warrants, but it's not always necessary. Heavy stacking (three or more position players) is absolutely necessary in GPPs.

Modest Stacking:
Football. No stacking to moderate stacking (QBs and receivers are most common) in cash games. Moderate stacking (again, most often QBs and receivers) is absolutely necessary in GPPs.

No Stacking:
Basketball. There has to be a rare circumstance, such as a team projected to score 115 to 130 points, to consider any stacking in cash games or even in GPPs.

Examples are the quarterback throwing a long pass to a wide receiver, or a baseball player hitting a home run with a teammate on base. If you've coupled those players on your roster, you get a bolt of fantasy points for two of your players from one big play. In football, this is a common lineup strategy in GPPs where you need lots of fantasy points to finish near the top of the leaderboard.

While there's some correlation in basketball (for instance, a player feeds an assist to a teammate who scores a basket), stacking usually isn't advisable. In basketball, teammates normally *take* fantasy points from one another. If one player scores 40 of his team's 110 points, that means that some of his teammates are getting fewer shots. Admittedly, there are rare occasions when stacking would be beneficial. If you knew a basketball game was going into overtime, it would be a great idea to have a couple of guys from each team, but that would require a crystal ball. A more realistic opportunity for stacking would be if a good fast-paced offensive team is facing a team that will accommodate that fast tempo, but also has a terrible defense. Then, you could rationalize having a couple of players from the favored team.

Lineup Style—There are two main approaches to building a daily fantasy NBA lineup. A common approach with the catchy label of "Studs and Scrubs" advocates picking a few (three is usually the right number) top-tier players and filling in with players who are lower-priced, but are scheduled to get more playing time for that game as they start in place of an injured or resting front-liner. The conventional Studs and Scrubs wisdom is the way to go in GPPs. The rub here, however, is the challenge of cherry-picking the scrubs who'll get 25 or 35 minutes of playing time and that means staying on top of real-world lineup changes.

Another method of basketball-lineup construction is the "Average Joes" roster, which is more suitable for cash-game contests, meaning the 50/50s, double-ups, and H2Hs. This is less challenging, because you're banking on a group of NBA starters simply playing their normal games to keep you in contention in the cash games. Again, you need to be sure that your guys are starting; assuming there's no problem there, you're looking for mid-priced players with low standard deviations, something that's easier to find in basketball than in, say, baseball.

Final Word

Clearly, DFS basketball is one of the more challenging of all the sports for a DFS beginner. For starters, it requires more focus and attention than any other daily fantasy sport. In football, and especially in baseball, one of your players can get zero points and you can still cash in a 50/50, double-up, or head-to-head. Not in basketball. If you slip on one player, the contest is finished for you.

In addition, because of the unrelenting tempo of the season and last-minute lineup changes, you have to stay on top of NBA news. In fact, some DFS hoops grinders monitor Twitter and set up automatic news alerts that get sent right to their mobile devices, so they don't miss anything.

All that being said, the NBA is an exciting game with a devoted following and daily fantasy has lots of potential to grow the league's audience and strengthen its hold on existing fans. For those who count themselves among the NBA's devotees and find that daily fantasy provides a little extra kick to the game, the sound advice is to approach DFS as entertainment and be prudent with your investment.

If free games are available, play those for a while or at low stakes until you get a feel for daily fantasy NBA. Take note of how many fantasy points it takes to hit the money in cash games and how many points it takes to hit the top 15% to 20% in GPPs.

Once you have a handle on how many fantasy points are necessary to cash, figure out how many points you need for each $1,000 of salary-cap money spent (points/$m) from each player at each position to make that total. By playing with the numbers, you'll begin to get a feel for assembling competitive lineups, even if you aren't a spreadsheet expert plumbing the deep well of NBA data.

Chapter 8

Hockey

More than any other daily fantasy sport, hockey is about correlation.

As discussed several times already, correlation is a statistical phenomenon where one player's performance impacts another on the stat sheets. Correlation between teammates—especially as it applies to "stacking" members of a single real-life sports team in your DFS lineup—can sometimes figure prominently in building a money-winning roster.

In basketball, correlation isn't much of a factor and, indeed, stacking is often considered undesirable.

In football, stacking is highly desirable in large guaranteed-prize-pool tournaments, but it's often best avoided in cash games.

In baseball, stacking hitters can be a viable lineup-building approach in cash games, as well as in GPPs against the right pitching match-up.

In hockey, however, because of the pervasive statistical connectivity among players, stacking is an absolute necessity in both cash games and tournaments, at least to some degree.

Not surprisingly, NHL daily fantasy contests are the most thinly played of the major sports. Hockey's exposure on national television has produced uneven results in terms of viewership and fan interest, although recent years have seen some improvements. Meanwhile, some major metropolitan newspapers in markets where there's no NHL franchise barely cover the league at all in their sports pages. So it should come as no surprise that in daily fantasy, hockey is a niche segment, though that can tend to make the competition even rougher, because the DFS hockey participants are more likely to be avid than casual fans. Anyone trying DFS hockey should be well-versed in the game, because the competition certainly will be.

Skating into DFS Hockey

The starting point for a DFS hockey participant is to examine the differences in the rules for lineup building and for accumulating points. Here is the comparison between FanDuel and DraftKings.

FanDuel Lineup (9 players)—2 centers, 2 left wingers, 2 right wingers, 2 defensemen, and 1 goalie. The website determines the players available at each position. Lineup players must be from three different NHL teams and no more than four players can be from the same team.

FanDuel Scoring—forwards/defensemen: goal 3, assist 2, plus/minus 1/-1, penalty minute 0.25, power-play point 0.5, shot on goal 0.4; goalies: win 3, goal against -1, save 0.2, shutout 2.

DraftKings Lineup (9 players)—2 centers, 3 wingers, 2 defensemen, 1 utility (center, winger, or defenseman), and 1 goalie. The website determines what players are available to play each position. Skaters, meaning non-goalies, must be from at least three different NHL teams.

DraftKings Scoring—all players: goal 3, assist 2, shot on goal 0.5, blocked shot 0.5, short-handed point bonus - goal/

assist 1, shootout goal 0.2, hat trick bonus 1.5; goalies: win 3, save 0.2, goal against -1, shutout bonus 2.

DraftKings Scoring Notes—Goalies receive points for all stats they accrue, including goals and assists. The goalie shutout bonus is credited to goalies if they complete the entire game with zero goals allowed in regulation plus overtime. Shootout goals will not prevent a shutout. Goalie must complete the entire game to get credit for a shutout.

When you examine the lineup rules, you'll notice that for the 2015-16 NHL season, DraftKings made no distinction between right and left wingers, while FanDuel did. Further, though it's not listed in the parameters set forth above, DraftKings allows multi-positional eligibility in hockey in the same way it does in baseball. So, it's possible that a hockey player may be eligible to play both winger and center and can be used in a DraftKings lineup at either of those positions.

Vin Narayanan, formerly a fantasy hockey writer for *USA Today,* points out the advantages of selecting players who are eligible as wingers, but who'll actually take the ice as centers. "In daily fantasy hockey, every goal results in multiple points being awarded, because there's going to be the actual scorer plus whoever gets an assist, and that's usually two other players on every goal," Narayanan said.

"You have to put a premium on centers because they're the playmakers and they're going to be involved in almost any scoring play, whether it's as the goal-scorer or as the player who provides an assist. Wingers, as the sniper on the offense, may get goals, but you can't count on them being in on every scoring play. The trick in DFS is to find players who may be playing as wingers, but are natural centers."

So, when playing on DraftKings, successfully hunting for

players with multi-positional eligibility could result in having more than two players who are natural centers. As Narayanan points out, that's an important edge; it can result in having more than two natural centers on your team and playmakers are more likely to be involved in scoring.

The Holy Goalie

The heart of a hockey lineup is the goalie position. Goalies are to hockey DFS lineups what quarterbacks are to DFS football and what pitchers are to DFS baseball. Goalies are routinely among the highest fantasy point-getters, if not *the* top fantasy scorer, in your lineup. And goalie points are much more reliable than even a top goal-scorer.

"That's where you spend your money," Narayanan said. "You're looking for goalies playing for teams that are big favorites, because you get that three-point bonus for a goalie win."

The way to find those teams, as usual, is to look at the Las Vegas odds. In hockey, the sports betting lines are similar to baseball. The money line indicates who the favorite is. A minus number indicates the favorite, and a plus number indicates the underdog. The higher the numbers, the bigger the favorite or the underdog. In addition, the Vegas odds include an over-under number, the linemaker's forecast of how many total goals will be scored in the game. So when shopping for goalies, the ideal choice would be one who plays for a team that's heavily favored in a game with a relatively low over-under total.

Perhaps the most challenging part about rostering an NHL goalie for your lineup is simply making sure that the net minder you select will actually be in between the pipes that night. This means checking websites that provide that kind of information, such as DailyFaceoff.com. However you manage to do it, always check the status of your goalie before the puck is dropped. If your guy doesn't start, your DFS lineup is finished.

In cash games, there's no profit in trying to go cheap on the goalie. Find a keeper you feel is reliable and will be playing for the team likelier to win. Then you can figure out the offense around him.

That brings up the question of what statistics are the best measures for a goalie. This is much debated, but goals-against average and save percentage are at the top of the list.

In large-field tournaments, though, you may not be able to play it safe on the goalie; the premier goalies may eat up too much of your salary cap. In a big field, you'll need points in bunches and that means loading up on as much firepower as possible, which will require those salary-cap dollars.

The solution could be a backup goalie on a good team playing against an inferior opponent. If you can find such a situation and a salary pricing inefficiency makes him a bargain, that's the type of goalie you want in a tournament.

Stacking Players and Team Stats

On offense, whether cash games or tournaments, you're looking for effective stacks. FanDuel allows for as many as four skaters from one NHL team, but requires the eight skaters be from three different real teams. DraftKings also requires the skaters be from at least three real teams, but has no cap on players from a single real team.

When you consider the lineup rules and combine that with the correlation involved in point accumulation, it becomes obvious why stacking is advisable. Here's an example using FanDuel scoring.

Let's say you select the entire front line of the Pittsburgh Penguins (a center and two wingers), plus a Pittsburgh defenseman. A goal is scored by the Penguin left winger on your roster in a normal 5-on-5 situation, meaning both teams were at full strength. The center and right winger in your line-up each get an assist on the score. In addition, your Pittsburgh defenseman happens to be on the ice when the goal is scored.

The scorer gets 3 fantasy points for the goal, plus 0.4 points for shot on goal (3.4). The center and right winger each get 2 points (4). And it turns out that all four of your players on the ice get credit for the plus/minus (4). That totals 11.4 points on one play.

When building lineups, several stacking permutations are possible: two sets of four skaters from two real teams and a goalie from a third team (this grouping would be allowed on FanDuel only); one set of four skaters from one real team and two skaters each from two other real teams; two sets of three skaters and one set of two skaters from three real teams; and four sets of two skaters each from four real teams are just some of the possible groupings. The selection depends on how many and which NHL teams you project as able to produce big offensive games that night. Among websites DFS participants can consult in order to locate line groupings for NHL teams, meaning wingers and centers who play together on shifts, is DailyFaceoff.com.

For NHL statistics, handy sources include the league's own website, NHL.com, and ESPN.com.

The first step when looking for offensive players is to examine team statistics, such as goals per game, shots on goal, 5-on-5 ratio, and power-play goals.

Goals per game is self-explanatory, and if you're completely unfamiliar with the NHL, it's certainly the place to start in order to figure out which teams have the best offenses. Both major DFS websites also reward shots on goal, so that's another important category to examine.

The 5-on-5 ratio is important for what it reveals about a team generally; it's also a good guide for directing your line-up stacks. The ratio speaks to relative team effectiveness when playing even-handed, which is the situation for much of the game.

For the 2014-15 regular season, the New York Rangers had the NHL's best 5-on-5 ratio of 1.32. That means for every 1 goal the opposition scored when both sides had five skaters on the ice, the Rangers scored 1.32 goals for an advantage of 32%. This statistic has special relevance in FanDuel, which rewards/penalizes plus-minus. When a team scores a goal, every player on the ice for that team earns a plus point. Every player on the ice for the team that yielded the goal racks up a minus. (Power plays, discussed below, don't count.) The 5-on-5 ratio was an indicator that the Rangers, as a team, were consistently on the better side of the plus-minus statistic. And if you're stacking on FanDuel, obviously the plus-minus reward/penalty could affect more than one of your players.

At the other end of the 5-on-5 spectrum for 2014-15, the Buffalo Sabres had a ratio of 0.61, which is a 39% disadvantage. So once that trend became obvious, you would have avoided Buffalo players.

Power-play goals is another statistic that's more relevant on FanDuel, with its bonus (0.5) for each power-play point scored. A power play occurs when one team commits a penalty and the offending player is sent to the penalty box for either two (most commonly) or five minutes. The opposing team gets to play with a one-man advantage for the duration of the penalty. For the 2014-15 regular season, the Washington Capitals had the most power-play goals, 70, while the hapless Sabres had the fewest, just 30.

DraftKings gives a 1-point bonus for both goals and assists on short-handed goals. So if playing on DraftKings, being aware of short-handed stats may be beneficial. Then again, since short-handed goals are relatively rare—the New York Islanders and the Winnipeg Jets were the 2014-15 regular-season leaders with 10 each—it's not a highly predictive outcome.

Once you identify the teams with the most effective offense, you can advance to the next step, looking at their first and second lines and the most productive players on those lines, as well as determining who plays on the first power-play line.

The Penalty-Point Controversy

One of the more controversial aspects of daily fantasy sports is embedded in the FanDuel hockey rules that award points for penalty minutes. Generally speaking, penalty minutes are a measure of a hockey player's lawlessness, at least in terms of the rules of the game. So it would seem, at least at first glance, that accumulating penalty minutes isn't a good thing, because the player sitting in the penalty box puts his team at a disadvantage.

Now, some hockey fans would argue to the contrary. Their opinion is that taking penalties for any number of reasons has benefit—protecting certain star players or loosening up other teams from checking too closely, for example.

This debate won't be decided here. But if you're looking for those penalty-minute points on FanDuel, it may influence you to select power forwards who can also score over snipers. So even on-ice enforcers have their place in the daily fantasy world, at least they did during the 2014-15 season at FanDuel.

Chapter 9

Golf

The daily fantasy sports industry may want to distance itself from traditional sports wagering for one obvious reason—DFS websites accept customers in 44 states (as of this writing) while unfettered betting on sports occurs in just one, Nevada—but that's the last thing that a DFS player should do, as he can certainly make use of the hard work done by Las Vegas oddsmakers in order to be a winner in daily fantasy. This is especially true in DFS golf.

Of the two major DFS websites, only DraftKings was offering daily fantasy golf in mid-2015. FanDuel does not offer golf, citing legal concerns.

What legal concerns? Marc Edelman, a New York law professor specializing in fantasy sports, wrote for the *Forbes* website that UIGEA requires that fantasy sports contests be determined by player performance in "multiple real-world sporting or other events" in order to fall within the parameters of the fantasy sports carve-out in the federal law. The concern voiced by those who question the practice of offering golf in DFS is that a single tournament doesn't qualify under the multiple-events limitation.

Whether it does or doesn't was immaterial to Pennsylvania policeman Brett Marino, who won DraftKing's Masters Tournament Millionaire Maker contest in 2015.

Marino's win was all the more incredible, because he had just one entry in the contest (it was a multi-entry contest where many participants enter several lineups), and the policeman didn't even pay the $27 entry fee to get into the contest. He won his way into the Millionaire Maker by acing a $5 satellite, thereby turning $5 into $1 million. And for good measure, on the same weekend, Marino also won a smaller fantasy golf contest for $4,000. The combined winnings of $1,004,000 made him the second-biggest money earner for the Masters, behind only the actual winner at Augusta National, Jordan Spieth, who pocketed $1.8 million.

Before his fairy-tale seven-figure Masters payday, the most Marino had ever won playing fantasy sports was a $16 profit on a $20 head-to-head contest.

Marino's story echoes that of a much more celebrated average-Joe-turned-millionaire off a meager investment. Chris Moneymaker, a 28-year-old Tennessee accountant, launched the poker boom when he won the 2003 World Series of Poker Main Event and $2.5 million after winning his way into the $10,000-buy-in event in a $40 online qualifier. Daily fantasy sports has yet to have its Moneymaker Moment, despite Cinderella stories like that of the cop from Phillipsburg, Pennsylvania, Brett Marino.

The difference?

In addition to the fortuity of Moneymaker's Dickensian name, the accountant's heroics were memorialized on ESPN. That amazing story is a big reason that some within the daily fantasy sports industry are eager to spread the game's appeal with a bit more flair and drama. For example, FanDuel CEO Nigel Eccles said his company is pushing hard for more DFS-inspired content, particularly on television.

So how can you replicate Brett Marino's spectacular fantasy

golf results? Here's how to stay out of the rough and put you near the top of the leaderboard.

The Vegas Connection

When picking teams of golfers in DFS, an important guide is the Las Vegas odds.

The first step is to compare the DFS golfer prices with the Vegas odds posted for winning an upcoming tournament. We'll use the 2015 Masters Tournament as an example.

The big event on DraftKings was the Millionaire Maker that cost $27 to enter. And as the name implied, the winner would earn a minimum of $1 million. Participants were required to assemble teams of six golfers working within a salary cap of $50,000.

During the days leading up to the tournament, star golfers Rory McIlroy and Jordan Spieth were the short-odds favorites in the Vegas sports books to win the tournament; both were 8-1.

In DraftKings' pricing, McIlroy was by far the most expensive golfer in the field at $14,900. That was $2,700 more than the next most expensive golfer, Bubba Watson, who had a salary-cap number of $12,200. In the Vegas odds, Watson was 10-1 to win.

So among the top three golfers listed in the Las Vegas odds, Spieth was the lowest priced at $11,900, and for a DFS participant taking the value-pricing approach for picking golfers, Spieth turned out to be easily the best buy.

Spieth, then just 21 years old, went on to win the tournament, racking up 28 birdies along the way and scoring 132.5 fantasy points for his owners.

Among the five golfers who were listed in the Vegas odds at

12-1 or shorter, the cheapest was Dustin Johnson at $10,500, and for DFS owners who were value hunting, he would be on the radar. As it turned out, the 6-foot-4 Johnson—one of golf's big boomers off the tee—turned out to be a great value pick, finishing tied for sixth with 18 birdies and three eagles.

If a savvy player researched just a little deeper, he would have found that the number-six golfer on the Vegas odds board was Jimmy Walker at 18-1 and on DraftKings, Walker's cap number was just $8,900. That was the second-cheapest Draft-Kings price among the top 18 golfers listed in the Vegas odds. But Walker, who was just coming off his fifth PGA win, didn't turn out to be such a bargain, finishing tied for 38th. His 65 fantasy points were just a so-so result.

Yet, a bargain-hunting DFS participant could have picked Johnson and Walker—two of the top-six tournament contenders according to the odds makers—for a combined expenditure of $19,400, and still have an average salary of $7,650 to spend on the remaining four golfers. That kind of cap room would have given a DFS participant the available salary to go after another premium player, such as veteran superstar Phil Mickelson or standout Englishman Justin Rose, a pair of golfers who cost under $10,000 in cap salary and who eventually tied for second in the 2015 Masters.

Now, that's not to say that selecting golfers simply by comparing salary-cap numbers to odds is a magic bullet for assembling a daily fantasy golf lineup. But it *is* an excellent way to create a frame of reference for a reasonable evaluation, especially for those new to fantasy golf.

Along with comparing cap salaries with the Vegas odds, another beginning step is to do a projection of which players are most likely to make the cut into the tournament finals. (In a typical four-day PGA tournament, the score of the 70th lowest player after the first two days becomes a demarcation. Players with that score or better advance past Day 2 to play in Days 3 and 4. The golfers whose scores exceed the cut-off are sent packing.)

So the reason for making the calculation about who's likely to make the "cut" may be obvious, but it's still worthy of emphasis. The DFS team owner can only accumulate points from golfers who are playing, and each golfer who fails to make the cut forfeits 36 holes of point opportunities.

In truth, it becomes difficult to make money in daily fantasy golf if any of the six players on a team fails to go the distance. So it's important to check the past performances of the golfers you're considering, to see what their stats are on making cuts. That statistic and many others can be found on PGATour.com.

Once you've narrowed your universe of golfers to those likely to make the cut, divide that group into birdie-makers and consistent par shooters. Again, you should be combing through the stats.

Right off the bat, dump the par shooters. The DraftKings scoring rules favor birdies, and especially eagles, over pars—and the rules don't penalize bogeys all that much (more on that angle coming up).

Consistency

Notice that in DFS golf scoring, the top 50 finishers accumulate points. It cannot be emphasized enough: To be in the hunt for those full-tournament points and to rack up individual-hole points on Days 3 and 4, a golfer has to at least make the cut. A golfer's cuts-made percentage is a key statistic.

Recent Performances

As anyone who has ever picked up a golf club knows, a lot of the game is confidence, even among the pros. So golfers who have been playing well recently are more likely to keep that frame of mind. Conversely, golfers who have been struggling are liabilities on a DFS roster. Thus, along with overall consistency, check on how the golfers you're considering have been faring recently.

Eagle/Birdie Shooters

An often-overlooked aspect of DFS golf is how the scoring system affects outcomes. Some golfers are erratic performers. They'll shoot a bogey on one hole and come back with a birdie on the next. But sometimes, the most erratic players can actually be huge point-getters.

For the 2015 Masters Tournament on DraftKings, a birdie was worth +3 points and an eagle was worth +8 points. A bogey was penalized one-half (-0.5) point and a double bogey was -1 point. Pars added one-half (+0.5) point.

So a golfer who offset very bad holes with very good ones actually did a daily fantasy owner more good than a steady golfer, even when those players' scorecards wound up with identical tallies at the end of the round.

Here's an example:

In the second round of the Masters, Dustin Johnson shot a 5-under 67. That was a superb round, but it was choppy. Johnson's 18 holes included two bogeys (-1) and a double-bogey (-1), but he offset the stinkers with three birdies (+9) and three eagles (+24). He added eight pars (+4). That totaled a +35 for those 18 holes, which was a hefty pickup for his owners.

On the first day of the tournament, Justin Rose carded an

identical 5-under par 67. But Rose was more consistent with six birdies (+18), one bogey (-½) and 11 pars (+5½). That added up to +23 points for 18 holes for Rose's owners.

So both players had the same totals on their scoreboards, a 67, but Dustin Johnson's owners collected 12 more points for the same 5-under-par score. When choosing your golf lineups, it's important to consider a golfer's track record for under-par scoring and how it matches up with the way the daily fantasy scoring rewards birdies and eagles.

Statistics

Golf statistics are certainly not as familiar to the average sports fan as stats in other sports, but there are some key ones to track. Among the more in-vogue golf statistics is "strokes gained." Strokes gained is a comparative metric developed by a Columbia University professor.

For instance, in putting, a baseline is calculated for how many strokes are taken on average per round on the PGA Tour. Then, an individual golfer's putting performance is compared to that baseline. If a golfer's average is less than the PGA Tour average, that's reflected in strokes gained.

The same is done with other parts of the golf game. Two of the more closely watched of these advanced metrics are strokes gained in putting and strokes gained tee-to-green. These statistics are available on PGATour.com.

The Course

When selecting football and baseball players, the DFS player has to be mindful of matchups. Is a star wide receiver going against a shutdown cornerback? Is the power-hitting left-hand-batting first baseman going against a left-handed pitcher with a nasty slider? In golf, the matchup is the course.

It will take a little drilling, but if a DFS player can understand a little about the course and the golfers being considered, that can be a significant edge. Back when Tiger Woods was dominating the Masters Tournament, one of his advantages was that he could reach the Par 5s in two strokes. Then, Augusta National was lengthened to take away from the big hitters and that edge was nullified to a great degree. But that's just one course. Other courses are advantageous to the big belters, and when one comes on the radar, a DFS player can use that information to an advantage.

Golf experts understand how different courses play to the strength and weaknesses of different golfers. DFS players can benefit if they have insight into this important dynamic or if they spend the time to match the course's characteristics to golfers who best match up with that layout by using driving (distance and accuracy) statistics, as well as other stats, that are found on PGATour.com.

DFS Golf Scoring/DraftKings

Here's an example of golf scoring for DraftKings for the 2015 Masters Tournament.

Each golfer accumulated points for the following: overall finish in the tournament; performances on individual holes (birdies/eagles), and superior performances over consecutive holes, within a single round, and throughout the tournament. Golfers were penalized for poor holes, such as bogeys and double-bogeys.

Tournament Finish Scoring

Points ranging from 30 for 1st to 1 for 41st-50th.

Per-Hole Scoring

Double eagle +20, eagle +8, birdie +3, par +0.5, bogey -0.5, double bogey -1, worse than double bogey -1.

Bonuses

Streak of three birdies or better (maximum one per round) +3, bogey-free round +3, all four rounds under 70 strokes +5, hole in one +10.

Chapter 10

Lineup Optimizers

This book contains many references to online tools designed to help DFS participants assemble competitive lineups, whether the goal is scoring enough points to finish in the money in cash games or making a run at the mega-prize in large-field guaranteed-prize-pool tournaments.

Online tools for daily fantasy analysis seem to multiply by the day, both in number and sophistication. Exactly when a DFS player reaches the point of diminishing returns and *so much* information becomes *too much* information is up to each individual to decide.

However, one tool that stands apart from other statistical aids is the so-called "lineup optimizer." Simply put, a lineup optimizer is a computer program that takes into account a host of variables in order to make your lineup for you.

There are many ways to set the parameters you want the optimizer to observe. You don't have to make any selections if you don't want to; you can start with zero players and the program will offer its "optimal" lineup for that day. You can also start with one player, perhaps a quarterback, and identify what website you're playing on, and the lineup optimizer will spit out the rest of a suggested roster that uses all or most of the salary cap. You might want to include a certain quarterback, running back, and wide receiver. You can also exclude certain players.

In baseball, for example, you might want to eliminate players whose games are likely to be affected by the rain that's forecast.

Once you've established your parameters, you click the "set lineup" button and presto! You have the best effort of someone's algorithm for building fantasy lineups.

It might feel a little like a 21st century turn on alchemy, the medieval faux science that attempted to turn base metals into gold. In fairness to the creators of the various online lineup optimizers, their programs are far from computerized voodoo. To the contrary, these are honest attempts to marry hard data with sharp mathematical approaches to derive the best possible combinations.

However, since so many websites offer lineup optimizers, it's a reasonable assumption that so far, no one has stumbled onto the one secret of turning lead into gold in daily fantasyland.

If there ever does come a time when these programs can spit out absolutely optimal lineups, there probably would have to be some changes to the rules to make outcomes less predictive, yet still allow DFS to be a game of skill.

Thankfully, computer programs can't completely account for the unpredictable nature of sports. Routinely, some light-hitting shortstop belts a grand slam or a no-name quarterback throws four TD passes and those guys didn't make it into the "optimal" lineup. So, lineup optimizers, used apart from any human judgment, are far from a silver bullet in making daily fantasy lineups, but their development bears watching.

For now, DFS beginner and intermediate players should understand two things about lineup optimizers.

First, they exist. If you were unaware of them before now, consider yourself informed. It's also worth knowing that DFS pros use lineup optimizers, either available on the Internet (sometimes for a fee) or computer models that they build themselves. Finding an online lineup optimizer is easy. Just type "lineup optimizer" into a search engine and take your pick. Two of the larger DFS-content websites, RotoGrinders and RotoWire, have optimizers, but there are plenty of others.

Second, while the websites that provide lineup optimizers stand behind the mathematical soundness of their products, if they're being completely honest, they'll concede that it's just one more tool for building a lineup. As already pointed out, optimizers aren't and never can be perfect, and that's a good thing. Lineup optimizers can't account for the human element in the real games, occasionally referred to as "randomness." Still, for anyone new to daily fantasy, a lineup optimizer is a reasonable starting point. For one thing, it can make a DFS participant aware of certain player combinations that fit under a salary cap that might not have been apparent, and for another, it can turn you on to some important fundamental DFS concepts.

In the end, though, what makes daily fantasy worth playing is that it's fun to build lineups using your own research, expertise, and wits. Beyond that, it's gratifying—and sometimes lucrative—to test those wits and expertise against other players, especially when you prevail!

Chapter 11

The Future

The emergence of daily fantasy sports has been a marvel. Yet despite the extraordinary surge in participation, revenue, and venture capital that's been invested in this new game, the future is hardly crystal clear. The view all depends on which end of the DFS telescope you look through.

Peer through the lens that makes things look bigger and you'll see tens of millions of paying customers who make playing DFS a routine part of how they enjoy sports. From this perspective, daily fantasy could conceivably become almost as big as the real games on which they're based.

But a look through the opposite end, where things appear smaller, reveals that the game's prospects could shrink for any number of reasons. The most obvious of those—after the turmoil that struck the daily fantasy industry just a few weeks into the 2015 NFL season—would be substantial changes in the legal or regulatory landscape.

The event that rocked the DFS world occurred when a DraftKings employee first accidently posted online sensitive data on September 27, an NFL Sunday, that was supposed to be published only after the games were completed (that data revealed to what degree, by percentage, specific NFL players were owned by DraftKings customers). On the same weekend, the same DraftKings employee, Ethan Haskell, won $350,000 on rival website FanDuel. What followed was intense scrutiny by media, public officials, regulators, attorneys general, and a flurry of lawsuits. Universally, there was a call for regulating the daily fantasy industry. But DFS could founder for other reasons: because casual players can't compete with the pros and get discouraged, or the novelty simply wears off.

Billion-Dollar Future

For now, daily fantasy is a sports-culture phenomenon. As daily fantasy sports experienced an extraordinary growth spurt from 2013 through 2015, Adam Krejcik, a financial analyst based at Eilers Research in Los Angeles whose research on the DFS industry has been ground-breaking, published projections that were startling.

In October 2014, Krejcik released a report that sifted through the available financial data for the two major daily fantasy websites, along with additional information from relevant sources. His white paper on the industry described three potential arcs for DFS growth through the year 2020: bearish (least optimistic), baseline (middle road), and bullish (most optimistic) forecasts. They were based on various outcomes in several categories, such as how successful DFS will be in attracting players, how much those customers will spend, and what the regulatory climate will turn out to be for daily fantasy.

In 2014, the combined revenue for FanDuel and DraftKings was $97 million. In the baseline forecast, Krejcik calculated that revenues would rise to about $1.4 billion by 2020. The high-end forecast was $2.6 billion. The low-end was about $470 million.

As we've seen, *revenue* represents 8%-9% of the total entry fees in the contests (the amount raked from the prize pool). But revenue doesn't equate to profit, and at the time of this writing, no major daily fantasy sports company had yet reported a profit. The biggest expense for DFS companies is marketing to attract customers, and it's unclear when revenue will catch up to those heavy expenses. During the 2015 football season, DraftKings and FanDuel were spending tens of millions on TV advertising.

In July 2015, Internet heavyweight Yahoo, which had been running traditional fantasy sports games for years, announced that it would offer its own daily fantasy contests. Krejcik predicted modest revenues for the Internet company in the near-term.

In one of the more eyebrow-raising projections, Krejcik reports that as early as 2016, using the middle-range forecast, total entry fees in North America would catch up to total sports wagers placed in all of Nevada's legal sports books, in the $4 billion to $5 billion range. Further, by 2020, also using the baseline projection, DFS entry fees would be about $14.5 billion, which would approximately triple Nevada's current sports-wagering handle.

As rosy as some of those numbers would suggest the future might be for DFS, veteran gaming-industry analyst turned activist investor Jason Ader has made even bolder optimistic predictions. Just a partial account of Ader's résumé shows that he's the CEO of SpringOwl Asset Management, the largest shareholder of bwin.party digital entertainment (known for its online-gaming business) and he's a shareholder and director of Las Vegas Sands Corp., owner of casinos in Las Vegas and Macau.

Speaking on CNBC in 2015, Ader said of daily fantasy sports, "That's the hot area. ... Fantasy sports is the biggest and hottest area in the gaming industry right now, no doubt about it."

Ader then dropped this bombshell: "The business has the potential to be as big as Macau over time." Although Macau's gaming industry cooled after a torrid start, it was still on pace to hit about $25 billion-$30 billion in revenues for 2015.

"When you consider the total Internet gaming revenue in the United Kingdom and Europe, taking in everything from Internet bingo to poker to sports wagering, that comes to more than twenty billion," Ader said in a later interview. "And as you consider daily fantasy five, ten years down the road, it could certainly be there."

While some may doubt that type of revenue is possible for daily fantasy in the foreseeable future, the enthusiasm for DFS expressed by an astute financial analyst like Ader is certainly attention-getting.

Appeal to Millennials

A primary reason cited by Ader for his optimism regarding daily fantasy sports is the game's appeal to Millennials, the generation whose coming of age coincided with the new century.

"The Millennial demographic hasn't embraced traditional gaming at all," Ader said. "When they go to Las Vegas, they go to the clubs, they'll drink those expensive cocktails, and they're spending money, but they're certainly not playing slot machines. For years now, casinos have been trying to figure out how they can attract younger gamers. Nothing has worked—until DFS cracked the code."

Daily fantasy braids interactivity, skill, and data, and packages it all in a technology with which Millennials are familiar, Ader said. "The spinning-reel slot machine is to daily fantasy sports what the buggy-whip business was to the automobile industry."

Adam Levitan, a daily fantasy sports expert who helps teach DFS "boot camps," echoes Ader's assessment. "My generation, I'm thirty-three, and the next generation, we're not interested in the mindless games like slots or roulette or craps. We're into skill games. That's why poker caught on," Levitan told me. "But with poker, people who weren't very good dropped out, because eventually they got tired of losing, and now the [poker] games are much tougher [to beat]. Now, daily fantasy sports has come along and we're seeing some overlap from people who used to play poker."

In addition, the predominant characteristics of daily fantasy sports are tailored to Millennial tastes. Their generation was weaned on games and diversions where success is determined by skill—whether fine motor or intellectual—and not on the roll of dice or the spin of a dial, like the games that were favored by preceding generations. The Internet, in placing vast volumes of information at the fingertips of Millennials, has removed barriers to previously hard-to-find facts and figures and instilled in this younger generation a respect for, and a reliance on, data. Also, a constant barrage of marketing and entertainment that emphasizes aspirational goals has encouraged an appetite for instant gratification. Finally, DFS all happens in the cyber world, an environment native to Millennials.

Daily fantasy sports is a gaming outlet that checks off all the boxes for Millennials. It's sports wagering for a hyperconnected generation that craves control, which is often elusive for many young people who find themselves adrift in uncertain economic times.

Vin Narayanan, formerly editor-in-chief at gaming news website Casino City and a one-time fantasy sports columnist at *USA Today*, said the enormous appeal that daily fantasy holds for Millennials, especially the more recent wave of that generation, is reminiscent of how online poker grabbed young people a few years ago. But daily fantasy may have an even stronger grip, Narayanan said, because it fits the newest gamers' "entertainment profile."

"One, daily fantasy has brevity and it's a bound event, meaning you know when it starts and when it ends," Naraynan said. "Two, it involves something they already love—sports. Poker was a game a lot of kids had to learn. Daily fantasy is based on something they believe they're already knowledgeable about. It's something that's both familiar and new for them. They've seen their parents play traditional fantasy sports, but at the same time, this is different. It's not their parents' fantasy sports."

Another interesting facet to daily fantasy has generally gone without much comment. The major DFS websites allow participation in the play-for-cash games at 18 years old, except in a few states where participants have to be 19. In contrast, even in those states where online gaming (poker and sometimes casino games) is legal—New Jersey, Nevada, and Delaware—the age limit for participation is 21.

The daily fantasy sports industry may contend that DFS is *not* gambling—or at least isn't defined as such in jurisdictions where the contests are allowed—and because of that distinction, any age comparison between daily fantasy and online gaming, including poker, is immaterial. Even without debating that issue, the indisputable point regarding Millennials is that since daily fantasy sports does allow 18-year-olds to play, the industry has a highly favorable recruiting opportunity to latch onto a youthful audience at a time when those consumers are both impressionable and just developing adult-level entertainment habits that last a lifetime.

It also bears mention that DFS, by virtue of its 18-year-old threshold, is inviting a clientele that's only just beginning to de-velop judgment in making financial decisions. When you con-sider that players are permitted to enter any number of games every day, some of which cost hundreds, even thousands, of dollars, it would appear some younger DFS players could be making financial decisions for substantial sums.

Regulation

That 18-year-olds are permitted to play daily fantasy sports contests for a lot of money on a daily basis may surprise peo-ple who might also wonder why government doesn't require a higher age limit. The reality is that the daily fantasy sports in-dustry has been operating with little regulatory oversight of any kind, and the restrictions on gambling activities simply don't apply to fantasy sports, whether it's the season-long or the daily variety. That situation may change soon.

Daily fantasy sports' legal standing comes from a coupling of two things: the famous carve-out in UIGEA and the fact that in most of America, fantasy sports is considered a game of skill and therefore legal. Lack of regulatory oversight has benefitted DFS operators in that they don't have the expense of compliance. Consumers benefit from that as well; they don't have to pay those costs that would get passed through to them in higher rake. On the other hand, DFS consumers have not had the protections that regulation may afford in areas such as contest integrity, segregation of player accounts from opera-tional accounts, and customer disputes.

Large-website operators understand that lack of regulation can actually be a huge problem for the industry. Before daily fantasy forced a firestorm of controversy in the fall of 2015, FanDuel CEO Nigel Eccles said that it's been a concern for him for a long time. "It's been on my mind right from the start, going back to 2009," Eccles said in an interview. "We knew as we got bigger that people would wonder, 'How can this be done with no regulation?' For instance, we have to make sure people are confident that kids are not playing. For any daily fantasy company, this is a subject that has to be at the top of the agenda."

"There are two main reasons why regulation comes into play: to collect taxes and to protect the public," said David Schwartz, director of the Center for Gaming Research at the University of Nevada Las Vegas.

Schwartz, who authored a comprehensive examination of gambling, *Roll the Bones: The History of Gambling*, made the point that government's interest in activities such as daily fantasy sports usually springs from culling revenues from it. "One of the first things that occurs to me is where is the money [being spent on daily fantasy] coming from," Schwartz said.

If government sees DFS as taking away from activities, such as casino gambling, which pay special taxes, the state may see daily fantasy as diverting revenues that would otherwise be a source of taxation.

"If it's money that people might have otherwise bet with an illegal bookie on sports," Schwartz said, "then [the DFS industry] can say that it's diminishing the influence of organized crime."

Richard Schuetz, a gaming-industry veteran who served on the California Gambling Control Commission, predicted that daily fantasy was flirting with big problems operating in an unregulated environment. "This type of business is all about managing risk," Schuetz said. "And for three, four, five million dollars, the daily fantasy people could have a very credible regulatory agency in place."

Schuetz used the example of mixed martial arts, a combat sport that not so long ago was banned in most jurisdictions. Then it helped craft a credible set of regulations for state licensing agencies to consider. Now MMA operates as a lucrative mainstream sport in all but a few jurisdictions.

FanDuel's Eccles said that his industry has to be prepared to offer solutions to regulatory questions. "It's the right thing to do for the protection of our players, as well as protecting the industry."

DraftKings officials have advocated self-regulation.

Paul Charchian, president of the Fantasy Sports Trade Association, said before the industry's troubles erupted, "The FSTA already has the beginnings of a framework in place now … a 'paid-operator' or 'paid-contest' charter that all of our [daily] contest operators must agree to." But after the criticism rained down on daily fantasy, the FSTA announced the formation of a self-policing group called the Fantasy Sports Control Agency.

At this writing, government involvement in the conduct of daily fantasy was being discussed in many states, with Pennsylvania, Illiniois, New Jersey, and Massachusetts being just some of them. Nevada decided DFS fell under sports gaming laws and insisted that DFS companies either be licensed or stop operating in the state. The question of DFS regulation moved from "if" to "how."

Enemies

As daily fantasy sports has grown, it has attracted both allies and enemies, and the influence of those friends and foes will help determine the shape of DFS in the years ahead.

Let's start with the enemies. Former U.S. Rep. Jim Leach,

the Iowa congressman who helped sponsor UIGEA with its fantasy sports carve-out, is representative of a social-values mindset that was blindsided by how the seemingly innocuous fantasy sports carve-out helped give rise to an enterprise it views as being akin to sports gambling, regardless of legal interpretation. Leach has said a number of times that the results are not what he envisioned when he allowed the fantasy sports carve-out into his bill and he's not happy about it. And social-values groups are also beginning to take notice of DFS.

In Louisiana, one of five states from which the big DFS websites do not allow participation, a so-called saints-and-sinners coalition successfully opposed an attempt to legalize fantasy sports, with the "sainted" Louisiana Family Forum ("an organization committed to defending faith, freedom, and the traditional family") and the "sinner" legal gaming interests resisting the effort.

As the fantasy sports industry tries to eliminate barriers in the other four states, Iowa, Washington, Arizona and Montana, pushback will almost certainly appear from the same type of coalition opposition. Plus, it's clear that commercial casinos are aggravated by the fact that they're saddled by a slew of regulations, and frequently special taxes, while the daily fantasy business gets a free pass, all the while contending that it's not gambling.

MGM Resorts International CEO Jim Murren expressed interest in entering the DFS arena at first, but his company held off, because of regulatory concerns.

"Clearly, this cannot be ignored, and it is gambling," Murren said of daily fantasy sports while speaking to reporters in April 2015. "We have not engaged in it as a commercial enterprise, because we haven't gotten comfort by our regulators that we should."

As time went on, Murren's complaints got louder. Murren said that those who contend DFS isn't gambling, such as sports league executives, are wrong. "I don't know how to run a football team," Murren said, "but I do know how to run a casino, and this is gambling."

So if commercial gaming interests see daily fantasy as competition, it's not unreasonable to expect that they might expend lobbying efforts to ensure that DFS deals with some of the same regulatory issues the bricks-and-mortar and legal online gambling industries already wrestle with. And commercial gaming companies believe (rightfully so) that they need the cover of regulation to enter the DFS business, as a precaution in protecting their casino licenses across the country.

The DFS industry quickly found out there was another player on the cultural landscape that was hostile: the mainstream media. Though the DFS industry has consistently put out the not-gambling mantra, some influential news organizations have hammered on DFS as a proxy for sports gambling. For instance, when Yahoo announced its entry into the daily fantasy market, the *Los Angles Times'* online article about it used the word "betting" eight times. It also sometimes managed to include betting and gambling in the same sentence, such as describing Yahoo Sports Daily Fantasy as a "betting service that could introduce tens of millions of people to legalized online sports gambling."

After the Ethan Haskell incident, the *New York Times* ran blistering articles about daily fantasy, labeling the combination of events a "scandal." Along with a string of critical news articles on DFS, the *New York Times* established itself as one of the most prominent media detractors of daily fantasy sports in its editorial "Rein In Online Fantasy Sports Gambling." Unfortunately, much of the mainstream coverage of DFS often featured factual inaccuracies, such as when the *New York Times* mistakenly referred to DFS entry fees as revenue, a faux pas that multiplied real revenue tenfold. The *Times* made the correction when the error was pointed out.

Allies

Daily fantasy also has some powerful friends.

DFS has recruited a number of allies as a result of business dealings to date and there is the cache of popular sentiment that has attached itself to fantasy sports in general. Professional sports organizations and media companies both have benefitted from the considerable advertising money DFS companies have been spending—estimated at about $100 million in 2014 and much more in 2015. Those same organizations and businesses would continue to benefit from the increased fan engagement that DFS provides. In the end, heightened fan interest means more money, directly or indirectly, for everyone—the sports leagues, teams, individual athletes, and media companies that broadcast games and provide content.

The list of sports leagues and teams that aren't in some sort of partnership or getting daily fantasy advertising dollars is almost shorter than the list of those who are.

The NBA has an equity position in FanDuel. Major League Baseball has the same in DraftKings.

FanDuel has advertising deals with 16 NFL teams (and has a FanDuel lounge in the Washington Redskins' stadium). DraftKings signed advertising agreements with 13 NFL teams, plus Madison Square Garden in New York City and the Staples Center in Los Angeles with DraftKings-branded fantasy lounges in both buildings.

FanDuel announced multi-year advertising deals with 15

NBA teams. DraftKings has nine NBA teams in its advertising corner and counts the NHL as a major advertising partner. DraftKings is also NASCAR's and Major League Soccer's official daily fantasy sports partner.

On the media side, FanDuel has received investment money from companies associated with NBC and Comcast and has a media partnership with CBS Sports. DraftKings landed a $150 million investment from Fox Sports, and has an agreement with ESPN that makes DraftKings the exclusive DFS provider on all ESPN platforms.

One of the few major players in the sports-media complex that was on the sidelines as this writing was the NFL, which hadn't linked arms with any daily fantasy company, although the majority of the league's teams have their own individual ad deals with either FanDuel or DraftKings. Plus Dallas Cowboys owner Jerry Jones and New England Patriots owner Robert Kraft are investors in DFS companies.

So, it's obvious that daily fantasy sports has lots of business connections that have a lot to gain from a successful maturation of the industry. Plus, a growing populist sentiment on its side is evidenced by the well over 50 million fantasy sports participants, although the vast majority of that number are involved in the season-long version.

Put it all together and a prohibition of daily fantasy is going to have strong opposition.

If someone does challenge daily fantasy sports, they'd better be prepared for a battle and not just from DFS interests, but also, perhaps, from some of their friends who've found a good fit in daily fantasy.

"Obviously, we're a daily game," said Bob Bowman, the president and CEO of MLB Advanced Media, about baseball. "So this is a sport that works really well with daily fantasy. The biggest drawback of the [traditional-style] fantasy game is that it's grueling. It's six months long, you have to put in 20 minutes a day if you want to win, and that's a big time commitment. With daily fantasy, it takes less time and you know a lot sooner than six months how you did."

In fact, that difference—the effort that goes into a season-long contest (dropping, adding, and trading for players), in contrast to the occasional random events that influence a daily contest—could be the foundation of a legal challenge based on the argument that the daily iteration of fantasy sports isn't nearly the game of skill that the traditional version is.

Major League Baseball has conducted mathematical research that it says illustrates that short-duration fantasy baseball is a contest where skill predominates and Bowman is unimpressed with the claim that the shorter time period diminishes the skill factor.

"Most Major League games take just two hours and forty-five minutes," Bowman said, "and they sure take a lot of skill. The time element is not the issue."

Protecting the Ecosystem

Apart from external legal challenges, some critics contend DFS may be doomed, because its "ecosystem" is endangered by an overarching flawed model of competition among the game's several layers of participants.

The flow of players into the relatively new daily fantasy game and the interaction and balance among beginner, intermediate, and skilled players are referred to as the DFS ecosystem.

In the ideal ecosystem, after a surge of new players enters daily fantasy sports for one reason or another, a substantial number remain in the game. Either they get good enough to become profitable or their losses are tolerable and the entertainment value derived from playing exceeds the cost. The ideal ecosystem also allows for casual players to become more skilled over time and perhaps evolve into experts, with some of them even making enough money that the profits amount to a livelihood. And occasionally, players go on to hit life-changing grand prizes and become celebrities within the DFS community.

Of course, daily fantasy is less than a zero-sum game, due to the rake the DFS websites take, and in the end, the fun aspect has to be appealing enough to keep a hold on players who consistently lose more than they win. The problem, as some see it, is that in the current DFS climate with its small cadre of super-skilled players, the consistent financial losses suffered by casual players will become so demoralizing that the newbies give up and never return.

Some advantage-gambling experts—gamblers who use approaches like mathematics and game theory to gain an advantage in games played either against the house or other players—have criticized daily fantasy sports for an over-reliance on "volume players." Volume players are the advantage players of daily fantasy sports who employ their own mathematical models to build optimal lineups. However, what differentiates such expert DFS players from, say, an expert poker player sitting down at a poker table in a casino is that the superior poker player is playing at just one table against a finite number of opponents. In daily fantasy, an expert player (or a group) can submit hundreds of entries in scores of contests conducted simultaneously, thus dominating thousands of less-skilled competitors.

The result, according to advantage players such as Ed Miller and Jeff Hwang, is that in short order, volume players will deplete the pool of casual players. Then, it's just experts pitting their computer models against one another. In such a narrative, daily fantasy becomes a fable that ends up badly for the sharks and fish alike.

Miller has called the current state of daily fantasy sports a "broken model."

"Right now, everything is in favor of the skill players," said Miller, who has written several highly respected poker books. "The skill players have all these advantages of being able to analyze the statistical data to pick the best players, they have the edge of understanding lineup construction, and they have an understanding of which players are underpriced. All these edges are cumulative and on top of that, the skilled players have the ability to enter contests dozens if not hundreds of times. Pretty soon, people are just going to stop playing."

Hwang, another poker author, made the same point about the fragility of the ecosystem. He concedes that DFS has strong appeal as a legal alternative to traditional sports wagering, which is largely illegal, but he questions whether the industry is sustainable.

"At some point—barring some drastic change in the product—I find it likely that DFS is going to run into a buzzsaw, where attrition rates are too high and the influx of new players will not be enough to mask the skill gap," Hwang wrote in an article.

And gambling experts aren't the only ones who wonder about the sharks devouring the fish and putting the brakes on daily fantasy sports. Financial analyst Adam Krejcik said essentially the same thing in his 2014 industry analysis.

"Our research suggests an increasing number of high-volume players are already having an adverse impact on casual user growth," Krejcik wrote in his 2014 white paper on the DFS industry.

None of this is lost on those within daily fantasy sports. DFS author Jonathan Bales also worries about keeping casual fans in the game. He said in an interview for this book that DFS marketing efforts shouldn't put so much emphasis on the massive guaranteed-prize-pool contests, because the GPPs are precisely where beginning players are at the greatest disadvantage.

"Once the websites get a new customer, there needs to be more education that steers new players to the fifty-fifties, the cash games, where they'll have a better chance to experience some success so they don't burn through their bankroll so quickly," Bales said.

FanDuel CEO Nigel Eccles recognizes the issue has to be addressed.

"Our mission is to bring the daily fantasy product to the mass market and the product is not going to be nearly as exciting if it stays as a niche," Eccles said. "As we think about our product development, we always think, 'How do we cater to that mass market?' In the short run, there may be a temptation to say, why don't we build a product for these high-volume guys to get that quick volume, but we don't see it that way. We want to go out to the mass market. We want to make sure they have a good experience. We try to steer newer players to fifty-fifty games where there's a fifty percent chance they'll have a good outcome—and if they already have some skill, significantly better than a fifty percent chance—and away from the really big tournaments where only the very best are going to win. And there are other things we can do to try to monitor predator behavior that goes after newer players."

As of this writing, FanDuel had placed some limitations on

the number of games a single player can enter, but those limitations are generous, and DraftKings has no entry limitations at all.

For its part, DraftKings offers beginner contests where participants can play against other beginners, defined as customers who have played in 50 contests or fewer in a given sport. Once participants hit the 50-contest threshold for a specific sport, the beginner contests are no longer available to them.

FanDuel offers Rookie League contests to new players, but you're eligible to play those for only 15 days after your initial deposit.

Root, Root, Root, but for Which Home Team?

Just a few years ago, daily fantasy sports was virtually unknown even among the most rabid fans, including the tens of millions who belonged to traditional fantasy leagues. Evidence that DFS was trudging along in near obscurity was in the numbers. As recently as 2012, FanDuel was lucky to get a few hundred people a day plunking down a few bucks here and there.

The numbers have certainly changed. By the 2014 NFL season, on a busy football Sunday, FanDuel had 343 servers humming along to support 100,000 concurrent users and processing nearly 100 entries and edits a second. The participation accelerated in 2015.

By the 2015 NFL season, mainstream sports programming was incorporating more DFS analysis and advice. Someday soon, a sports channel may even have an as-it-happens telecast of a spectacular daily fantasy championship where a winner is crowned and handed a check for several million dollars.

DraftKings has been edging toward providing more and

more of its own content both in text and on videos. Matt Kalish, one of DraftKings' co-founders, said greater media exposure—whether it comes from conventional third-party outlets or the DFS industry itself—is needed to make daily fantasy part of the fabric of the sports landscape.

"There's tremendous opportunity in mainstream media," Kalish said in an interview. "At first, we saw the networks begin to incorporate references to daily fantasy in their programming that was more broadly about (traditional) fantasy. But we're at the point where there's an appetite for other types of daily fantasy-type entertainment."

Kalish said that DraftKings has ambitions to pursue its own content creation. "We're not just doubling down, we're going to go in ten-times on content."

The goal is to steer the Monday-morning water-cooler conversation, which so far has typically been about what happened on the scoreboard, toward what happened in the universe of DFS.

"For the first time this year, it's starting to happen. We see it in golf," Kalish said, pointing to the $1 million golf prizes up for grabs on DraftKings during the four major golf tournaments in 2015 that received attention both in niche and mainstream media. "The popularity of daily fantasy golf was a big surprise and there was tremendous buzz.

"It's the network effect," Kalish continued. "We're at the point where everyone at least knows someone who plays daily fantasy. So there's a bond if you're having that sports conversation at the water cooler or on the bus going to work. People love to debate which players they like before the fact. Then after it's over, they want to talk about who came through for them and who let them down."

So as daily fantasy sports evolves and more fans become

invested in the contests that go beyond the scoreboard, what will that mean for the games, and how will it change what it means to be a fan?

Trent Dilfer, the winning quarterback for the Baltimore Ravens in Super Bowl XXXV and now an analyst for ESPN, said he saw the changes coming when he was still playing and fantasy football was still played in the traditional format.

"Toward the end of my playing career, I was beginning to get a sense of the pulse of the fans on this fantasy issue," said Dilfer. "Where it used to be that you'd go into another town, say to play the New York Giants, all you'd get were hisses and boos. Stuff like, 'You guys suck! We're going to kick your ass!' Then that started to change.

"When I was with the [Seattle] Seahawks, you'd go into a place like New York and now you'd hear from the fans, 'I hope you guys lose, but I hope *you* have a great game. I'm starting you on my fantasy team.'"

In recent years, Dilfer said, the shift in fan focus has become even more noticeable.

"Now I have fans coming up to me and instead of talking about the game, I notice they tend to talk about specific players. They're nice enough not to be obvious and ask me who to play in fantasy, but you can tell that the focus is more on players from all over the league."

Anita Marks is a veteran radio sports-talk host on ESPN in New York, a member of the New York Giants broadcast team, and writes about fantasy football for The Bleacher Report website. Marks said fans frequently ask her about her favorite teams and she explains to them that as a journalist, she really doesn't have personal favorites apart from supporting the teams in whatever city she happens to be working.

But then there are her fantasy team players. Marks was

asked once about a photo of herself in a radio studio wearing a Mets cap. The cap, she explained, had little to do with the team and everything to do with her favorite fantasy baseball pitcher, the Mets' Matt Harvey.

"As more and more people get involved in fantasy sports, it's inevitable what's going to happen. Increasingly, fans are going to identify with players more than teams," Marks said. "And the reason is obvious. You get so tied into a player, you connect so much with a player who is going to provide you with the points to win your daily or your weekly fantasy contest."

Marks went on to explain that this is good for the leagues, referencing how, for decades, wagering interest helped drive football fans to the NFL and can do the same for DFS.

"When the Kansas City Chiefs are playing the Cleveland Browns, look at the TV ratings outside those specific cities. You look at a place like New York and there are decent ratings for that game. How come? Because there are a bunch of people in New York with Kansas City plus two and a half. Or in the case of fantasy sports, they have [Chiefs running back] Jamaal Charles on their fantasy team and they need another thirty yards from him to win their daily fantasy contest."

FanDuel's Eccles points out that fan engagement in DFS drives interest in games that they'd otherwise ignore. Not only do they watch more games, they watch them longer, because a late-game base hit or basket or reception can decide a contest. In all, DFS-engaged fans consume 40% more sports content, both in events and news, according to FanDuel research.

That argument was convincing to the NBA, which took an equity stake in FanDuel.

"If you're a fan of a particular team and that particular team is not necessarily winning on the court, you may or may not be engaged," said Sal LaRocca, the NBA's president of global operations and merchandising. "But if you have a daily fantasy team and there are players on your team that are from other teams, you would be potentially interested in researching them or watching that player play, and just be more interested in the league [overall] ... and developing fans is something that any sports league would have a keen interest in."

There was a time when sports-league officials and team owners marched off to Washington, D.C., to vehemently warn against what has been described as "the game within a game." Back in the 1970s, the game-within-a-game referred to the pointspread and the leagues pushed Congress to outlaw sports wagering.

Art Rooney, the late Pro Football Hall of Fame owner of the Pittsburgh Steelers, described the supposed threat of the game-within-a-game like this: "More fans would have a financial stake in the [pointspread] outcome of the game and hence little or no interest in its competitive value."

That's changed, too. In a complete about-face, sports leagues now see benefit in the game-within-a-game that daily fantasy provides, arguing there's no chance results would or could be rigged, because they consist of so many moving parts.

Trent Dilfer is ambivalent about how daily fantasy will potentially influence fan experience. He's concerned that daily fantasy football may warp a fan's view of the bigger picture. Diminished, Dilfer fears, will be the whole point of the game itself: final scores and winning a Super Bowl.

"I do like that more people are watching, but I certainly don't like what [daily fantasy] is doing to the fans," Dilfer said. "It bothers me in a situation where, say, [a running back] catches a pass for five yards and fails to get the first down and his team has to punt, but the reaction of some fans of that team is that they're still happy with the play, because it's a PPR (point-per-reception) contest and they just got the points for the catch and the yards."

Academicians who study sports and fan attitudes said a shift in fan views was already occurring due to traditional fantasy sports, but that the changes will be more pronounced with the rise of daily fantasy.

"It's getting to the point where fans can tell you what their players did in a game, but not the outcome of the game itself," said Joris Drayer, an associate professor of sports business at Temple University who co-authored a research report, *Gambling and Fantasy: An Examination of the Influence of Money on Fan Attitudes and Behaviors.* "Now, fans are thinking, 'I can be that guy who wins the hundred thousand on Sunday—and that changes a fan.'"

In the short run, increased fan engagement is appealing to sports leagues and may have economic benefits, such as more subscriptions to premium content, such as TV season passes to out-of-market games. However, if the bonds that tie fans to their favorite teams are loosened, the question is how that could affect traditional revenue streams, such as purchases of team merchandise or even attendance at games.

In answer to that question, some sports organizations are trying to show that live-attendance numbers and following fantasy teams don't have to be mutually exclusive, that the two can be merged. Football stadiums for the Jacksonville Jaguars and San Francisco 49ers have already pioneered the creation of fantasy football lounges for fantasy fans at the games. DraftKings sponsors fantasy lounges in the stadiums of the Dallas Cowboys, New England Patriots, and Kansas City Chiefs. When the Minnesota Vikings move in 2016, their new stadium will engender another giant step in that direction.

"The entire stadium will be fantasy friendly and then there

will be a fantasy sports club," said Fantasy Sports Trade Association president Paul Charchian, a consultant on the project. "They'll have a whole section of the stadium that's just for fantasy and will accommodate fantasy players. So we're seeing that teams are recognizing that until now, you had an either-or proposition of following your fantasy team or going to the stadium. The Vikings want to be one of the first teams to meaningfully change how that works."

In some ways, fantasy sports, particularly the daily version, is a way for fans to liberate themselves from what has been the constraints of rooting for the home team.

"It gives a fan some control," said University of Alabama professor Andy Billings, whose research includes how sport, mass-media, and consumption habits come together. "Fantasy sports gives a long-suffering fan whose team isn't doing well the chance to say, 'I'm done with this particular team, but I'm not done with the sport.'"

Also, it gives fans an opportunity to actively prove what they've believed about themselves all along, that *they* can manage a team better than real-life sports executives, and get paid for doing it.

FanDuel's Eccles said that he doesn't believe home-team loyalty will be supplanted by fantasy team interests, but it's common sense for fantasy players to have a shared loyalty.

"Obviously, sometimes you come into conflicts whenever your home team is playing against your [fantasy] quarterback. And that can become a very difficult situation where you're shooting for a high score in a game," Eccles said during a panel discussion. "But the thing I say to people is, 'Look, your fantasy team is *your* team, *you* picked it.' So, sometimes it's … a team you picked against a team picked by a billionaire you don't know."

Dan Okrent, the journalist and historian credited with inventing Rotisserie Baseball, has seen his own interest in fantasy sports wane and is ambivalent about where daily fantasy, with its potentially far more intoxicating appeal, will take sports fans.

"The positive side to all this is that some fans who follow, say, the Philadelphia Phillies used to know just the stars on that one team, but now they know the twenty-fifth player on the San Diego Padres," Okrent said. "And that part of it is good, because it gets people more attached to the game of baseball, rather than to just the local team. But the bad thing about it is that with the daily fantasy element, the involvement is so intense, it can lead to an actual detachment from the local team, because now your interest is just focused on the individual players. And what's worse is that the players you're connected to today aren't even going to be the players you're connected to tomorrow."

In that way, daily fantasy sports may be an apt metaphor for the tenor of 21st century America, where so many things that were once counted on to provide a sense of permanency—homes, jobs, relationships—are now assumed to be short-term, even ephemeral.

In terms of sports, daily fantasy has the potential to profoundly shift fan loyalty away from a communal, almost tribal, act of faith to a far more personal and singular experience rooted in self-interest.

"We're number one!" is on the cusp of giving way to simply, "I won!" or even "*I'm* number one!"

Uncertain is whether sports, and the fans who love them, will be better off for the change.

Epilogue

Every August, NFL greats from the past are inducted into the Pro Football Hall of Fame for their contributions to the game. But if entry into the Hall were truly based on exceptional contributions, there would already be a bust of the late Charles K. McNeil at the pro-football shrine in Canton, Ohio. McNeil, a graduate of the University of Chicago and a one-time math teacher, is the man credited with inventing what we now call the "pointspread," that magic number that makes every team equal to every other team—in a betting sense.

Although the major sports organizations may never admit it, gambling, as a primary ingredient in heightened fan interest, is a key reason why major-league sports have become both an enormous cultural influence and a mega-business in America. That's been especially true for the NFL, whose ascendancy as America's number-one sport came soon after the pointspread became the favored way to bet on sporting events. Still, the connection between the professional sports leagues' prosperity and gambling has been an inconvenient reality that those leagues have tried to sidestep as they preach about "the integrity of the game."

Daily fantasy sports changes all that.

Because of the new nexus of federal and state laws (in most cases), together with the belief that the complexity of fantasy sports renders efforts to illicitly manipulate outcomes pointless, the leagues not only tolerate, but have embraced, DFS.

Why wouldn't they? DFS drives the same type of heightened fan interest that traditional gambling has for many years. The notion that sports fans can have an interest in a game that goes beyond the scoreboard (enthusiasm based on *self*-interest) is now something the major sports organizations can finally promote. And that's very good news for the daily fantasy industry.

That said, daily fantasy's quick burst out of the starting blocks doesn't mean it can last over the long run.

For starters, no one—not even executives of the largest DFS companies—believes that daily fantasy can continue operating in a regulatory vacuum.

In addition, there's already a concern that the game's skill-based nature could also be its undoing, as highly proficient players entering huge numbers of DFS contests might kill the game's appeal for casual players.

Also, a reasonable equilibrium has to be found for the commission DFS websites charge for participating in their contests. So far, the norm has been 8%-10%, with some of the more popular contests as high as 13%. Such percentages make the games extremely difficult to beat in the long run.

Daily fantasy sports is poised to be transformational in how fans relate to the games they love. However, in the process, those who control the industry need to keep in mind the most important virtue of any game—fair play.

In fall 2015, just as this book was about to go to press, regulation, proficiency, and commissions were a distant second on the DFS agenda. Instead, the industry was obsessed with a more immediate concern: acquiring new customers. And thanks to all the venture capital raised earlier in the year, the two major DFS websites saturated television sports programming with advertising as the 2015 NFL season began.

Daily fantasy's two heavyweights wanted attention, and they got it. The ad campaigns attracted millions of new customers, but also caught the eye of mainstream news organizations that found the arguments that DFS was "not gambling" unpersuasive. Many of those news organizations, which previously had been oblivious to daily fantasy's growing popularity, had little difficulty quickly ginning up outrage over the upstart cyber companies run by 30-something entrepreneurs.

By and large, these same news organizations also routinely criticized legalized gambling, especially the traditional casino industry, and often contended that any economic benefits accrued from the expansion of gambling were offset by social harm. This time, however, Big News had an ally in the very same Big Gaming industry that it typically railed against. Traditional gambling companies had been irked by daily fantasy from the very start, for a number of reasons.

First, DFS had done what Big Gaming has failed to do: exploit cyberspace for gaming purposes.

Second, DFS managed to attract Millennials, at which Big Gaming has also failed miserably.

And third, Big Gaming considers DFS competition with an unfair advantage: the lack of strict regulation and sometimes onerous taxation. As we've seen, daily fantasy has been operating out of the reach of government oversight. Plus, it's been unencumbered by the special taxes that politicians are always eager to pile onto gaming operations, whether bricks-and-mortar or Internet.

As a result, Big News, with its influential megaphone, and Big Gaming, with longtime ties to politicians, were powerful voices that lawmakers, regulators, and attorneys general had no

choice but to listen to when daily fantasy made itself an issue
with its advertising harangue.

Then the DFS industry handed its enemies a gift. On Sept.
27, 2015, daily fantasy's version of Mrs. O'Leary's cow kicked
over the lantern that set ablaze the DFS world (the cow is said
to have started the small barn fire that turned into the confla-
gration that burned down Chicago in 1871). Just three weeks
into the 2015 NFL season during a slate of Sunday games, a
mid-level DraftKings employee, Ethan Haskell, published data
by mistake on the DraftKings website that was supposed to
remain confidential until all the games were finished. The data
reflected to what degree various NFL players were included in
the lineups of DraftKings customers.

While such data can be helpful in assembling lineups, its
release was a relatively small miscue in itself. Unfortunately for
the industry, that same weekend Haskell won $350,000 playing
at rival FanDuel. At best, it was an awkward coincidence. At
worst, it appeared that an industry insider had exercised a significant advantage over regular customers. Even though Fan-
Duel, DraftKings, and a law firm hired by DraftKings quickly
investigated to see if Haskell had used the confidential information to help win at FanDuel, and all three determined that
he hadn't, suspicion—like the Chicago fire—was soon out of
control. The data release was referred to as a "scandal" in major news stories and Haskell's win was called "insider trading."
When it came to light that employees of DFS companies routinely played on competing websites, the daily fantasy industry
immediately forbade the practice.

The advertising onslaught, the Haskell leak, and the potential for insider abuses prompted more intense questioning from
governments and law enforcement regarding whether DFS was
justified in calling itself "not gambling." Having opened the

2015 NFL season as a shooting-star industry, the daily fantasy business was fighting for its life before the football campaign was even half over.

Assuming daily fantasy survives the critical attention it received during the 2015 NFL season—and it will—there are many lessons the industry should heed and act on. Here are the top ten.

1. *Regulation.* Whether regulation is imposed by governmental entities or it becomes the province of an independent body with firm oversight authority (such as bar associations), the DFS industry needs to move toward such oversight. Crafting a set of rules through a trade organization that has no authority to effectively censure and punish violators is unlikely to satisfy government, law enforcement, and Big News.

2. *Taxation.* Winning daily fantasy customers already receive normal tax-reporting documentation, much like casino customers who hit a jackpot on a slot machine. But if state permissions become the rule for DFS companies, the industry better be prepared for the special taxes frequently imposed on gaming businesses, whether regular casinos or legal online gaming websites.

3. *Internal Technological and Personnel Controls.* The daily fantasy industry's processes for safeguarding sensitive data should be submitted to regulatory scrutiny and subject to regular monitoring. Employees with access to such information should also be carefully screened and monitored.

4. *Know Your Customer.* When legal online gaming began in New Jersey, Nevada, and Delaware, operators had to establish stringent protocols for making sure potential customers were exactly who they said they were, particularly that they were of legal age and within the state's borders while participating. Daily fantasy should ensure that its protocols for identifying

customers are just as rigorous. For instance, one DFS website operator, CBS Sportsline, requires that customers, in order to withdraw money, must supply personal information, such as Social Security and driver's-license numbers, plus an attached scan of the license.

5. *Revisiting Age Limitations.* At least through the beginning of the 2015 NFL season, the age limit for playing on many daily fantasy websites was 18. The age for participating in other types of legalized online gaming, including poker, has been 21. Despite the industry's insistence about the differences between DFS and gambling, daily fantasy should be preemptive in warding off criticism that it preys on a demographic that's too young to fully form judgments about playing contests for cash.

6. *Responsible Gaming.* When the American Gaming Association came into existence in the 1990s, its first top executive, Frank Fahrenkopf, encouraged casino executives to concede that their product could have adverse societal impacts and that their industry needed to help mitigate them through research, education, and exclusion policies. Big Gaming now has a wealth of data with which to defend itself when attacked, plus a legacy of promoting responsible gaming. The DFS industry needs to do the same by employing social scientists, treatment specialists, and other experts to do honest appraisals of the effects of DFS and, in instances where customers need help, suggest where to get it.

7. *Consumer Protection.* Both as part of regulation and in crafting internal company policies, the industry must assure customers a level playing field. That includes making sure player deposits are held in segregated accounts and not comingled with operating funds; publicizing the remedies for technological malfunctions that affect contests; and spelling out how dis-

putes are resolved, preferably by an independent party.

8. *Honing a Sustainable Model.* Where money is involved, suspicion abounds. The fallout from the revelation that daily fantasy employees were playing in contests on other websites illustrates how the industry must do more to assure government, law enforcement, and customers that its contests aren't predatory schemes where the most accomplished and prolific players win the lion's share of prizes. The specter of daily fantasy's own 1% gobbling most of the prize money hurts DFS in the eyes of policy-makers and portends a short life for the industry. A sample of remedies to make DFS more friendly for casual players includes: enforcing strict limits on entries by a single player in a given contest; forbidding the use of technological enhancements, such as software (scripting) that enables bulk lineup entries and last-minute changes; and restricting prolific players to certain tiers of contests where they compete against one another. To help casual players protect themselves, companies could and should provide databases of their users with a reasonable amount of public data, minimally showing total contests played by user name.

9. *Honest Messaging.* Anyone who has watched a TV sports channel knows the typical daily fantasy advertising pitch: "Win big money! Just pick a fantasy sports team!" A more honest approach would be to de-emphasize dreams of windfalls and, instead, promote enhanced fan engagement. In the end, most players will derive entertainment value from playing daily fantasy, not make a profit. In addition, DFS should be more transparent about the reality of the heavily advertised sign-up bonuses (as covered in Chapter 3).

10. *Slow the Roll.* The strategy behind incessant advertising campaigns during the 2015 NFL season was understandable in part; the two major players believe that once customers get used

to a specific website, they're likely to stick with it. Thus, each struggled to attract as many customers as possible. That might or might not be true. A less cynical perspective of winning the hearts and wallets of consumers is to offer a superior product (easier user interface) and a better deal (lower rake). Over time, companies with the better product will grow organically—because they deserve to, not because they yelled the loudest.

Appendix

Daily Fantasy Tax Reporting

The ramifications of taxes as they impact gamblers are a big mystery to most people. Many tax preparers aren't knowledgeable about gambling issues, even if they're sharp in all other areas. In addition, the IRS offers surprisingly few details to instruct gamblers how to navigate the tax maze, and what it does say can be broad, ambiguous, obscure, or even contradictory. (It's possible this was done intentionally, in order to fit most gambling issues within general guidelines. It's also likely that the cumbersome tax bureaucracy has been slow to keep up with changing times.)

To make matters worse, fantasy sports is so new, and potentially controversial in terms of its legal status (is it gambling or isn't it?), that it will certainly generate its own tax implications.

But one thing is clear: Income is income, no matter where it comes from. This means that winnings, over and above losses, from fantasy sports must be reported to the IRS, whether this activity is gambling, a hobby, or a full-scale legitimate business.

Luckily, there's help in maneuvering through the potentially treacherous waters of taxes and DFS. Patrick Guinan, a Certified Public Accountant in Philadelphia and head of

DailyFantasyTaxes.com, advises fantasy sports participants on how they should report and file their DFS winnings.

In short, if you have net winnings of more than $600 from any daily fantasy sports site, you'll be sent IRS Form W-9, requiring your Social Security number and home address. When the time comes, you'll also receive Form 1099-MISC with the amount of your winnings of more than $600 shown in Box 3.

Guinan stresses that taxpayers are required to report net earnings of even $1, but anything over $600 is reported to the IRS.

On most returns, net winnings are reported on Line 21 of the 1040 tax form as "Other Income." But what about the losses? This is where the proverbial can of worms gets opened. Reporting losses is different for casual players or hobbyists compared to professional DFS participants and whether you itemize or take the standard deduction. Self-employment (Social Security) taxes are also a consideration. And then there are state taxes (for example, states such as Pennsylvania and New Jersey don't have itemized deductions, while others do). However, no matter how you file, you definitely need to keep track of how often you participate and how much you win and lose, as well as keep good records of your activities.

Jean Scott, author of the bestselling *Frugal* series of gambling books, is an expert on gambling and taxes. Together with Marissa Chien, an Enrolled Agent and high-stakes advantage gambler, she's written three editions of *Tax Help for Gamblers*. This is the best book on gambling and taxes, an indispensable resource for helping fantasy sports participants stay square with the IRS.

Glossary

As is the case in any game of skill, it's important to consistently try to get better at daily fantasy sports. That means reading the Internet websites, blogs, and forums that are certain to multiply as DFS becomes more popular.

To help make you more fluent in the language of DFS, here are some common terms. This Glossary is generally arranged alphabetically, but in cases where more general terms have logical subset terms, those are grouped together.

Auction Draft—A type of fantasy draft in which participants bid on various athletes. Often, each fantasy owner receives a fixed amount of points. Those points often represent an actual cash value, say $1 per point. Fantasy owners bid on athletes to build rosters, while staying within the limits of the allotted points that each fantasy team is permitted. Such drafts are sometimes used in season-long contests, but they are rare, if they exist at all, in daily fantasy sports.

Buy-in—The amount of money it costs to enter a daily fantasy sports contest. Most of the buy-in goes toward the prize pool that will be paid out to the participants. A smaller percentage of the buy-in is kept by the website for administering and overseeing the contest.

Cashing/Cash—You cash when you finish high enough in a daily fantasy contest to win a prize. You "min cash" (short for minimum cash) when you finish just high enough in a tournament to win the smallest amount of money offered in the prize-payout schedule.

Cash Games—The general term given to daily fantasy contests where participants are usually trying to double, or approximately double, their buy-in. There are several varieties of cash games.

- *50/50:* In these contests, 50% of the field qualifies for a prize. The prize is usually slightly less than double the buy-in, because of the commission taken by the website. For instance, a $10 buy-in with a lineup that earns enough points to qualify for a prize usually returns a total of $18, for an $8 profit.
- *Double Up:* In these contests, all players who cash get double their buy-in, but slightly less than half the field will cash. In that way, the website makes its profit.
- *Head-to-head (H2H):* In these contests, the field is limited to just two participants; the winner takes all, less the website's commission.

Ceiling—The potential upper limit in fantasy points of what an athlete can be expected to score.

Chalk—The favorite in any wagering event. In horse racing, the chalk is the horse that leaves the starting gate with the lowest odds. In DFS, the chalk is the highest-priced player or one of the highest-priced players at a given position.

DFS—The common initialism for daily fantasy sports.

Dollars/Point (or dollars per point, or $/Point)—
One measurement of an athlete's value in daily fantasy sports. A player who costs $3,000 and produces (or is projected to produce) 10 fantasy points per game has a $/point value of $300 per point. A player who costs $3,000 and scores 20 fantasy points has achieved a Dollars/Point value of $150 per point. The lower an athlete's Dollars/Point value, the better; the daily fantasy owner is getting more value for the cap salary expended on the player.

Donkey—A daily fantasy player who makes poor decisions and is perceived as throwing away money. The same term is prevalent in poker and has the same meaning in that game.

Fade—In general, "fade" means avoid. In poker, fading a card means avoiding having a card come out that will beat you. In DFS, fading means avoiding a player who will be commonly owned, because whatever good he does for you, he's doing for a lot of your competitors.

Field—The total number of entrants in a daily fantasy sports contest.

Fish—Weaker participants in a daily fantasy sports contest. Often, fish are newer or less experienced players.

Floor—The potential lower limit in fantasy points of what an athlete can be expected to score.

Freeroll—A DFS contest in which the participants are not required to pay a fee, but there's still a prize pool. Freerolls are sometimes offered by a DFS website to individual players for frequent participation or to a larger group of participants as a promotion.

FPPG (Average of Fantasy Points Per Game)—If an athlete in the first five games of the season scores 10, 8, 6, 12, and 8 points, his FPPG is 8.8 (44 points divided by 5).

GPP (Guaranteed Prize Pool tournament)—These popular DFS contests offer a top-heavy prize structure, so that the highest finishers make a great deal of money, but only 15%-20% of the participants get any prize at all. The prize pool is guaranteed by the website. For example, in a $100,000 GPP, the website is committed to pay out $100,000 in prizes regardless of how many participants buy in. GPPs are the highest-profile daily fantasy sports contests and sometimes attract thousands of players, resulting in so-called "life-changing" top prizes.

GPP Player—An athlete who is worthy of consideration in a GPP tournament, due to a great deal of upside potential, but who also has the potential of getting very few points on a bad day. A GPP Player is generally considered a bad choice for cash games, because of his performance volatility.

Grinder—A daily fantasy sports participant who plays regularly in order to grind out a profit. Grinders often consider themselves DFS pros.

Hedge—To choose lineups in multiple daily fantasy contests that offset each other and mitigate risk. Theoretically, hedging can reduce the overall financial risk to a DFS participant.

Liquidity—The number of participants available to participate in daily fantasy games. A great deal of liquidity is considered desirable: Having a large number of interested participants allows a website to offer a wide range of contests at various price points. So far, NFL contests generate the greatest liquidity.

Lock—That point in time when DFS participants can no longer make changes to their lineups or rosters. The lock time for daily fantasy sports rosters is usually the same time as the actual sports games begin.

Min (minimum) Salary—The lowest salary a daily fantasy website offers on players.

Multi-entry Contest—A daily fantasy sports tournament that allows an individual participant to enter the contest more than once. The multiple entries can be different lineups, the same lineup, or a combination of different and the same. DFS pros sometimes enter dozens of lineups in contests that accept thousands of entries.

Multiple Position Eligibility (MPE)—The categorizing of individual athletes on certain daily fantasy websites. For example, on some websites, baseball player Chris Davis may be listed as both a first baseman and an outfielder. As a result, a DFS participant can use Davis in a lineup at either 1B or OF. Some websites assign just one position to a player.

Multiplier—A daily fantasy contest in which the prize is some multiple of the buy-in. For instance, in a triple-up with a buy-in of $25, all entrants who qualify for cash prizes receive $75. In addition to triples, a variety of multipliers are available on various websites for prizes that are 4 times, 5 times, and 10 times the buy-ins. The higher the multiple, the more difficult it is to cash.

Overlay—This occurs when the prize pool promised by the website exceeds the total money contributed by the participants. Overlays are considered advantageous situations for DFS participants.

Pay Up—Using a proportionately large amount of salary-cap allowance on a single athlete, due to the belief that his performance will justify the high cost.

Payout Structure/Prize Structure (Schedule)—The amount of money paid to DFS participants who qualify for a prize. The payout/prize structure/schedule is posted as part of the rules for the contest.

Pivot—To change an opinion on a player, often as a result of breaking news.

PPR (point-per-reception)—A scoring system in fantasy football, either season-long or daily, that credits a football player with points for pass receptions in addition to the yards gained on the catches.
> *Full PPR:* A football player credited with one point for each reception.
> *Half PPR:* A football player credited with one-half (0.5) point for each reception.

Positive Expected Value (+EV)—A term common to gambling, especially in games of skill, where participants believe they can hold an advantage over the casino, the house, or another player. In DFS, positive expected value is associated with tournament overlays where the guaranteed prize pool exceeds the fees that the players contribute.

Prize Pool—The total amount of money available to be distributed as prizes to the participants in a daily fantasy contest.

Punt—To place less value on a specific position within your lineup. Let's assume that, on a given day, all the catchers in all the scheduled MLB games are below-average offensive performers, and there's no reasonable expectation that any of them will produce a meaningful amount of fantasy points. A DFS participant may elect to use the least amount of salary cap as possible, or "punt" the catcher position.

Qualifier/Satellite/Survivor/Step—These are contests, often at modest buy-ins, in which the prize is an entry into still another contest where the eventual prize is of substantial value. For instance, a DFS participant may enter a $2-buy-in satellite with 10 other players where the prize is entry into a subsequent $20-buy-in contest.

Rake/Margin/Commission—The fee that daily fantasy sports websites charge participants for playing the contests.

Regression/Reversion (to the Mean)—A mathematical phenomenon that describes how an anomalous set of statistics eventually returns to an established norm. For instance, if a baseball player has a five-year career batting average of .250, and the overall mean for all major league batters for a season is .250, a reasonable expectation for that batter would be a season-long average of about .250, given some allowance for a standard deviation. However, if through the first one-third of a season that same batter is hitting .400, a reversion or regression to the mean is highly likely and, statistically, he could be expected to hit less than .400 for the remainder of the season, as his batting average regresses closer to the mean.

Roster/Lineup—These terms are used interchangeably in daily fantasy sports. Rosters or lineups indicate the team of players a DFS participant selects in a daily fantasy sports contest. In traditional season-long fantasy contests, there's often a distinction between roster (the total pool of players on a fantasy owner's team) and lineup (that group of players chosen to be in action at a given time). Typically, however, that distinction doesn't exist in daily fantasy sports.

Salary Cap—The total amount of fictitious money available to daily fantasy participants to select rosters or lineups of athletes. For example, if the salary cap for a given NFL daily fantasy contest is $50,000, a DFS participant must assemble a lineup (usually for nine positions) in which the total of the fictitious salaries for the players chosen does not exceed $50,000.

Salary Cap Draft (a.k.a. Cap Draft)—A fantasy sports draft that establishes an upper-end limit of a fictitious money amount used as a parameter for assembling each roster. Athletes available to be chosen are assigned notional salaries and fantasy contest participants have to stay within the overall limit (i.e., the salary cap) when assembling their rosters or lineups.

Sharks—Stronger participants in a daily fantasy contest, usually with more experience and better player-evaluation skills.

Shorting—This terms comes from the stock market when investors are betting on a stock to go down rather than up. In DFS, it means to avoid (see "fade") a certain player, sometimes because of a likelihood that the athlete will be popularly held, thus minimizing his effectiveness in larger tournaments.

Snake Draft—The type of draft that fans are accustomed to seeing in the NFL's annual draft of college players. Fantasy team owners select players in an arranged order and when a team owner selects a certain player, no other owner can chose that athlete. The owner with the first pick in the first round has the last pick in the second round. The owner with the last pick in the first round has the first pick in the second round. This type of draft is exceedingly common in season-long fantasy sports, but exceedingly rare in daily fantasy sports.

Stacking—Including two or more players from the same team in a daily fantasy lineup. A typical stacking strategy in daily fantasy football would be a quarterback and wide receiver from the same team. In that way, a single big play involving those two players would deliver a windfall of fantasy points.

Staking—Exactly what it sounds like: One person bankrolls another person, presumably a more accomplished DFS practitioner, in exchange for a share of the profits, assuming there are any.

Synergy—Similar to stacking, except that the term is used more commonly in reference to DFS baseball lineups. In applying a synergy strategy, a DFS owner includes two or more MLB players who bat in either consecutive order or in close proximity. In that way, if one or two players on the same team get on base and a third batter drives his teammates home, the DFS owner who has packed his lineup with all three players benefits from fantasy points for both the RBIs and the runs scored on a single hit.

Tilt—Another term that has gained popularity through poker. In poker, it means losing one's composure and subsequently engaging in ill-advised play. In DFS, tilt means much the same, i.e., suffering anxiety because your roster does poorly, something that you can watch as it happens. While one cannot adversely affect the DFS contest in progress while on tilt (as in poker), one needs to keep his or her emotions in check and not rush into more DFS contests while in an agitated state.

Train—More than one entry of the identical roster in the same daily fantasy sports contest. Some tournaments permit a participant to enter more than one roster (multi-entry). Some DFS participants enter the identical roster many times to either win a bigger overall share of the prize pool or, in qualifying tournaments, to win more qualifiers or "tickets" into a subsequent bigger tournament.

Value Player/Value Pick—A player whose fantasy salary is relatively low compared to higher expectations for how many points he can or could produce.

Tracking Bonuses

As discussed in this book, it's important to take advantage of all sign-up offers and their attending bonuses.

LasVegasAdvisor.com is a subsidiary of Huntington Press, the leading publisher of gambling books (including this one), and a respected source for expert analysis of gambling games and playing strategies. As an extension of this book, LasVegasAdvisor.com stays up to date on bonus offers from all of the operating DFS sites and provides the pros and cons of each.

About the Author

As a former reporter and editor covering both sports and news for the *Philadelphia Inquirer* and *Baltimore Sun*, Bill Ordine has been following daily fantasy sports since its inception. In addition to studying the business side of the exploding industry, Ordine has interviewed some of the game's biggest winners and most recognized theorists to become one of DFS' most noted authorities. At the *Inquirer*, Ordine was one of the lead journalists on a reporting team that was a finalist for the 1997 Pulitzer Prize for Spot News Reporting. His previous book, authored with writing partner Ralph Vigoda, was *Fatal Match*, an account of the murder of Olympic wrestler David Schultz by millionaire John du Pont.

About Huntington Press

Huntington Press is a specialty publisher of Las Vegas- and gambling-related books and periodicals, including the award-winning consumer newsletter, *Anthony Curtis' Las Vegas Advisor*.

Huntington Press
3665 Procyon Avenue
Las Vegas, Nevada 89103
E-mail: books@huntingtonpress.com